Mastering Apache Cassandra 3.x
Third Edition

An expert guide to improving database scalability and availability without compromising performance

Aaron Ploetz
Tejaswi Malepati
Nishant Neeraj

BIRMINGHAM - MUMBAI

Mastering Apache Cassandra 3.x
Third Edition

Commissioning Editor: Pravin Dhandre
Acquisition Editor: Divya Poojari
Content Development Editor: Chris D'cruz
Technical Editor: Suwarna Patil
Copy Editor: Safis Editing
Project Coordinator: Nidhi Joshi
Proofreader: Safis Editing
Indexer: Mariammal Chettiyar
Graphics: Tom Scaria
Production Coordinator: Arvindkumar Gupta

First published: October 2013
Second Edition: March 2015
Third Edition: October 2018

Production reference: 1311018

Published by Packt Publishing Ltd.
Livery Place
35 Livery Street
Birmingham
B3 2PB, UK.

ISBN 978-1-78913-149-9

www.packtpub.com

`mapt.io`

Mapt is an online digital library that gives you full access to over 5,000 books and videos, as well as industry leading tools to help you plan your personal development and advance your career. For more information, please visit our website.

Why subscribe?

- Spend less time learning and more time coding with practical eBooks and Videos from over 4,000 industry professionals

- Improve your learning with Skill Plans built especially for you

- Get a free eBook or video every month

- Mapt is fully searchable

- Copy and paste, print, and bookmark content

Packt.com

Did you know that Packt offers eBook versions of every book published, with PDF and ePub files available? You can upgrade to the eBook version at `www.packt.com` and as a print book customer, you are entitled to a discount on the eBook copy. Get in touch with us at `customercare@packtpub.com` for more details.

At `www.packt.com`, you can also read a collection of free technical articles, sign up for a range of free newsletters, and receive exclusive discounts and offers on Packt books and eBooks.

Foreward

Being asked to write the next edition of *Mastering Apache Cassandra* was a bit of a tall order. After all, writing a master-level book sort of implies that I have mastered whatever subject the book entails, which, by proxy, means that I should have mastered Apache Cassandra in order to be asked to author such a book. Honestly, that seems pretty far from the truth.

I feel privileged to have been a part of the Apache Cassandra community since 2012. I've been helping out by answering questions on Stack Overflow since then, as well as submitting Jira tickets, and the first of my patches to the project a couple of years later. During that time I've also written a few articles (about Apache Cassandra), managed to be selected as a DataStax MVP (most valuable professional) a few times, and have presented at several NoSQL events and conferences.

Talking with other experts at those events has humbled me, as I continue to find aspects of Apache Cassandra that I have yet to fully understand. And that is really the best part. Throughout my career, I have found that maintaining a student mentality has allowed me to continue to grow and get better. While I have managed to develop an understanding of several aspects of Apache Cassandra, there are some areas where I still feel like I am very much a student. In fact, one of the reasons I asked my good friend and co-worker Tejaswi Malepati to help me out with this book, is that there are aspects of the Apache Cassandra ecosystem that he understands and can articulate better than I.

Ultimately, I hope this book helps you to foster your own student mentality. While reading, this book should inspire you to push the bounds of your own knowledge. Throughout, you will find areas in which we have offered tips. These pointers are pieces of advice that can provide further context and understanding, based on real-world experience. Hopefully, these will help to point you in the correct direction and ultimately lead to resolution.

Thank you, and enjoy!

Aaron Ploetz

Lead Engineer, Target Corp. and Cassandra MVP.

Contributors

About the authors

Aaron Ploetz is the NoSQL Engineering Lead for Target, where his DevOps team supports Cassandra, MongoDB, and Neo4j. He has been named a DataStax MVP for Apache Cassandra three times and has presented at multiple events, including the DataStax Summit and Data Day Texas. Aaron earned a BS in Management/Computer Systems from the University of Wisconsin-Whitewater, and an MS in Software Engineering from Regis University. He and his wife, Coriene, live with their three children in the Twin Cities area.

I'd like to thank my wife, Coriene, for all of her support through this endeavor. Sometimes, I think she is more excited about my authoring projects than I am.

Tejaswi Malepati is the Cassandra Tech Lead for Target. He has been instrumental in designing and building custom Cassandra integrations, including web-based SQL interface and data validation frameworks between Oracle and Cassandra. Tejaswi earned a master's degree in computer science from the University of New Mexico, and a bachelor's degree in Electronics and Communication from Jawaharlal Nehru Technological University in India. He is passionate about identifying and analyzing data patterns in datasets using R, Python, Spark, and Cassandra.

A very special thanks to Aaron Ploetz, who provided me with this opportunity to be a co-author. Also, I am grateful to my family, friends, and team for their constant encouragement in completing my first book.

Nishant Neeraj is an independent software developer with experience in developing and planning out architectures for massively scalable data storage and data processing systems. Over the years, he has helped to design and implement a wide variety of products and systems for companies, ranging from small start-ups to large multinational companies. Currently, he helps drive WealthEngine's core product to the next level by leveraging a variety of big data technologies.

About the reviewers

Sourav Gulati has been associated with the software industry for more than 8 years. He started his career with Unix/Linux and Java then moved to the Big data and NoSQL space. He has been designing and implementing Big data solutions for last few years. He is also the co-author of Apache Spark 2.x for Java Developers published by *Packt*. Apart from the IT world, he likes to play lawn tennis and likes to read about mythology.

Ahmed Sherif is a data scientist who has been working with data in various roles since 2005. He started off with BI solutions and transitioned to data science in 2013. In 2016, he obtained a master's in Predictive Analytics from Northwestern University, where he studied the science and application of ML and predictive modeling using both Python and R. Lately, he has been developing ML and deep learning solutions on the cloud using Azure. In 2016, his first book, *Practical Business Intelligence,* was published by Packt. He currently works as a technology solution professional in data and AI for Microsoft.

Amrith Ravindra is a machine learning (ML) enthusiast who holds degrees in electrical and industrial engineering. While pursuing his Master's, he delved deeper into the world of ML and developed a love for data science. Graduate level courses in engineering gave him the mathematical background to launch himself into a career in ML. He met Ahmed Sherif at a local data science meetup in Tampa. They decided to put their brains together to write a book on their favorite ML algorithms. He hopes that this book will help him to achieve his ultimate goal of becoming a data scientist and actively contributing to ML.

Valentina Crisan is a product architecture consultant in the big data domain and a trainer for big data technologies (Apache Cassandra, Apache Hadoop architecture, and Apache Kafka). With a background in computer science, she has more than 15 years' experience in telecoms, architecting telecoms, and value-added service solutions, and has headed technical teams over a number of years. Passionate about the opportunities cloud and data could bring in different domains, for the past 4 years, she has been delivering training courses for big data architectures and works in different projects related to these domains.

Swathi Kurunji is a software engineer at Actian Corporation. She has a PhD in computer science from the University of Massachusetts, Lowell, USA. She has worked as a software development intern with IT companies including EMC and SAP. At EMC, she gained experience on Apache Cassandra data modeling and performance analysis. She worked with Wipro Technologies in India as a project engineer managing application servers. She has experience with database systems, such as Apache Cassandra, Sybase IQ, Oracle, MySQL, and MS Access. Her interests include software design and development, big data analysis, the optimization of databases, and cloud computing. She has previously reviewed Cassandra *Data Modeling and Analysis published by* Packt.

I would like to thank my husband and my family for all their support.

Packt is searching for authors like you

If you're interested in becoming an author for Packt, please visit `authors.packtpub.com` and apply today. We have worked with thousands of developers and tech professionals, just like you, to help them share their insight with the global tech community. You can make a general application, apply for a specific hot topic that we are recruiting an author for, or submit your own idea.

Table of Contents

Preface

This book is intended to help you understand the Apache Cassandra NoSQL database. It will describe procedures and methods for configuring, installing, and maintaining a high-performing Cassandra cluster. This book can serve as a reference for some of the more obscure configuration parameters and commands that may be needed to operate and maintain a cluster. Also, tools and methods will be suggested for integrating Cassandra with Apache Spark, as well as practices for building Java applications that use Cassandra.

Who this book is for

This book is intended for a DBA who is responsible for supporting Apache Cassandra clusters. It may also benefit full-stack engineers at smaller companies. While these individuals primarily build applications, they may also have to maintain and support their Cassandra cluster out of necessity.

What this book covers

Chapter 1, *Quick Start*, walks the reader through getting started with Apache Cassandra. As the title suggests, explanations will be brief in favor of guiding the reader toward quickly standing up an Apache Cassandra single-node cluster.

Chapter 2, *Cassandra Architecture*, covers the ideas and theories behind how Apache Cassandra works. These concepts will be useful going forward, as an understanding of Cassandra's inner workings can help in building high-performing data models.

Chapter 3, *Effective CQL*, introduces the reader to the CQL. It describes building appropriate data models and how to leverage CQL to get the most out of your cluster.

Chapter 4, *Configuring a Cluster*, details the configuration files and settings that go into building an Apache Cassandra Cluster. In addition, this chapter also describes the effects that some of the settings have, and how they can be used to keep your cluster running well.

Chapter 5, *Performance Tuning*, discusses the extra settings, configurations, and design considerations that can help to improve performance or mitigate issues.

Chapter 6, *Managing a Cluster*, goes into detail when describing the nodetool utility, and how it can be used for operations on an Apache Cassandra cluster. Adding and removing nodes is covered, as well as taking and restoring from backups.

Chapter 7, *Monitoring*, describes how to integrate a technology stack that provides a window into an Apache Cassandra cluster's history and performance metrics.

Chapter 8, *Application Development*, takes the reader through design considerations around coding Java applications to work with an Apache Cassandra cluster.

Chapter 9, *Integration with Apache Spark*, talks about installing and using Apache Spark in order to analyze and discover value in your data.

Appendix A, *References*, In this chapter you will find links present for various references present throughout the book.

To get the most out of this book

This book assumes that you have access to hardware on which you can install, configure, and code against an Apache Cassandra instance. Having elevated admin or sudo privileges on the aforementioned machine will be essential to carrying out some of the tasks described.

This book is written from the perspective of running Apache Cassandra on a macOS or Linux instance. As OS-specific system administration is not within the scope of this book, readers who are new to Linux may find value in seeking out a separate tutorial prior to attempting some of the examples.

The Java coding examples will be easier to do from within an integrated developer environment (IDE), with Apache Maven installed for dependency management. You may need to look up additional resources to ensure that these components are configured properly. Several IDEs have a plugin that allows for direct integration with Apache Maven.

Download the example code files

You can download the example code files for this book from your account at www.packt.com. If you purchased this book elsewhere, you can visit www.packt.com/support and register to have the files emailed directly to you.

You can download the code files by following these steps:

1. Log in or register at www.packt.com.
2. Select the **SUPPORT** tab.
3. Click on **Code Downloads & Errata**.
4. Enter the name of the book in the **Search** box and follow the onscreen instructions.

Once the file is downloaded, please make sure that you unzip or extract the folder using the latest version of:

- WinRAR/7-Zip for Windows
- Zipeg/iZip/UnRarX for Mac
- 7-Zip/PeaZip for Linux

The code bundle for the book is also hosted on GitHub at https://github.com/PacktPublishing/Mastering-Apache-Cassandra-3.x-Third-Edition. In case there's an update to the code, it will be updated on the existing GitHub repository.

We also have other code bundles from our rich catalog of books and videos available at https://github.com/PacktPublishing/. Check them out!

Conventions used

There are a number of text conventions used throughout this book.

CodeInText: Indicates code words in text, database table names, folder names, filenames, file extensions, pathnames, dummy URLs, user input, and Twitter handles. Here is an example: "This will store the PID of the Cassandra process in a file named cassandra.pid in the local/cassandra directory."

A block of code is set as follows:

```
<dependencies>
 <dependency>
   <groupId>com.datastax.cassandra</groupId>
   <artifactId>cassandra-driver-core</artifactId>
   <version>3.6.0</version>
 </dependency>
</dependencies>
```

Any command-line input or output is written as follows:

```
cassdba@cqlsh> use packt;
cassdba@cqlsh:packt>
```

Bold: Indicates a new term, an important word, or words that you see on screen. For example, words in menus or dialog boxes appear in the text like this.

 Warnings or important notes appear like this.

 Tips and tricks appear like this.

Get in touch

Feedback from our readers is always welcome.

General feedback: If you have questions about any aspect of this book, mention the book title in the subject of your message and email us at customercare@packtpub.com.

Errata: Although we have taken every care to ensure the accuracy of our content, mistakes do happen. If you have found a mistake in this book, we would be grateful if you would report this to us. Please visit www.packt.com/submit-errata, selecting your book, clicking on the Errata Submission Form link, and entering the details.

Piracy: If you come across any illegal copies of our works in any form on the internet, we would be grateful if you would provide us with the location address or website name. Please contact us at copyright@packt.com with a link to the material.

If you are interested in becoming an author: If there is a topic that you have expertise in and you are interested in either writing or contributing to a book, please visit authors.packtpub.com.

Reviews

Please leave a review. Once you have read and used this book, why not leave a review on the site that you purchased it from? Potential readers can then see and use your unbiased opinion to make purchase decisions, we at Packt can understand what you think about our products, and our authors can see your feedback on their book. Thank you!

For more information about Packt, please visit `packt.com`.

1
Quick Start

Welcome to the world of **Apache Cassandra**! In this first chapter, we will briefly introduce Cassandra, along with a quick, step-by-step process to get your own single-node cluster up and running. Even if you already have experience working with Cassandra, this chapter will help to provide assurance that you are building everything properly. If this is your first foray into Cassandra, then get ready to take your first steps into a larger world.

In this chapter, we will cover the following topics:

- Introduction to Cassandra
- Installation and configuration
- Starting up and shutting down Cassandra
- **Cassandra Cluster Manager (CCM)**

By the end of this chapter, you will have built a single-node cluster of Apache Cassandra. This will be a good exercise to help you start to see some of the configuration and thought that goes into building a larger cluster. As this chapter progresses and the material gets more complex, you will start to connect the dots and understand exactly what is happening between installation, operation, and development.

Introduction to Cassandra

Apache Cassandra is a highly available, distributed, partitioned row store. It is one of the more popular NoSQL databases used by both small and large companies all over the world to store and efficiently retrieve large amounts of data. While there are licensed, proprietary versions available (which include enterprise support), Cassandra is also a top-level project of the Apache Software Foundation, and has deep roots in the open source community. This makes Cassandra a proven and battle-tested approach to scaling high-throughput applications.

High availability

Cassandra's design is premised on the points outlined in the *Dynamo: Amazon's Highly Available Key-value Store* paper (`https://www.allthingsdistributed.com/files/amazon-dynamo-sosp2007.pdf`). Specifically, when you have large networks of interconnected hardware, something is always in a state of failure. In reality, every piece of hardware being in a healthy state is the exception, rather than the rule. Therefore, it is important that a data storage system is able to deal with (and account for) issues such as network or disk failure.

Depending on the **Replication Factor** (**RF**) and required consistency level, a Cassandra cluster is capable of sustaining operations with one or two nodes in a failure state. For example, let's assume that a cluster with a single data center has a keyspace configured for a RF of three. This means that the cluster contains three copies of each row of data. If an application queries with a consistency level of one, then it can still function properly with one or two nodes in a down state.

Distributed

Cassandra is known as a **distributed database**. A Cassandra cluster is a collection of nodes (individual instances running Cassandra) all working together to serve the same dataset. Nodes can also be grouped together into logical data centers. This is useful for providing data locality for an application or service layer, as well as for working with Cassandra instances that have been deployed in different regions of a public cloud.

Cassandra clusters can scale to suit both expanding disk footprint and higher operational throughput. Essentially, this means that each cluster becomes responsible for a smaller percentage of the total data size. Assuming that the 500 GB disks of a six node cluster (RF of three) start to reach their maximum capacity, then adding three more nodes (for a total of nine) accomplishes the following:

- Brings the total disk available to the cluster up from 3 TB to 4.5 TB
- The percentage of data that each node is responsible for drops from 50% down to 33%

Additionally, let's assume that before the expansion of the cluster (from the prior example), the cluster was capable of supporting 5,000 operations per second. Cassandra scales linearly to support operational throughput. After increasing the cluster from six nodes to nine, the cluster should then be expected to support 7,500 operations per second.

Partitioned row store

In Cassandra, rows of data are stored in tables based on the hashed value of the partition key, called a **token**. Each node in the cluster is assigned multiple token ranges, and rows are stored on nodes that are responsible for their tokens.

Each keyspace (collection of tables) can be assigned a RF. The RF designates how many copies of each row should be stored in each data center. If a keyspace has a RF of three, then each node is assigned primary, secondary, and tertiary token ranges. As data is written, it is written to all of the nodes that are responsible for its token.

Installation

To get started with Cassandra quickly, we'll step through a single-node, local installation.

The following are the requirements to run Cassandra locally:

- A flavor of Linux or macOS
- A system with between 4 GB and 16 GB of **random access memory** (**RAM**)
- A local installation of the **Java Development Kit** (**JDK**) version 8, latest patch
- A local installation of Python 2.7 (for cqlsh)
- Your user must have sudo rights to your local system

While you don't need to have sudo rights to run Apache Cassandra, it is required for some of the operating system configurations.

Apache Cassandra 3.11.2 breaks with JDK 1.8.0_161. Make sure to use either an older or newer version of the JDK.

Head to the Apache download site for the Cassandra project (`http://cassandra.apache.org/download/`), choose 3.11.2, and select a mirror to download the latest version of Cassandra. When complete, copy the `.tar` or `.gzip` file to a location that your user has read and write permissions for. This example will assume that this is going to be the `~/local/` directory:

```
mkdir ~/local
cd ~/local
cp ~/Downloads/apache-cassandra-3.11.2-bin.tar.gz  .
```

Untar the file to create your `cassandra` directory:

```
tar -zxvf apache-cassandra-3.11.2-bin.tar.gz
```

Some people prefer to rename this directory, like so:

```
mv apache-cassandra-3.11.2/ cassandra/
```

Configuration

At this point, you could start your node with no further configuration. However, it is good to get into the habit of checking and adjusting the properties that are indicated as follows.

cassandra.yaml

It is usually a good idea to rename your cluster. Inside the `conf/cassandra.yaml` file, specify a new `cluster_name` property, overwriting the default `Test Cluster`:

```
cluster_name: 'PermanentWaves'
```

The `num_tokens` property default of `256` has proven to be too high for the newer, 3.x versions of Cassandra. Go ahead and set that to `24`:

```
num_tokens: 24
```

To enable user security, change the `authenticator` and `authorizer` properties (from their defaults) to the following values:

```
authenticator: PasswordAuthenticator
authorizer: CassandraAuthorizer
```

Cassandra installs with all security disabled by default. Even if you are not concerned with security on your local system, it makes sense to enable it to get used to working with authentication and authorization from a development perspective.

By default, Cassandra will come up bound to `localhost` or `127.0.0.1`. For your own local development machine, this is probably fine. However, if you want to build a multi-node cluster, you will want to bind to your machine's IP address. For this example, I will use `192.168.0.101`. To configure the node to bind to this IP, adjust the `listen_address` and `rpc_address` properties:

```
listen_address: 192.168.0.101
rpc_address: 192.168.0.101
```

If you set `listen_address` and `rpc_address`, you'll also need to adjust your seed list (defaults to `127.0.0.1`) as well:

```
seeds: 192.168.0.101
```

I will also adjust my `endpoint_snitch` property to use `GossipingPropertyFileSnitch`:

```
endpoint_snitch: GossipingPropertyFileSnitch
```

cassandra-rackdc.properties

In terms of NoSQL databases, Apache Cassandra handles multi-data center awareness better than any other. To configure this, each node must use `GossipingPropertyFileSnitch` (as previously mentioned in the preceding `cassandra.yaml` configuration process) and must have its local data center (and `rack`) settings defined. Therefore, I will set the `dc` and `rack` properties in the `conf/cassandra-rackdc.properties` file:

```
dc=ClockworkAngels
rack=R40
```

Starting Cassandra

To start Cassandra locally, execute the Cassandra script. If no arguments are passed, it will run in the foreground. To have it run in the background, send the -p flag with a destination file for the **Process ID (PID)**:

```
cd cassandra
bin/cassandra -p cassandra.pid
```

This will store the PID of the Cassandra process in a file named cassandra.pid in the local/cassandra directory. Several messages will be dumped to the screen. The node is successfully running when you see this message:

```
Starting listening for CQL clients on localhost/192.168.0.101:9042
(unencrypted).
```

This can also be verified with the nodetool status command:

```
bin/nodetool status

Datacenter: ClockworkAngels
===========================
Status=Up/Down
|/ State=Normal/Leaving/Joining/Moving
--  Address        Load       Tokens  Owns (effective)  Host ID      Rack
UN  192.168.0.101  71.26 KiB 24       100.0%            0edb5efa...  R40
```

Cassandra Cluster Manager

If you want an even faster way to install Cassandra, you can use an open source tool called CCM. CCM installs Cassandra for you, with very minimal configuration. In addition to ease of installation, CCM also allows you to run multiple Cassandra nodes locally.

First, let's clone the CCM repository from GitHub, and cd into the directory:

```
git clone https://github.com/riptano/ccm.git
cd ccm
```

Next, we'll run the setup program to install CCM:

```
sudo ./setup.py install
```

To verify that my local cluster is working, I'll invoke `nodetool status` via `node1`:

```
ccm node1 status

Datacenter: datacenter1
========================
Status=Up/Down
|/ State=Normal/Leaving/Joining/Moving
--  Address      Load Tokens          Owns (effective)  Host ID       Rack
UN  127.0.0.1    100.56 KiB 1         66.7%             49ecc8dd...   rack1
UN  127.0.0.2     34.81 KiB 1         66.7%             404a8f97...   rack1
UN  127.0.0.3     34.85 KiB 1         66.7%             eed33fc5...   rack1
```

To shut down your cluster, go ahead and send the `stop` command to each node:

```
ccm stop node1
ccm stop node2
ccm stop node3
```

Note that CCM requires a working installation of Python 2.7 or later, as well as a few additional libraries (`pyYAML`, `six`, `ant`, and `psutil`), and local IPs `127.0.0.1` through `127.0.0.3` to be available. Visit `https://github.com/riptano/ccm` for more information.

> Using CCM actually changes many of the commands that we will follow in this book. While it is a great tool for quickly spinning up a small cluster for demonstration purposes, it can complicate the process of learning how to use Cassandra.

A quick introduction to the data model

Now that we have a Cassandra cluster running on our local machine, we will demonstrate its use with some quick examples. We will start with cqlsh, and use that as our primary means of working with the Cassandra data model.

Using Cassandra with cqlsh

To start working with Cassandra, let's start the **Cassandra Query Language** (**CQL**) shell . The shell interface will allow us to execute CQL commands to define, query, and modify our data. As this is a new cluster and we have turned on authentication and authorization, we will use the default `cassandra` and `cassandra` username and password, as follows:

```
bin/cqlsh 192.168.0.101 -u cassandra -p cassandra

Connected to PermanentWaves at 192.168.0.101:9042.
[cqlsh 5.0.1 | Cassandra 3.11.2 | CQL spec 3.4.4 | Native protocol v4]
Use HELP for help.
cassandra@cqlsh>
```

First, let's tighten up security. Let's start by creating a new superuser to work with.

New users can only be created if authentication and authorization are properly set in the `cassandra.yaml` file:

```
cassandra@cqlsh> CREATE ROLE cassdba WITH PASSWORD='flynnLives' AND
LOGIN=true and SUPERUSER=true;
```

Now, set the default `cassandra` user to something long and indecipherable. You shouldn't need to use it ever again:

```
cassandra@cqlsh> ALTER ROLE cassandra WITH
PASSWORD='dsfawesomethingdfhdfshdlongandindecipherabledfhdfh';
```

Then, exit cqlsh using the `exit` command and log back in as the new `cassdba` user:

```
cassandra@cqlsh> exit
bin/cqlsh 192.168.0.101 -u cassdba -p flynnLives

Connected to PermanentWaves at 192.168.0.101:9042.
[cqlsh 5.0.1 | Cassandra 3.11.2 | CQL spec 3.4.4 | Native protocol v4]
Use HELP for help.
cassdba@cqlsh>
```

Now, let's create a new keyspace where we can put our tables, as follows:

```
cassdba@cqlsh> CREATE KEYSPACE packt WITH replication =
  {'class': 'NetworkTopologyStrategy', 'ClockworkAngels': '1'}
  AND durable_writes = true;
```

For those of you who have used Cassandra before, you might be tempted to build your local keyspaces with `SimpleStrategy`. `SimpleStrategy` has no benefits over `NetworkTopologyStrategy`, and is limited in that it cannot be used in a plural data center environment. Therefore, it is a good idea to get used to using it on your local instance as well.

With the newly created keyspace, let's go ahead and `use` it:

```
cassdba@cqlsh> use packt;
cassdba@cqlsh:packt>
```

The cqlsh prompt changes depending on the user and keyspace currently being used.

Now, let's assume that we have a requirement to build a table for video game scores. We will want to keep track of the player by their `name`, as well as their `score` and `game` on which they achieved it. A table to store this data would look something like this:

```
CREATE TABLE hi_scores (name TEXT, game TEXT, score BIGINT,
    PRIMARY KEY (name,game));
```

Next, we will `INSERT` data into the table, which will help us understand some of Cassandra's behaviors:

```
INSERT INTO hi_scores (name, game, score) VALUES ('Dad','Pacman',182330);
INSERT INTO hi_scores (name, game, score) VALUES
('Dad','Burgertime',222000);
INSERT INTO hi_scores (name, game, score) VALUES ('Dad','Frogger',15690);
INSERT INTO hi_scores (name, game, score) VALUES ('Dad','Joust',48150);
INSERT INTO hi_scores (name, game, score) VALUES
('Connor','Pacman',182330);
INSERT INTO hi_scores (name, game, score) VALUES ('Connor','Monkey
Kong',15800);
INSERT INTO hi_scores (name, game, score) VALUES ('Connor','Frogger',4220);
INSERT INTO hi_scores (name, game, score) VALUES ('Connor','Joust',48850);
INSERT INTO hi_scores (name, game, score) VALUES ('Avery','Galaga',28880);
INSERT INTO hi_scores (name, game, score) VALUES
('Avery','Burgertime',1200);
INSERT INTO hi_scores (name, game, score) VALUES ('Avery','Frogger',1100);
INSERT INTO hi_scores (name, game, score) VALUES ('Avery','Joust',19520);
```

Now, let's execute a CQL query to retrieve the scores of the player named `Connor`:

```
cassdba@cqlsh:packt> SELECT * FROM hi_scores WHERE name='Connor';
 name    | game        | score
---------+-------------+--------
 Connor  |     Frogger | 4220
 Connor  |       Joust | 48850
 Connor  | Monkey Kong | 15800
 Connor  |      Pacman | 182330
(4 rows)
```

That works pretty well. But what if we want to see how all of the players did while playing the `Joust` game, as follows:

```
cassdba@cqlsh:packt> SELECT * FROM hi_scores WHERE game='Joust';

InvalidRequest: Error from server: code=2200 [Invalid query]
message="Cannot execute this query as it might involve data filtering and
thus may have unpredictable performance. If you want to execute this query
despite the performance unpredictability, use ALLOW FILTERING"
```

As stated in the preceding error message, this query could be solved by adding the `ALLOW FILTERING` directive. Queries using `ALLOW FILTERING` are notorious for performing poorly, so it is a good idea to build your data model so that you do not use it.

Evidently, Cassandra has some problems with that query. We'll discuss more about why that is the case later on. But, for now, let's build a table that specifically supports querying high scores by `game`:

```
CREATE TABLE hi_scores_by_game (name TEXT, game TEXT, score BIGINT,
  PRIMARY KEY (game,score)) WITH CLUSTERING ORDER BY (score DESC);
```

Now, we will duplicate our data into our new query table:

```
INSERT INTO hi_scores_by_game (name, game, score) VALUES
('Dad','Pacman',182330);
INSERT INTO hi_scores_by_game (name, game, score) VALUES
('Dad','Burgertime',222000);
INSERT INTO hi_scores_by_game (name, game, score) VALUES
('Dad','Frogger',15690);
INSERT INTO hi_scores_by_game (name, game, score) VALUES
('Dad','Joust',48150);
INSERT INTO hi_scores_by_game (name, game, score) VALUES
('Connor','Pacman',182330);
INSERT INTO hi_scores_by_game (name, game, score) VALUES ('Connor','Monkey
Kong',15800);
```

```
INSERT INTO hi_scores_by_game (name, game, score) VALUES
('Connor','Frogger',4220);
INSERT INTO hi_scores_by_game (name, game, score) VALUES
('Connor','Joust',48850);
INSERT INTO hi_scores_by_game (name, game, score) VALUES
('Avery','Galaga',28880);
INSERT INTO hi_scores_by_game (name, game, score) VALUES
('Avery','Burgertime',1200);
INSERT INTO hi_scores_by_game (name, game, score) VALUES
('Avery','Frogger',1100);
INSERT INTO hi_scores_by_game (name, game, score) VALUES
('Avery','Joust',19520);
```

Now, let's try to query while filtering on game with our new table:

```
cassdba@cqlsh:packt> SELECT * FROM hi_scores_by_game
                            WHERE game='Joust';

 game  | score | name
-------+-------+---------
 Joust | 48850 |  Connor
 Joust | 48150 |     Dad
 Joust | 19520 |   Avery
(3 rows)
```

As mentioned previously, the following chapters will discuss why and when Cassandra only allows certain PRIMARY KEY components to be used in the WHERE clause. The important thing to remember at this point is that in Cassandra, tables and data structures should be modeled according to the queries that they are intended to serve.

Shutting down Cassandra

Before shutting down your cluster instances, there are some additional commands that should be run. Again, with your own, local node(s), these are not terribly necessary. But it is a good idea to get used to running these, should you ever need to properly shut down a production node that may contain data that people actually care about.

First, we will disable gossip. This keeps other nodes from communicating with the node while we are trying to bring it down:

```
bin/nodetool disablegossip
```

Next, we will disable the native binary protocol to keep this node from serving client requests:

```
bin/nodetool disablebinary
```

Then, we will drain the node. This will prevent it from accepting writes, and force all in-memory data to be written to disk:

```
bin/nodetool drain
```

With the node drained, we can kill the PID:

```
kill 'cat cassandra.pid'
```

We can verify that the node has stopped by tailing the log:

```
tail logs/system.log
```

```
INFO   [RMI TCP Connection(2)-127.0.0.1] 2018-03-31 17:49:05,789
StorageService.java:2292 - Node localhost/192.168.0.101 state jump to
shutdown
INFO   [RMI TCP Connection(4)-127.0.0.1] 2018-03-31 17:49:49,492
Server.java:176 - Stop listening for CQL clients
INFO   [RMI TCP Connection(6)-127.0.0.1] 2018-03-31 17:50:11,312
StorageService.java:1449 - DRAINING: starting drain process
INFO   [RMI TCP Connection(6)-127.0.0.1] 2018-03-31 17:50:11,313
HintsService.java:220 - Paused hints dispatch
INFO   [RMI TCP Connection(6)-127.0.0.1] 2018-03-31 17:50:11,314
Gossiper.java:1540 - Announcing shutdown
INFO   [RMI TCP Connection(6)-127.0.0.1] 2018-03-31 17:50:11,314
StorageService.java:2292 - Node localhost/192.168.0.101 state jump to
shutdown
INFO   [RMI TCP Connection(6)-127.0.0.1] 2018-03-31 17:50:13,315
MessagingService.java:984 - Waiting for messaging service to quiesce
INFO   [ACCEPT-localhost/192.168.0.101] 2018-03-31 17:50:13,316
MessagingService.java:1338 - MessagingService has terminated the accept()
thread
INFO   [RMI TCP Connection(6)-127.0.0.1] 2018-03-31 17:50:14,764
HintsService.java:220 - Paused hints dispatch
INFO   [RMI TCP Connection(6)-127.0.0.1] 2018-03-31 17:50:14,861
StorageService.java:1449 - DRAINED
```

Summary

In this chapter, we introduced Apache Cassandra and some of its design considerations and components. These aspects were discussed and a high level description of each was given, as well as how each affects things like cluster layout and data storage. Additionally, we built our own local, single-node cluster. CCM was also introduced, with minimal discussion. Some basic commands with Cassandra's nodetool were introduced and put to use.

With a single-node cluster running, the cqlsh tool was introduced. We created a keyspace that will work in a plural data center configuration. The concept of query tables was also introduced, as well as running some simple read and write operations.

In the next chapter, we will take an in-depth look at Cassandra's underlying architecture, and understand what is key to making good decisions about cluster deployment and data modeling. From there, we'll discuss various aspects to help fine-tune a production cluster and its deployment process. That will bring us to monitoring and application development, and put you well on your way to mastering Cassandra!

2
Cassandra Architecture

In this chapter, we will discuss the architecture behind Apache Cassandra in detail. We will discuss how Cassandra was designed and how it adheres to the **Brewer's CAP** theorem, which will give us insight into the reasons for its behavior. Specifically, this chapter will cover:

- Problems that Cassandra was designed to solve
- Cassandra's read and write paths
- The role that horizontal scaling plays
- How data is stored on-disk
- How Cassandra handles failure scenarios

This chapter will help you to build a good foundation of understanding that will prove very helpful later on. Knowing how Apache Cassandra works under the hood helps for later tasks around operations. Building high-performing, scalable data models is also something that requires an understanding of the architecture, and your architecture can be the difference between an unsuccessful or a successful cluster.

Why was Cassandra created?

Understanding how Apache Cassandra works under the hood can greatly improve your chances of running a successful cluster or application. We will reach that understanding by asking some simple, fundamental questions. What types of problems was Cassandra designed to solve? Why does a **relational database management system** (**RDBMS**) have difficulty handling those problems? If Cassandra works this way, how should I design my data model to achieve the best performance?

RDBMS and problems at scale

As the internet grew in popularity around the turn of the century, the systems behind internet architecture began to change. When good ideas were built into popular websites, user traffic increased exponentially. It was not uncommon in 2001 for too much web traffic being the reason for a popular site being slow or a web server going down. Web architects quickly figured out that they could build out multiple instances of their website or application, and distribute traffic with load balancers.

While this helped, some parts of web architectures were difficult to scale out, and remained bottlenecks for performance. Key among them was the database. This problem was further illustrated by Dr. Eric Brewer and Dr. Armando Fox, in their 1999 paper *Harvest, Yield, and Scalable Tolerant Systems* (http://lab.mscs.mu.edu/Dist2012/lectures/HarvestYield.pdf). This paper was key in describing how large-scale systems would have to be built in the future, in that achieving only two of **consistency**, **availability**, and [network] **partition tolerance** were possible at any one time. The points discussed in Brewer and Fox's paper would go on to be commonly referred to as Brewer's CAP theorem.

This is significant, because when a relational database receives so much traffic that it cannot serve requests, there is little that can be done. Relational databases are both highly-available and consistent, at the expense of not being tolerant to network interruptions (partitions). This is ultimately due to their single-instance, monolithic design.

Perhaps the only way to give relational databases more resources to work with was to scale vertically. This meant adding things such as RAM, CPU cores, and disks to the existing machine instance. While vertical scaling helped to alleviate some of the problems presented by the web scale, it was limited by how many resources the single server architecture could support. It wouldn't be long before vertical scaling was revealed as a band-aid, and the problem would soon present itself again.

NoSQL databases largely came about as new and innovative ways to solve this problem. The key idea was that data could be distributed across multiple instances—providing more resources to a distributed dataset, simply by adding more instances. This practice became known as horizontal scaling. This design required selecting network partition tolerance as an early design choice. Whether more importance was to be placed on data consistency or high availability was largely driven by whichever problem the system architects were trying to solve.

Cassandra and the CAP theorem

Many of the design ideas behind Apache Cassandra were largely influenced by Amazon Dynamo. It embraced partition-tolerance to be able to scale horizontally when needed, as well as to reduce the likelihood of an outage due to having a single point of failure. Cassandra also prefers to serve its data in a highly-available fashion, and embraces the concept of eventual consistency:

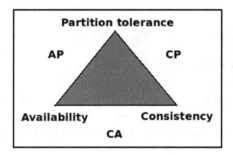

Figure 2.1: A graphical representation of Brewer's CAP theorem, using sides of a triangle to represent the combination of the different properties of consistency, availability, and partition tolerance

When data is written, it is replicated to multiple instances. During this process, it is possible that one (or more) of the replica writes could fail. Reads for this data would then return stale or dirty results. However, one of the design choices for Cassandra was that the possibility of serving stale data outweighed the risk of a request failing. This clearly gives Cassandra a CAP designation as an **AP** database.

Cassandra's ring architecture

An aspect of Cassandra's architecture that demonstrates its AP CAP designation is in how each instance works together. A single-instance running in Cassandra is known as a **node**. A group of nodes serving the same dataset is known as a **cluster** or **ring**. Data written is distributed around the nodes in the cluster. The partition key of the data is hashed to determine it's **token**. The data is sent to the nodes responsible for the token ranges that contain the hashed token value.

 The consistent hashing algorithm is used in many distributed systems, because it has intrinsic ways of dealing with changing range assignments. You can refer to *Cassandra High Availability* by Strickland R. (2014), published by Packt.

The partition key (formerly known as a **row key**) is the first part of PRIMARY KEY, and the key that determines the row's token or placement in the cluster. PRIMARY KEY components will be further discussed in the Chapter 3, *Effective CQL* .

Each node is also assigned additional, ancillary token ranges, depending on the replication factor specified. Therefore, data written at an RF of three will be written to one primary node, as well as a secondary and tertiary node.

Partitioners

The component that helps to determine the nodes responsible for specific partitions of data is known as the partitioner. Apache Cassandra installs with three partitioners. You can refer to Apache Cassandra 3.0 for DSE 5.0, *Understanding the Architecture*. Retrieved on 20180404 from: https://docs.datastax.com/en/cassandra/3.0/cassandra/architecture/archTOC.html. Partitioners differ from each other in both efficiency and data-distribution strategy.

ByteOrderedPartitioner

ByteOrderedPartitioner sorts rows in the cluster lexically by partition key. Queried results are then returned ordered by that key. Tokens are calculated by the hexadecimal value of the beginning of the partition key.

When we discuss data modeling and CQL later on, the ability to order a result set by a partition key may seem like a good idea. But there are several problems with this partitioner. Foremost among them is that data distribution typically suffers.

RandomPartitioner

RandomPartitioner was the default partitioner prior to Apache Cassandra 1.2. Tokens are calculated using a MD5 hash of the complete partition key. Possible token values range from zero to (2^{127}) - 1. For additional information you can refer to Saha S. (2017). *The Gossip Protocol - Inside Apache Cassandra*. Retrieved on 20180422 from: https://www.linkedin.com/pulse/gossip-protocol-inside-apache-cassandra-soham-saha/

Murmur3Partitioner

`Murmur3Partitioner` is an improvement in efficiency over `RandomPartitioner`, and is currently the default partitioner. The **murmur3** hashing algorithm is more efficient, because Cassandra does not really need the extra benefits provided by a cryptographic hash (MD5). Possible token values range from $-(2^{63})$ to $(2^{63})-1$.

Important points about Apache Cassandra's partitioners:

- A partitioner is configured at the cluster level. You cannot implement a partitioner at the keyspace or table level.
- Partitioners are not compatible. Once you select a partitioner, it cannot be changed without completely reloading the data.
- Use of `ByteOrderedPartitioner` is considered to be an anti-pattern.
- `Murmur3Partitioner` is an improvement on the efficiency of `RandomPartitioner`.

`Murmur3Partitioner` is the default partitioner, and should be used in new cluster builds.

> `ByteOrderedPartitioner` and `RandomPartitioner` are still delivered with Apache Cassandra for backward compatibility, providing older implementations with the ability to upgrade.

Single token range per node

Prior to Apache Cassandra 1.2, nodes were assigned contiguous ranges of token values. With this approach, token ranges had to be computed and configured manually, by setting the `initial_token` property in `cassandra.yaml`. A possible token distribution (using `Murmur3Partitioner`) with single token ranges assigned per node is as follows:

Node #	Start token	End token
0	5534023222112865485	-9223372036854775808
1	-9223372036854775807	-5534023222112865485
2	-5534023222112865484	-1844674407370955162
3	-1844674407370955161	1844674407370955161
4	1844674407370955162	5534023222112865484

Table 2.1: An example of the token range assignments for a five-node cluster, where each node is assigned responsibility for a single, contiguous token range

With one node responsible for a single, contiguous token range, nodes would follow each other in the ring. When rows are written to the node determined by the hashed token value of their partition key, their remaining replicas are written to ancillary ranges on additional nodes. The additional nodes designated to hold secondary ranges of data are determined by walking the ring (or data center, depending on replication strategy) in a clockwise direction:

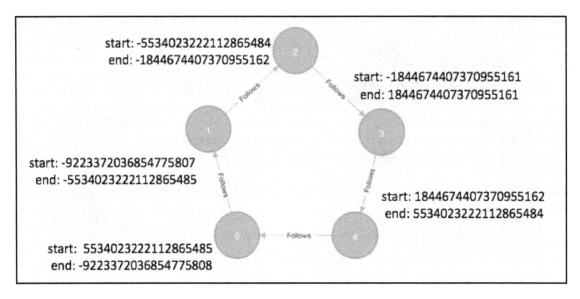

Figure 2.2: A five-node cluster (non-vnodes) illustrating how one node follows another based on their start and end token ranges

For example, consider the `hi_scores_by_game` table from the previous chapter. As that table uses `game` as its partition key, data stored in that table will be written to a node based on the hash of the value it has for `game`. If we were to store data for the `Pacman` game, its hashed token value would look like this:

```
cassdba@cqlsh:packt&gt; SELECT game, token(game)
    FROM hi_scores_by_game WHERE game=Pacman;

game         | system.token(game)
-------------+----------------------
    Pacman   | 4538621633640690522
```

The partition key value of `Pacman` hashes to a token of `4538621633640690522`. Based on the figures depicting the preceding five-node cluster, node four is primarily responsible for this data, as the token falls between `1844674407370955162` and `5534023222112865484`.

Now let's assume that the `packt` keyspace has the following definition:

```
CREATE KEYSPACE packt WITH replication =
  {'class': 'NetworkTopologyStrategy', 'ClockworkAngels': '3'}
  AND durable_writes = true;
```

If all five of the nodes are in the `ClockworkAngels` data center, then the nodes responsible for the two additional replicas can be found by traversing the ring in a clockwise manner. In this case, node zero is responsible for the second replica of the `Pacman` high score data, and node one is responsible for the third replica.

> `NetworkTopologyStrategy` also takes logical rack definition into account. When determining additional replica placement, this strategy will attempt to place replicas on different racks, to help maintain availability in the event of a rack failure scenario.

Vnodes

Newer versions of Apache Cassandra have an option to use virtual nodes, better known as **vnodes**. Using vnodes, each node is assigned several non-contiguous token ranges. This helps the cluster to better balance its data load:

Node #	Token ranges
0	79935 to -92233, -30743 to -18446, 55341 to 67638
1	-92232 to -79935, -61488 to 61489, 43043 to 55340
2	-79934 to -67638, -43041 to -30744, 67639 to 79935
3	-67637 to -55340, 61490 to 18446,18447 to 30744
4	-55339 to -43042, -18445 to -61489, 30745 to 43042

Table 2.2: An example of the token range distribution for a five-node cluster using vnodes. Each node is assigned responsibility for three, non-contiguous token ranges. Smaller numbers were used in this example for brevity.

While the application of virtual nodes may seem more chaotic, it has several benefits over single, manually-specified token ranges per node:

- Provides better data distribution over manually-assigned tokens.
- More numerous, multiple token ranges per node allows multiple nodes to participate in bootstrapping and streaming data to a new node.
- Allows for automatic token range recalculation. This is useful when new nodes are added to the cluster, to prevent the existing nodes from needing to be reconfigured and bounced (restarted).

Cassandra 3.0 uses a new token-allocation algorithm that allows the distribution of data to be optimized for a specific keyspace. Invoking this algorithm is only possible when using vnodes and `Murmur3Partitioner`. It requires that a keyspace be specified for the `allocate_tokens_for_keyspace` property in the `cassandra.yaml` file. You can refer to Apache Software Foundation (2016). Documentation: *Adding, replacing, moving and removing nodes*, retrieved on 20180418 from: `http://cassandra.apache.org/doc/latest/operating/topo_changes.html`.

Cassandra's write path

Understanding how Cassandra handles writes is key to knowing how to build applications on top of it. The following is a high-level diagram of how the Cassandra write path works:

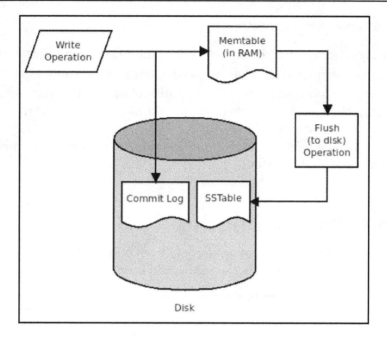

Figure 2.3: An illustration of the Cassandra write path, showing how writes are applied both to in-memory and on-disk structures

When a write operation reaches a node, it is persisted in two places. There is an in-memory structure known as a **memtable**, which gets the write. Additionally, the new data is written to the commit log, which is on-disk.

 The commit log is Cassandra's way of enforcing durability in the case of a *plug-out-of-the-wall* event. When a node is restarted, the commit log is verified against what is stored on-disk and replayed if necessary.

Once a flush of the memtable is triggered, the data stored in memory is written to the sorted string table files (**SSTables**) on-disk. The data is sorted by token value in memory, and then written to disk in sequential order. This is why Cassandra is known for its log-based, append-only storage engine.

Some quick notes about the write path:

- Data is sorted inside SSTables by token value, and then by clustering keys.
- SSTables are immutable. They are written once, and not modified afterward.
- Data written to the same partition key and column values does not update. The existing row is made obsolete (not deleted or overwritten) in favor of the timestamp of the new data.
- Data cannot be deleted. Deletes are considered to be writes, and are written as structures called **tombstones**.

Cassandra's read path

The Cassandra read path is somewhat more complex. Similar to the write path, structures in-memory and on-disk structures are examined, and then reconciled:

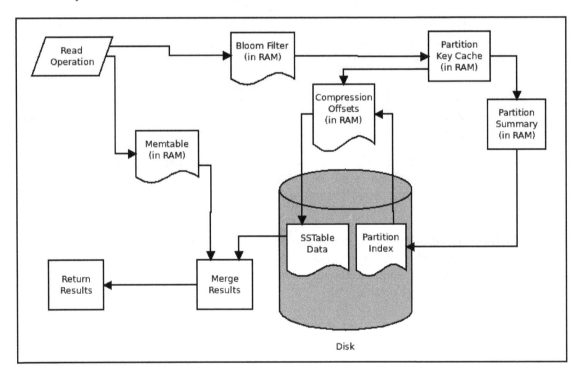

Figure 2.4: An illustration of the Cassandra read path, illustrating how the different in-memory and on-disk structures work together to satisfy query operations

As shown in the preceding figure, a node handling a read operation will send that request on two different paths. One path checks the memtables (in RAM) for the requested data.

If row-caching is enabled (it is disabled by default), it is checked for the requested row, followed by the bloom filter. The bloom filter (Ploetz, et-al 2018) is a probability-based structure in RAM, which speeds up reads from disk by determining which SSTables are likely to contain the requested data.

If the response from the bloom filter is negative, the partition key cache is examined. Unlike the row cache, the partition key cache is enabled by default, and its size is configurable (it defaults to the smaller value of either 5% of available heap or 100 MB). If the requested partition key is located within the partition key cache, its result is then sent to the compression offset. The compression offset is a dictionary/map that contains the on-disk locations for all partition data (SSTables).

If the partition key cache does not contain the requested key, the request is routed to the partition summary instead. There the requested key is examined to obtain a range of partitions for the key, which is then sent to the partition index. The partition index contains all of the partition keys which the node is responsible for. This, in conjunction with the resultant compression offset, will lead to the appropriate SSTable(s) on-disk. The appropriate values are then read, merged with any results obtained from the memtables, and the resultant dataset is returned.

Some structures in the read path are predicated on a negative search result from a prior step. Requesting data that does not exist still consumes compute resources, and may even exhibit higher read latencies than queries for data that does exist.

Some quick notes about the read path:

- Data is read sequentially from disk, and will be returned in that order. This can be controlled by the table's definition.
- Rows can persist across multiple SSTable files. This can slow reads down, so eventually SSTable data is reconciled and the files are condensed during a process called **compaction**.
- When data is read, its obsoleted or deleted values are read as well, and disregarded. Therefore data models allowing for multiple in-place writes and/or deletes will not perform well.

On-disk storage

When rows are written to disk, they are stored in different types of file. Let's take a quick look at these files, which should be present after what we did in Chapter 1, *Quick Start*.

 If you have not followed the examples from Chapter 1, *Quick Start*, that's okay. But some of the data to follow may be different for you.

SSTables

First of all, let's cd over to where our table data is stored. By default, keyspace and table data is stored in the data/ directory, off of the $CASSANDRA_HOME directory. Listing out the files reveals the following:

```
cd data/data/packt/hi_scores-d74bfc40634311e8a387e3d147c7be0f
ls -al
total 72
drwxr-xr-x  11 aploetz aploetz   374 May 29 08:28 .
drwxr-xr-x   6 aploetz aploetz   204 May 29 08:26 ..
-rw-r--r--   1 aploetz aploetz    43 May 29 08:28 mc-1-big-
CompressionInfo.db
-rw-r--r--   1 aploetz aploetz   252 May 29 08:28 mc-1-big-Data.db
-rw-r--r--   1 aploetz aploetz    10 May 29 08:28 mc-1-big-Digest.crc32
-rw-r--r--   1 aploetz aploetz    16 May 29 08:28 mc-1-big-Filter.db
-rw-r--r--   1 aploetz aploetz    27 May 29 08:28 mc-1-big-Index.db
-rw-r--r--   1 aploetz aploetz  4675 May 29 08:28 mc-1-big-Statistics.db
-rw-r--r--   1 aploetz aploetz    61 May 29 08:28 mc-1-big-Summary.db
-rw-r--r--   1 aploetz aploetz    92 May 29 08:28 mc-1-big-TOC.txt
```

The mc-1-big-TOC.txt file is the table of contents file for the directory. Listing its contents essentially shows the same list of files as we have previously. Some of the other files match up with parts of the Cassandra read path:

- mc-1-big-Index.db: Primary key index (matches partition keys to their data file positions)
- mc-1-big-Summary.db: Partition summary
- mc-1-big-CompressionInfo.db: Compression offsets
- mc-1-big-Filter.db: Bloom filter
- mc-1-big-Digest.crc32: Contains a **Cyclic Redundancy Check** (CRC) or **checksum** value for the uncompressed file chunks

The last file is `mc-1-big-Data.db`, which contains the data for the table. Listing out the contents of the file with a system tool, such as cat, will be cumbersome to read. So we will examine this file using some of the tools that come with Apache Cassandra.

How data was structured in prior versions

In Apache Cassandra versions 0.4 to 2.2, SSTable data was structured by row key. A row key kept a map of columns underneath it with their values. These columns were sorted by their column key. If you consider the key/value map structure from Java, it's easy to think of it as a map of a map.

As an example, consider the following CQL query from the previous chapter. Recall that it retrieves video game high-score data for a player named `Connor`:

```
cassdba@cqlsh:packt&gt; SELECT * FROM hi_scores WHERE name='Connor';
 name    | game         | score
---------+--------------+---------
 Connor  |      Frogger |    4220
 Connor  |        Joust |   48850
 Connor  | Monkey Kong  |   15800
 Connor  |       Pacman |  182330
(4 rows)
```

This CQL query and result set make sense in the way it is shown, mainly for those of us who have a background in relational databases. But this is not how the data is stored on-disk. In Apache Cassandra versions 1.2 to 2.2, CQL is simply a layer that abstracts the SSTable structure. If you were using Apache Cassandra 2.1 or earlier, this data could be viewed with the command-line interface tool, also known as `cassandra-cli`:

```
bin/cassandra-cli 192.168.0.101 -u cassdba -pw flynnLives
Connected to: "Rush" on 192.168.0.101/9160
Welcome to Cassandra CLI version 2.1.13
The CLI is deprecated and will be removed in Cassandra 2.2.  Consider
migrating to cqlsh.
CQL is fully backwards compatible with Thrift data; see
http://www.datastax.com/dev/blog/thrift-to-cql3
Type 'help;' or '?' for help.
Type 'quit;' or 'exit;' to quit.
[cassdba@unknown] use packt;
Authenticated to keyspace: packt
[default@packt] get hi_scores['Connor'];
Using default limit of 100
Using default cell limit of 100
-------------------
RowKey: Connor
```

```
=&gt; (name=Frogger:, value=, timestamp=1527640087988234)
=&gt; (name=Frogger:score, value=000000000000107c,
timestamp=1527640087988234)
=&gt; (name=Joust:, value=, timestamp=1527640087990162)
=&gt; (name=Joust:score, value=000000000000bed2,
timestamp=1527640087990162)
=&gt; (name=Monkey Kong:, value=, timestamp=1527640087986113)
=&gt; (name=Monkey Kong:score, value=0000000000003db8,
timestamp=1527640087986113)
=&gt; (name=Pacman:, value=, timestamp=1527640087984003)
=&gt; (name=Pacman:score, value=000000000002c83a,
timestamp=1527640087984003)
1 Rows Returned.
```

A few things to note here:

- We defined the partition key as the name column, which does not seem to be present here. But the get query works by simply retrieving data for RowKey of Connor.
- The game column was defined as our clustering key. Again, game itself is not present here, but we can see that the score recorded for each game seems to be keyed by the game's title (such as name=Frogger:score, value=000000000000107c, timestamp=1527640087988234).
- The CLI informs us that one row has been returned. As far as the storage layer is concerned, all cells (column keys and their values) constitute a single row.

The most important thing to remember from this example is that all data underneath a particular partition key is stored together. This is an important lesson that we will draw upon heavily in the next chapter.

How data is structured in newer versions

In versions of Apache Cassandra from 3.0 on, the underlying data is structured slightly differently. The Cassandra storage engine was rewritten as a part of this release, providing several benefits.

Consider the CQL query used as the basis for the prior example, where we queried our the hi_scores table for the player named Connor. If we were to look at the underlying data using the sstabledump tool, it would look something like this:

```
tools/bin/sstabledump
data/data/packt/hi_scores-73a9df80637b11e8836561ec0efea4b2/mc-1-big-Data.db
[ {
  "partition" : {
```

```
      "key" : [ "Connor" ],
      "position" : 0
    },
    "rows" : [
      {
        "type" : "row",
        "position" : 44,
        "clustering" : [ "Frogger" ],
        "liveness_info" : { "tstamp" : "2018-05-29T12:28:07.988225Z" },
        "cells" : [
          { "name" : "score", "value" : 4220 }
        ]
      },
      {
        "type" : "row",
        "position" : 44,
        "clustering" : [ "Joust" ],
        "liveness_info" : { "tstamp" : "2018-05-29T12:28:07.990283Z" },
        "cells" : [
          { "name" : "score", "value" : 48850 }
        ]
      },
      {
        "type" : "row",
        "position" : 66,
        "clustering" : [ "Monkey Kong" ],
        "liveness_info" : { "tstamp" : "2018-05-29T12:28:07.986579Z" },
        "cells" : [
          { "name" : "score", "value" : 15800 }
        ]
      },
      {
        "type" : "row",
        "position" : 94,
        "clustering" : [ "Pacman" ],
        "liveness_info" : { "tstamp" : "2018-05-29T12:28:07.984499Z" },
        "cells" : [
          { "name" : "score", "value" : 182330 }
        ]
      }
    ]
}
```

It's important to note from this JSON output that the data for `Connor` is divided into a hierarchy of three distinct sections: `partitions`, `rows`, and `cells`. Whereas before there were simply partitions containing cells of data, rows are now a first-class citizen in the Cassandra world. In this way, CQL is no longer an abstraction, but rather a fairly accurate representation of how the data is stored. This will be discussed in more detail in the next chapter.

 Even with the new storage engine, it is still important to note that all data underneath a particular partition key is stored together.

Additional components of Cassandra

Now that we have discussed the read and write paths of an individual Apache Cassandra node, let's move up a level and consider how all of the nodes work together. Keeping data consistent and serving requests in a way that treats multiple machines as a single data source requires some extra engineering. Here we'll explore the additional components which make that possible.

Gossiper

Gossiper is a peer-to-peer communication protocol that a node uses to communicate with the other nodes in the cluster. When the nodes gossip with each other, they share information about themselves and retrieve information on a subset of other nodes in the cluster. Eventually, this allows a node to store and understand state information about every other node in the cluster.

Each node's gossiper runs once per second (Saha 2017) and initiates communication with up to three other nodes. The gossip protocol first runs when the node is attempting to join the cluster. As a new node contains no information on the current network topology, it must be preconfigured with a list of current live nodes or `seeds` to help it start the communication process.

We will discuss the concept of seed nodes in Chapter 4, *Configuring a Cluster*. The most important thing to remember about them, is that they help new nodes discover the rest of the cluster's network topology when joining. All nodes are considered to be peers in Cassandra, and the seed-node designation does not change that.

You can view the currently perceived gossip state of any node using the `nodetool` utility on any node. The following command demonstrates what this looks like with a three-node cluster:

```
bin/nodetool gossipinfo

/192.168.0.101
  generation:1524418542
  heartbeat:462
  STATUS:14:NORMAL,-9223372036854775808
  LOAD:205:161177.0
  SCHEMA:10:ea63e099-37c5-3d7b-9ace-32f4c833653d
  DC:6:ClockworkAngels
  RACK:8:R40
  RELEASE_VERSION:4:3.11.2
  RPC_ADDRESS:3:192.168.0.101
  NET_VERSION:1:11
  HOST_ID:2:0edb5efa-de6e-4512-9f5d-fe733c7d448c
  RPC_READY:20:true
  TOKENS:15:&lt;hidden&gt;
/192.168.0.102
  generation:1524418547
  heartbeat:249
  STATUS:14:NORMAL,-3074457345618258603
  LOAD:205:49013.0
  SCHEMA:10:ea63e099-37c5-3d7b-9ace-32f4c833653d
  DC:6:ClockworkAngels
  RACK:8:R40
  RELEASE_VERSION:4:3.11.2
  RPC_ADDRESS:3:192.168.0.102
  NET_VERSION:1:11
  HOST_ID:2:404a8f97-f5f0-451f-8b72-43575fc874fc
  RPC_READY:27:true
  TOKENS:15:&lt;hidden&gt;
/192.168.0.103
  generation:1524418548
  heartbeat:248
  STATUS:14:NORMAL,3074457345618258602
  LOAD:205:54039.0
  SCHEMA:10:ea63e099-37c5-3d7b-9ace-32f4c833653d
  DC:6:ClockworkAngels
```

```
RACK:8:R40
RELEASE_VERSION:4:3.11.2
RPC_ADDRESS:3:192.168.0.103
NET_VERSION:1:11
HOST_ID:2:eed33fc5-98f0-4907-a02f-2a738e7af562
RPC_READY:26:true
TOKENS:15:&lt;hidden&gt;
```

As you can see, the gossip state of each node contains a wealth of information about it. Things such as status, data load, host ID, and schema version are readily visible. This is a good way to quickly gain an understanding of one node's view of the cluster.

> Remember, each node maintains its own view of the cluster's gossip state. While it should be the same on all nodes, it sometimes is not. It is entirely possible that some nodes can see certain nodes as down when other nodes do not. The `nodetool gossipinfo` command can be a valuable tool when troubleshooting firewall or network issues.

Snitch

Cassandra uses a component known as the snitch to direct read and write operations to the appropriate nodes. When an operation is sent to the cluster, it is the snitch's job (Williams 2012) to determine which nodes in specific data centers or racks can serve the request.

Most snitches that ship with Apache Cassandra are both data center- and rack-aware. That is, they are capable of viewing (predetermined) groups of nodes in the cluster as **logical data centers**. Additionally, the data centers can be further divided into logical racks.

> The term **logical** is used here because the data centers may or may not be physically separate from each other. That is, nodes in a single physical data center can be split into smaller data centers, and the snitch will enforce data-replication for each separately.

The replication of data per keyspace is defined in the keyspace definition using the configuration properties of `NetworkTopologyStrategy`. This can be seen in the following example keyspace definition:

```
CREATE KEYSPACE packt WITH replication = {
    'class': 'NetworkTopologyStrategy',
    'ClockworkAngels': '3',
    'PermanentWaves': '2'
};
```

In the previous example, we'll assume the use of `GossipingPropertyFileSnitch`, and that we have a number of nodes in our cluster assigned to our `ClockworkAngels` data center and some assigned to our `PermanentWaves` data center. When a write operation occurs on any of the tables stored in the `packt` keyspace, the snitch will ensure that three replicas of that data are written to the `ClockworkAngels` data center. Likewise, two replicas of the data will be written to the `PermanentWaves` data center.

As previously mentioned, the nodes in a data center can be further divided into racks. Let's assume that our `ClockworkAngels` data center has six nodes. To maintain the maximum amount of availability possible, we could divide them up like this:

```
Data center: ClockworkAngels
Node             Rack
========================
192.168.255.1    East_1
192.168.255.2    West_1
192.168.255.3    West_1
192.168.255.4    East_1
192.168.255.5    West_1
192.168.255.6    East_1
```

 Nodes in a data center are ordered by primary token range, not necessarily by IP address. This example was ordered by IP for simplicity.

Let's assume that our write has a partition key that hashes out to a primary range owned by `192.168.255.2`, which is in the `West_1` rack. The snitch will ensure that the first replica is written to `192.168.255.2`. Since our keyspace has an RF of three, the snitch will then walk the ring (clockwise by token ranges) to place the remaining replicas. As there are multiple racks, it will try to spread the replicas evenly across them. Therefore, it will place the second replica on `192.168.255.3`, which is in a different rack. As both racks are now covered from an availability perspective, the third replica will be placed on the next node, regardless of rack designation.

When working with physical data centers, entire racks have been known to fail. Likewise, entire availability zones have been known to fail in the cloud. Therefore, it makes sense to define logical racks with physical racks or **Availability Zones** (**AZs**) whenever possible. This configuration strategy provides the cluster with its best chance for remaining available in the event of a rack/AZ outage.

When defining your cluster, data center, and rack topology, it makes sense to build a number of nodes that evenly compliment your RF. For instance, with an RF of three, the snitch will spread the data evenly over a total of three, six, or nine nodes, split into three racks.

Phi failure-detector

Apache Cassandra uses an implementation of the **Phi Failure-Accrual** algorithm. The basic idea is that gossip between nodes is measured on a scale that adjusts to current network conditions. The results are compared to a preconfigured, static value (`phi_convict_threshold`) that helps a node decide whether another node should be marked as down. `phi_convict_threshold` will be discussed in later chapters.

Tombstones

Deletes in the world of distributed databases are hard to do. After all, how do you replicate nothing? Especially a key for nothing which once held a value. Tombstones are Cassandra's way of solving that problem.

As Cassandra uses a log-based storage engine, deletes are essentially writes. When data is deleted, a structure known as a **tombstone** is written. This tombstone exists so that it can be replicated to the other nodes that contained the deleted replica.

Discussion about tombstones tends to be more prevalent in Cassandra application-developer circles. This is primarily because their accumulation in large numbers can be problematic. Let's say that data is written for a specific key, then deleted, and then written and deleted three more times, before being written again. With the writes for that key being stored sequentially, SSTable data files that back that key will contain five possible values and four tombstones. Depending on how often that write pattern continues, there could be thousands of tombstoned and obsoleted stored across multiple files for that key. When that key is queried, there is essentially an accumulation of garbage that must be overlooked to find the actual, current value.

Accumulation of tombstones will result in slower queries over time. For this reason, use cases that require a high amount of delete activity are considered an anti-pattern with Apache Cassandra.

 The Apache Cassandra configuration has settings for warnings and failure thresholds regarding the number of tombstones that can be returned in a query.

Tombstones are eventually removed, but only after two specific conditions are met:

- The tombstone has existed longer than the table's defined `gc_grace_seconds` period
- Compaction runs on that table

The `gc_grace_seconds` stipulation exists to give the tombstone ample time to either replicate, or be fixed by a repair operation. After all, if tombstones are not adequately replicated, a read to a node that is missing a tombstone can result in data ghosting its way back into a result set.

Hinted handoff

When a node reports another as down, the node that is still up will store structures, known as **hints**, for the down node. Hints are essentially writes meant for one node that are temporarily stored on another. When the down node returns to a healthy status, the hints are then streamed to that node in an attempt to re-sync its data.

 As storage is finite, hints will be stored for up to three hours, by default. This means that a down node must be brought back within that time frame, or data loss will occur.

With Apache Cassandra versions older than 3.0, hints were stored in the hints table of the system keyspace. The problem with this approach is that once the stored hints were replayed, they were then deleted. This frequently led to warnings and failures due to tombstone accumulation. Apache Cassandra version 3.0 and up moved to a file-based system of hint storage, thus avoiding this problem so long as the `hints` directory has disk space available.

Compaction

As previously mentioned, once SSTable files are written to disk, they are immutable (cannot be written to again). Additional writes for that table would eventually result in additional SSTable files. As this process continues, it is possible for long-standing rows of data to be spread across multiple files. Reading multiple files to satisfy a query eventually becomes slow, especially when considering how obsolete data and tombstones must be reconciled (so as not to end up in the result set).

Apache Cassandra's answer to this problem is to periodically execute a process called **compaction**. When compaction runs, it performs the following functions:

- Multiple data files for a table are merged into a single data file
- Obsoleted data is removed
- Tombstones that have outlived the table's `gc_grace_seconds` period are removed

There are two different compaction strategies available with Apache Cassandra: `SizeTieredCompactionStrategy` and `LeveledCompactionStrategy`. These will be detailed in a later chapter. Compaction is configured on a per-table basis, and its configuration includes thresholds for determining how often compaction is run.

Cassandra does a good job of figuring out when compaction needs to be run. The best approach is to let it do what it needs to do. If it should be run sooner, then the configuration should be altered on the table in question. Forcing compaction (via the command line) to run outside of its configured thresholds has been known to drastically delay future compaction times.

Repair

Sometimes data replicas on one or more Cassandra nodes can get out of sync. There are a variety of reasons for this, including prior network instability, hardware failure, and nodes crashing and staying down past the three-hour hint window. When this happens, Apache Cassandra comes with a repair process that can be run to rectify these inconsistencies.

The repair process does not run on its own, and must be executed manually. Tools such as Reaper for Apache Cassandra allow for some automation, including scheduling cluster repairs.

Conditions that can cause data inconsistencies essentially do so by introducing factors that increase the entropy of the stored replicas. Therefore, Apache Cassandra employs an **anti-entropy** repair mechanism, which uses a binary Merkle tree to locate inconsistent replicas across different nodes. Discrepancies are then rectified by streaming the correct data from another node.

Merkle tree calculation

Merkle trees are created from the bottom up, starting with hashes of the base or leaf data. The leaf data is grouped together by partition ranges, and then it is hashed with the hash of its neighboring leaf to create a singular hash for their parent. Parents are hashed together with neighboring parents (to create their parents), until (Kozliner 2017) all have been combined into a single hash, known as the root. Based on the hash value of the root for a token range, the Merkle trees of different nodes can be quickly compared.

A Merkle tree calculation can consume high amounts of resources (CPU, disk I/O) on a node, which can result in temporary query timeouts as the node continues to try to serve requests. For this reason, it is best to run repairs during times when client requests are low. The Merkle tree calculation part of the repair processes can be monitored with `nodetool compactionstats`, where it will display as a **validation compaction**.

Let's walk through a quick example. Assume that we've added high scores for more users, we're running a repair on the `hi_scores` table, and we're only concerned about the token range of -9223372036854775807 to -7686143364045646507. We'll query our the `hi_scores` table for our users whose token value for `name` (our partition key) falls within that range:

```
cassdba@cqlsh&gt; SELECT DISTINCT name,token(name) FROM packt.hi_scores
   WHERE token(name) &gt;= -9223372036854775807
   AND token(name) &lt;= -7686143364045646507;

 name   | system.token(name)
--------+--------------------
 Connor | -8880179871968770066
    Rob | -8366205352999279036
    Dad | -8339008252759389761
   Ryan | -8246129210631849419

(4 rows)
```

Executing a range query on a partition key is only possible when also using the `token` function, as shown previously.

Now let's compute a hash (MD5 is used for this example) for all data within each partition:

Connor: h(dCo) = c13eb9350eb2e72eeb172c489faa3d7f

Rob: h(dRo) = 97ab517e5418ad2fe700ae45b0ffc5f3

Dad: h(dDa) = c9df57b434ad9a674a242e5c70587d8b

Ryan: h(dRy) = 9b961a89e744c86f5bffc1864b166514

To build a Merkle tree for this data, we start by listing each partition of hashed data separately, as leaf nodes. Then we will backtrack toward our root node by applying the hash function, `h()`, while combining our data recursively:

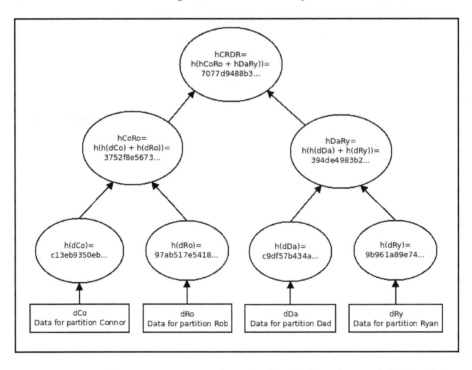

Figure 2.5: An example Merkle tree calculation for a node's token range containing four partitions of data. This illustrates how they are hashed and combined to compute the hash of the root (hCRDR).

Once the data for the partitions is hashed, it is then combined with its neighbor nodes to generate their parent node:

$$hCoRo = h(h(dCo) + h(dRo)) = 3752f8e5673ce8d4f53513aa2cabad40$$

$$hDaRy = h(h(dDa) + h(dRy)) = 394de4983b242dcd1603eecc35545a6d$$

Likewise, the final hash for the root node can be calculated as *Root node = hCRDR = h(hCoRo + hDaRy) = 7077d9488b37f4d39c908eb7560f2323*.

We can then perform this same Merkle tree calculation on another node (which is also responsible for the token range of -9223372036854775807 to -7686143364045646507). If all of the underlying data is consistent (and affirms our state of anti-entropy), they should all respond with a root node hash of *7077d9488b37f4d39c908eb7560f2323*. If one or more of them does not, the up-to-date node then prepares to stream a subset of the affected range of data to fix the inconsistency.

Streaming data

Once discrepancies are identified via Merkle trees, data files are streamed to the node containing the inconsistent data. Once this streaming completes, the data should be consistent across all replicas.

> Repair streams consume network resources that can also interfere with a node's ability to serve requests. Repair progress can be monitored using the `nodetool netstats` command.

Read repair

Read repair is a feature that allows for inconsistent data to be fixed at query time. `read_repair_chance` (and `dclocal_read_repair_chance`) is configured for each table, defaulting to 0.1 (10% chance). When it occurs (only with read consistency levels higher than ONE), Apache Cassandra will verify the consistency of the replica with all other nodes not involved in the read request. If the requested data is found to be inconsistent, it is fixed immediately.

Do note that read repairs do not occur when read consistency is set to ONE or LOCAL_ONE. Also, reads at a consistency level of all will force a read repair to happen 100% of the time. However, these read repairs do incur latency, which is why they are typically set to low percentages.

> Sometimes a single partition or key will be all that is inconsistent. If you find yourself in this situation, forcing a read repair is a simple task via cqlsh. If the number of inconsistent rows is a manageable number, you can fix them by setting your consistency level to all, and querying each of them.

Security

One criticism of NoSQL data stores is that security is often an afterthought. Cassandra is no exception to this view. In fact, Apache Cassandra will install with all security features initially disabled. While clusters should be built on secured networks behind enterprise-grade firewalls, by itself this is simply not enough. There are several features that Cassandra provides that can help to tighten up security on a cluster.

Authentication

Apache Cassandra allows for user authentication to be set up. Similar to other Cassandra components, users and their (encrypted) credentials are stored in a table inside the cluster. Client connections are required to provide valid username/password combinations before being allowed access to the cluster. To enable this functionality, simply change the authenticator property in the cassandra.yaml file from its default (AllowAllAuthenticator) to PasswordAuthenticator:

```
authenticator: PasswordAuthenticator
```

> Once you have created your own DBA-level superuser account for administrative purposes, you should never use the default cassandra user again. This is because the Cassandra user is the only user that has special provisions in the code to query the system_auth tables at a consistency level higher than ONE (it uses QUORUM). This means that the default Cassandra user may not be able to log in if multiple nodes are down.

When user authentication is enabled, Cassandra will create the system_auth keyspace. When using PasswordAuthenticator, CassandraRoleManager must also be used.

Authorization

With authentication set up, additionally enabling user authorization allows each user to be assigned specific permissions to different Cassandra objects. In Apache Cassandra versions 2.2 and up, users are referred to as **roles**. With authorization enabled, roles can be assigned the following permissions via CQL:

- ALTER: Change table or keyspace definitions
- AUTHORIZE: Grant or revoke specific permissions to other users
- CREATE:: Create new tables or keyspaces
- DESCRIBE: Retrieve definitions of a table or keyspace
- DROP: Delete specific tables or keyspaces
- EXECUTE: Run functions in a specific keyspace
- MODIFY: Run DELETE, INSERT, UPDATE, or TRUNCATE commands on a specific table
- SELECT: Query a specific table
- ALL PERMISSIONS: No restricted access on specific tables or keyspaces

The following are some examples:

```
GRANT SELECT ON KEYSPACE item TO item_app_readonly;
GRANT MODIFY ON KEYSPACE store TO store_app_user;
GRANT ALL PERMISSIONS ON KEYSPACE mobile TO mobile_admin;
```

Managing roles

As role-management is part of the user security backend, it requires PasswordAuthenticator to be enabled before its functionality is activated. The role system allows you to assign permissions to a role, and then GRANT access to that role for another user/role. As mentioned in the previous section, role management is new as of Apache Cassandra 2.2, and can greatly simplify user-management and permission-assignment.

Here is an example:

```
CREATE ROLE cassdba WITH SUPERUSER=true AND LOGIN=true AND
PASSWORD='bacon123';
CREATE ROLE supply_chain_rw WITH LOGIN=true AND PASSWORD='avbiuo2t48';
```

Client-to-node SSL

Enabling client-to-node **Secure Socket Layer** (**SSL**) security has two main benefits. First, each client connecting to the cluster must present a valid certificate that matches a certificate or **Certificate Authority** (**CA**) in the node's Java KeyStore. Second, upon successful connection (and cert validation), all traffic between the client and node will be encrypted.

Node-to-node SSL

Enabling node-to-node SSL security is designed to prevent a specific avenue of attack. A node will not be allowed to join the cluster, unless it presents a valid SSL certificate in its Java KeyStore and the Java TrustStore matches with the other nodes in the cluster. When this level of security is active, it will encrypt communication between the nodes over port `7001`.

Node-to-node SSL may seem unnecessary, but without it, an internal attacker could join a rogue node to your cluster. Then once it has bootstrapped, it will shut the node down and its data directories will contain at least some of your data. If you don't enable node-to-node SSL, this can be done without having to know any of the admin passwords to authenticate to the cluster.

Summary

In this chapter, we discussed many aspects of Apache Cassandra. Some concepts may not have been directly about the Cassandra database, but concepts that influenced its design and use. These topics included Brewer's CAP theorem data-distribution and- partitioning; Cassandra's read and write paths; how data is stored on-disk; inner workings of components such as the snitch, tombstones, and failure-detection; and an overview of the delivered security features.

This chapter was designed to give you the necessary background to understand the remaining chapters. Apache Cassandra was architected to work the way it does for certain reasons. Understanding why will help you to provide effective configuration, build high-performing data models, and design applications that run without bottlenecks. In the next chapter, we will discuss and explore CQL, and explain why it has certain limitations, and how to unleash its power.

3
Effective CQL

In this chapter, we will examine common approaches to data modeling and interacting with data stored in Apache Cassandra. This will involve us taking a close look at the Cassandra Query Language, otherwise known as **CQL**. Specifically, we will cover and discuss the following topics:

- The evolution of CQL and the role it plays in the Apache Cassandra universe
- How data is structured and modeled effectively for Apache Cassandra
- How to build primary keys that facilitate high-performing data models at scale
- How CQL differs from SQL
- CQL syntax and how to solve different types of problems using it

Once you have completed this chapter, you should have an understanding of why data models need to be built in a certain way. You should also begin to understand known Cassandra anti-patterns and be able to spot certain types of bad queries. This should help you to build scalable, query-based tables and write successful CQL to interact with them.

In the parts of this chapter that cover data modeling, be sure to pay extra attention. The data model is the most important part of a successful, high-performing Apache Cassandra cluster. It is also extremely difficult to change your data model later on, so test early, often, and with a significant amount of data. You do not want to realize that you need to change your model after you have already stored millions of rows. No amount of performance-tuning on the cluster side can make up for a poorly-designed data model!

An overview of Cassandra data modeling

Understanding how Apache Cassandra organizes data under the hood is essential to knowing how to use it properly. When examining Cassandra's data organization, it is important to determine which version of Apache Cassandra you are working with. Apache Cassandra 3.0 represents a significant shift in the way data is both stored and accessed, which warrants a discussion on the evolution of CQL.

Before we get started, let's create a keyspace for this chapter's work:

```
CREATE KEYSPACE packt_ch3 WITH replication =
  {'class': 'NetworkTopologyStrategy', 'ClockworkAngels':'1'};
```

To preface this discussion, let's create an example table. Let's assume that we want to store data about a music playlist, including the band's name, albums, song titles, and some additional data about the songs. The CQL for creating that table could look like this:

```
CREATE TABLE playlist (
 band TEXT,
 album TEXT,
 song TEXT,
 running_time TEXT,
 year INT,
 PRIMARY KEY (band,album,song));
```

Now we'll add some data into that table:

```
INSERT INTO playlist (band,album,song,running_time,year)
  VALUES ('Rush','Moving Pictures','Limelight','4:20',1981);
INSERT INTO playlist (band,album,song,running_time,year)
  VALUES ('Rush','Moving Pictures','Tom Sawyer','4:34',1981);
INSERT INTO playlist (band,album,song,running_time,year)
  VALUES ('Rush','Moving Pictures','Red Barchetta','6:10',1981);
INSERT INTO playlist (band,album,song,running_time,year)
  VALUES ('Rush','2112','2112','20:34',1976);
INSERT INTO playlist (band,album,song,running_time,year)
  VALUES ('Rush','Clockwork Angels','Seven Cities of Gold','6:32',2012);
INSERT INTO playlist (band,album,song,running_time,year)
  VALUES ('Coheed and Cambria','Burning Star IV','Welcome
Home','6:15',2006);
```

Cassandra storage model for early versions up to 2.2

The original underlying storage for Apache Cassandra was based on its use of the Thrift interface layer. If we were to look at how the underlying data was stored in older (pre-3.0) versions of Cassandra, we would see something similar to the following:

```
Rowkey: Rush

  Column Key: 2112 | 2112
    running_time: 20:34
    year: 1976

  Column Key: Clockwork Angels | Seven Cities of Gold
    running_time: 6:32
    year: 2012

  Column Key: MovingPictures | Limelight
    running_time: 4:20
    year: 1981

  Column Key: MovingPictures | Red Barchetta
    running_time: 6:10
    year: 1981

  Column Key: MovingPictures | Tom Sawyer
    running_time: 4:34
    year: 1981
```

```
Rowkey: Coheed and Cambria

  Column Key: Burning Star IV | Welcome Home
    running_time: 6:15
    year: 2006
```

Figure 3.1: Demonstration of how data was stored in the older storage engine of Apache Cassandra. Notice that the data is partitioned (co-located) by its row key, and then each column is ordered by the column keys.

As you can see in the preceding screenshot, data is simply stored by its row key (also known as the **partitioning key**). Within each partition, data is stored ordered by its column keys, and finally by its (non-key) column names. This structure was sometimes referred to as a **map of a map**. The innermost section of the map, where the column values were stored, was called a **cell**. Dealing with data like this proved to be problematic and required some understanding of the Thrift API to complete basic operations.

When CQL was introduced with Cassandra 1.2, it essentially abstracted the Thrift model in favor of a SQL-like interface, which was more familiar to the database development community. This abstraction brought about the concept known as the **CQL row**. While the storage layer still viewed from the simple perspective of partitions and column values, CQL introduced the row construct to Cassandra, if only at a logical level. This difference between the physical and logical models of the Apache Cassandra storage engine was prevalent in major versions: 1.2, 2.0, 2.1, and 2.2.

Cassandra storage model for versions 3.0 and beyond

On the other hand, the new storage engine changes in Apache Cassandra 3.0 offer several improvements. With version 3.0 and up, stored data is now organized like this:

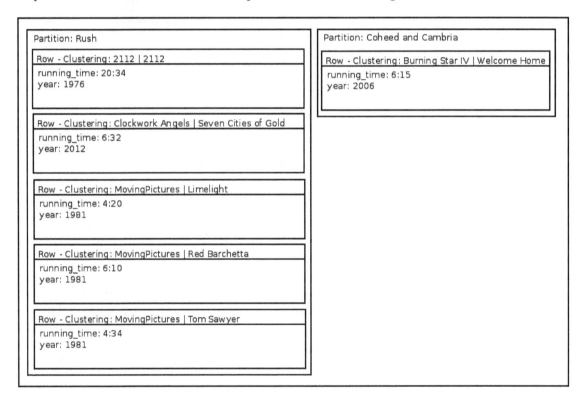

Figure 3.2: Demonstration of how data is stored in the new storage engine used by Apache Cassandra 3.0 and up. While data is still partitioned in a similar manner, rows are now first-class citizens.

The preceding figure shows that, while data is still partitioned similarly to how it always was, there is a new structure present. The row is now part of the storage engine. This allows for the data model and the Cassandra language drivers to deal with the underlying data similar to how the storage engine does.

> An important aspect not pictured in the preceding screenshot is the fact that each row and column value has its own timestamp.

In addition to rows becoming first-class citizens of the physical data model, another change to the storage engine brought about a drastic improvement. As Apache Cassandra's original data model comes from more of a key/value approach, every row is not required to have a value for every column in a table.

The original storage engine allowed for this by repeating the column names and clustering keys with each column value. One way around repeating the column data was to use the WITH COMPACT STORAGE directive at the time of table creation. However, this presented limitations around schema flexibility, in that columns could no longer be added or removed.

> Do not use the WITH COMPACT STORAGE directive with Apache Cassandra version 3.0 or newer. It no longer provides any benefits, and exists so that legacy users have an upgrade path.

With Apache Cassandra 3.0, column names and clustering keys are no longer repeated with each column value. Depending on the data model, this can lead to a drastic difference in the disk footprint between Cassandra 3.0 and its prior versions.

> I have seen as much as a 90% reduction in disk footprint by upgrading from Cassandra 2.x to Cassandra 3.0 and as little as 10% to 15%. Your experience may vary, depending on the number of columns in a table, size of their names, and primary key definition.

Data cells

Sometimes structures for storing column values are referred to as **cells**. Queries to Cassandra essentially return collections of cells. Assume the following table definition for keeping track of weather station readings:

```
CREATE TABLE weather_data_by_date (
  month BIGINT,
  day BIGINT,
  station_id UUID,
  time timestamp,
  temperature DOUBLE,
  wind_speed DOUBLE,
  PRIMARY KEY ((month,day),station_id,time));
```

In this model, the month and day keys are used to make up a composite partition key. The clustering keys are station_id and time. In this way, for each partition, the number of cells will be equal to the total unique combinations of tuples:

- station_id, time, temperature
- station_id, time, wind_speed

Understanding a cell comes into play when building data models. Apache Cassandra can only support 2,000,000,000 cells per partition. When data modelers fail to consider this, partitions can become large and ungainly, with query times eventually getting slower. This is why data models that allow for unbound row growth are considered to be an anti-pattern.

The maximum of 2,000,000,000 cells per partition is a hard limit. But, practically speaking, models that allow that many cells to be written to a single partition will become slow long before that limit is reached.

cqlsh

The cqlsh tool, which is also known as **CQL shell**, installs with Cassandra and should be used to control security, keyspace, and table definitions. Not to be confused with the old Cassandra-CLI (the deprecated Cassandra command-line interface), cqlsh will be your primary interface into controlling your Cassandra data model and analyzing cluster metadata.

If you do not have Apache Cassandra or cqlsh installed locally, you can use `pip` (Python's package manager) to accomplish this quickly: `pip install cqlsh`.

Logging into cqlsh

You will find `cqlsh` in the `/bin` directory of your Cassandra home directory. You can start it by invoking it with a host IP address to connect to and any flags required by your cluster or session to connect:

```
cqlsh <host_ip> <port> [flags/options]
```

In the interest of getting users on the correct path, we'll show you how to log into a cluster secured with both `auth` and `ssl` via cqlsh:

```
bin/cqlsh 192.168.0.101 -u cassdba -p flynnLives --ssl

Connected to PermanentWaves at 192.168.0.101:9042.
[cqlsh 5.0.1 | Cassandra 3.11.2 | CQL spec 3.4.4 | Native protocol v4]
Use HELP for help.
cassdba@cqlsh>
```

 The `--ssl` flag is not required if your cluster does not use client-to-node SSL. Also, versions of Apache Cassandra earlier than 2.1 did not require the `--ssl` flag, even to connect to a secured cluster. With these older versions, an SSL connection is completely dependent on your ability to properly set up your `cqlshrc` file.

Problems connecting to cqlsh

If you navigate to the well-known developer Q&A site, Stack Overflow (`www.stackoverflow.com`), and run a search query for connect on the cqlsh tag, you'll notice something astounding. About 25% of all cqlsh questions are about people having problems using it to connect to their cluster. Given this prevailing issue, a discussion on connecting to cqlsh is warranted.

There are three common scenarios in which you might be trying to connect to your cluster, and how cqlsh will show you a failure.

Local cluster without security enabled

This is the easiest scenario. It's also the least secure, so you shouldn't get into the habit of setting things up this way (which is what too much of running on your own machine can do):

```
bin/cqlsh
```

This is the only scenario where executing cqlsh without any parameters may work, and only if you have not configured your local Cassandra node to bind to anything but the home IP address of 127.0.0.1. cqlsh also uses 127.0.0.1 by default, so this will not work in a remote or multiple-node scenario.

 cqlsh connects via the native binary protocol and uses port 9042 by default. With Cassandra versions 2.0 and earlier, cqlsh connects via Thrift and uses port 9160. In both cases, you should not have to specify the port with cqlsh.

Remote cluster with user security enabled

When connecting to a remote cluster that uses authentication and authorization, you should have to provide the IP address of the host, along with a valid username and password:

```
bin/cqlsh 192.168.0.101 -u cassdba -p flynnLives
```

If you have trouble connecting to a remote cluster via cqlsh, try to figure out what it is using as its broadcast address, like this:

```
grep broadcast_ conf/cassandra.yaml

# broadcast_address: 1.2.3.4
broadcast_address: 192.168.0.101
# set broadcast_rpc_address to a value other than 0.0.0.0.
# rpc_address. If rpc_address is set to 0.0.0.0, broadcast_rpc_address must
broadcast_rpc_address: 192.168.0.101
#    Uses public IPs as broadcast_address to allow cross-region
```

Remote cluster with auth and SSL enabled

In this scenario, you will have to tell cqlsh where to find a SSL certificate to present at connection time. This is done in your $HOME/.cassandra/cqlshrc file. A common cqlshrc file used for connecting to a client-to-node SSL enabled cluster may look like this:

```
cat cqlshrc

[connection]
factory = cqlshlib.ssl.ssl_transport_factory

[ssl]
certfile = /home/aploetz/.cassandra/permanentWaves.pem
validate = false
```

Creation of the permanentWaves.pem file is demonstrated in the next section.

With that configuration in place, execute cqlsh providing the IP address of the host, along with a valid username and password and the --ssl flag:

```
bin/cqlsh 192.168.0.101 -u cassdba -p flynnLives --ssl
```

The most important thing to understand about cqlsh is that it connects to Apache Cassandra in the same way that an application does. Therefore, many of the same principles that apply to Cassandra client applications apply to cqlsh.

Connecting with cqlsh over SSL

Both client-to-node and node-to-node SSL require creation of a certificate for use with Cassandra. These certificates must also be added into Java keyStores (a keyStore and a trustStore). However, cqlsh is written in Python, and does not use a Java keyStore. Therefore, the certificate must be converted and exported into a PKCS12 (public key certificate standards) certificate file for use with cqlsh. Creating the certificate and connecting with it via cqlsh can be accomplished with some simple steps, which we will cover here.

Converting the Java keyStore into a PKCS12 keyStore

For this step, it's a good idea to copy the node's keyStore to a location where the following is applicable:

- You have full access or ownership of it
- You aren't risking corrupting the original

For this example, I'll copy it to the `.cassandra` directory underneath my home `dir` (which you may need `sudo` access to do):

```
sudo cp conf/keystore ~/.cassandra/keystore
```

Now, converting the Java keyStore into a PKCS12 keyStore can easily be done:

```
cd ~/.cassandra
keytool -importkeystore -srckeystore keystore -destkeystore p12keystore -
deststoretype PKCS12 -srcstorepass keystorepassword -deststorepass
keystorepassword
```

This will produce a `PKCS12` format keyStore file named `p12keystore`.

Exporting the certificate from the PKCS12 keyStore

Here, you will need the OpenSSL toolkit, and use it to create a **Privacy Enhanced Mail (PEM)** file:

```
openssl pkcs12 -in p12keystore -nokeys -out permanentWaves.pem -passin
pass:keystorepassword
```

This will produce a PEM file containing the certificate from the original keyStore.

Modifying your cqlshrc file

Connecting over SSL via cqlsh requires the use of the `cqlshrc` file. As indicated in the previous section, your `cqlshrc` file should be adjusted to reference the PEM file created in the prior step:

```
[connection]
factory = cqlshlib.ssl.ssl_transport_factory

[ssl]
certfile = /home/aploetz/.cassandra/permanentWaves.pem
validate = false
```

Along with specifying the PEM file in the `[ssl]` section, you will also need to specify whether the certificate should be validated at connection time. This feature is used for two-way SSL. Additionally, you will need to define `factory` in the `[connection]` section. Using the delivered `ssl_transport_factory` will suffice.

Testing your connection via cqlsh

With the certificate converted and exported, and your `cqlshrc` file updated, you should now be able to connect to your client-to-node SSL enabled cluster:

```
bin/cqlsh 192.168.0.101 -u cassdba -p flynnLives --ssl
```

Getting started with CQL

With some quick definitions of CQL data modeling and cqlsh completed, now we'll take a look at CQL. The basic commands for creating data structures (keyspaces, tables, and so on) will be covered right away, with command complexity increasing as we build more useful structures.

Creating a keyspace

Keyspaces are analogous to the logical databases of the relational world. A keyspace contains tables, which are usually related to each other by application, use case, or development team. When defining a keyspace, you also have the ability to control its replication behavior, specifying pairs of data center names and a numeric **Replication Factor (RF)**.

Creating a keyspace is a simple operation and can be done like this:

```
CREATE KEYSPACE [IF NOT EXISTS] <keyspace_name>
 WITH replication =
 {'class': '<replication_strategy>',
  '<data_center_name>':'<replication_factor>'}
 AND durable_writes = <true/false>;
```

Here is the detailed explanation of the preceding query:

- `keyspace_name`: Valid keyspace names must be composed of alphanumeric characters and underscores.
- `replication_strategy`: Either `SimpleStrategy` or `NetworkTopologyStrategy`.
- `data_center_name`: Valid only for `NetworkTopologyStrategy`, must be the name of a valid data center. If using `SimpleStrategy`, specify `replication_factor`.
- `replication_factor`: A numeric value representing the number of replicas to write for the key with which it is paired.
- `durable_writes`: A Boolean indicating whether writes should be written to the commit log. If not specified, this defaults to `true`.

 Names for keyspaces, tables, columns, and custom structures in Apache Cassandra must be alphanumeric. The only exception to that rule is that an underscore (_) is the only valid special character that can be used.

Single data center example

The following example will create the `packt_ch3` keyspace. When a write occurs, one replica will be written to the cluster. Writes will also be sent to the commit log for extra durability:

```
CREATE KEYSPACE IF NOT EXISTS packt_ch3
  WITH replication =
  {'class': 'NetworkTopologyStrategy', 'ClockworkAngels':'1'}
  AND durable_writes = true;
```

 `SimpleStrategy` isn't very useful, so my advice is not to use it. It's a good idea to get into the habit of using `NetworkTopologyStrategy`, as that's the one that should be used in production. `SimpleStrategy` offers no advantages over `NetworkTopologyStrategy`, and using `SimpleStrategy` can complicate converting into a multi-data center environment later.

Multi-data center example

The following example will create the `packt_ch3b` keyspace, as long as it does not already exist. When a write occurs, two replicas will be written to the `ClockworkAngels` data center, and three will be written to the `PermanentWaves` and `MovingPictures` data centers. Writes will also be sent to the commit log for extra durability:

```
CREATE KEYSPACE packt_ch3_mdc
  WITH replication = {'class': 'NetworkTopologyStrategy',
    'ClockworkAngels':'2', 'MovingPictures':'3', 'PermanentWaves':'3'}
  AND durable_writes = true;
```

Once you have created your keyspace, you can use it to avoid having to keep typing it later. Notice that this will also change your Command Prompt:

```
cassdba@cqlsh> use packt_ch3 ;
cassdba@cqlsh:packt_ch3>
```

Creating a table

Data in Cassandra is organized into storage structures known as tables. Some older documentation may refer to tables as column families. If someone refers to column families, it is safe to assume that they are referring to structures in older versions of Apache Cassandra:

```
CREATE TABLE [IF NOT EXISTS] [keyspace_name.]<table_name>
  <column_name> <column_type>,
  [additional <column_name> <column_type>,]
  PRIMARY KEY ((<partition_key>[,additional
<partition_key>])[,<clustering_keys]);
[WITH <options>];
```

Simple table example

For a small table with simple query requirements, something like this might be sufficient:

```
CREATE TABLE users (
  username TEXT,
  email TEXT,
  department TEXT,
  title TEXT,
  ad_groups TEXT,
  PRIMARY KEY (username));
```

Clustering key example

Let's say that we wanted to be able to offer up the same data, but to support a query for users by department. The table definition would change to something like this:

```
CREATE TABLE users_by_dept (
  username TEXT,
  email TEXT,
  department TEXT,
  title TEXT,
  AD_groups TEXT,
  PRIMARY KEY ((department),username))
WITH CLUSTERING ORDER BY (username ASC)
  AND COMPACTION = {'class':'LeveledCompactionStrategy',
  'sstable_size_in_mb':'200'};
```

As the preceding table will be read more than it will be written to (users queried more often than they are added), we also designate use of `LeveledCompactionStrategy`.

The default compaction strategy is `SizeTieredCompactionStrategy`, which tends to favor read and write patterns that are either even (50% read, 50% write) or more write-heavy.

For a later example, let's write some data to that table:

```
INSERT INTO users_by_dept(department,username,title,email) VALUES
('Engineering','Dinesh','Dev Lead','dinesh@piedpiper.com');
INSERT INTO users_by_dept(department,username,title,email) VALUES
('Engineering','Gilfoyle','Sys Admin/DBA','thedarkone@piedpiper.com');
INSERT INTO users_by_dept(department,username,title,email) VALUES
('Engineering','Richard','CEO','richard@piedpiper.com');
INSERT INTO users_by_dept(department,username,title,email) VALUES
('Marketing','Erlich','CMO','erlichb@aviato.com');
INSERT INTO users_by_dept(department,username,title,email) VALUES
('Finance/HR','Jared','COO','donald@piedpiper.com');
```

Composite partition key example

Solving data model problems attributed to unbound row growth can sometimes be done by adding another partition key. Let's assume that we want to query security entrance logs for employees. If we were to use a clustering key on a new column named time to one of the preceding examples, we would be continually adding cells to each partition. So we'll build this `PRIMARY KEY` to partition our data by `entrance` and `day`, as well as cluster it on `checkpoint_time` and `username`:

```
CREATE TABLE security_log (
  entrance TEXT,
  day BIGINT,
  checkpoint_time TIMESTAMP,
  username TEXT,
  email TEXT,
  department TEXT,
  title TEXT,
  PRIMARY KEY ((entrance,day),checkpoint_time,username))
WITH CLUSTERING ORDER BY (checkpoint_time DESC, username ASC)
AND default_time_to_live=2592000;
```

The preceding table will store data sorted within each partition by both `checkpoint_time` and `username`. Note that, since we care more about the most recent data, we have designated the clustering on `checkpoint_time` to be in descending order. Additionally, we'll assume we have a requirement to only keep security log data for the last 30 days, so we'll set `default_time_to_live` to 30 days (`2592000` seconds).

Table options

There are several options that can be adjusted at table-creation time. Most of these options are present on all tables. If they are omitted from table creation, their default values are assumed. The following are a few of the table options:

- Clustering order specifies the column(s) and direction by which the table data (within a partition) should be stored on disk. As Cassandra stores data written sequentially, it's also faster when it can read sequentially, so learning how to utilize clustering keys in your models can help with performance:

```
CLUSTERING ORDER BY (<clustering_key_name <ASC|DESC>)
```

- This setting represents the false positive probability for the table's bloom filter. The value can range between `0.0` and `1.0`, with a recommended setting of `0.1` (10%):

```
bloom_filter_fp_chance = 0.1
```

- The `caching` property dictates which caching features are used by this table. There are two types of caching that can be used by a table: **key caching** and **row caching**. Key caching is enabled by default. Row caching can take up larger amounts of resources, so it defaults to disabled or `NONE`:

```
caching = {'keys': 'ALL', 'rows_per_partition': 'NONE'}
```

- This property allows for the addition of `comment` or description for the table, assuming that it is not clear from its name:

```
comment = ''
```

- This enables the table for **Change Data Capture** (**CDC**) logging and `cdc` defaults to `FALSE`:

```
cdc = FALSE
```

- A map structure that allows for the configuration of the compaction strategy, and the properties that govern it:

```
compaction = {'class':
'org.apache.cassandra.db.compaction.LeveledCompactionStrategy'}
```

Apache Cassandra 3.0 ships with three compaction strategies:

- `SizeTieredCompactionStrategy`: This is the default strategy, and works well in most scenarios, specifically write-heavy throughput patterns. It works by finding similarly-sized SSTable files and combining them once they reach a certain size. If you create a table without configuring compaction, it will be set to the following options:

```
compaction = {'class':
'org.apache.cassandra.db.compaction.SizeTieredCompactionStrategy',
 'max_threshold': '32', 'min_threshold': '4'}
```

Under these settings, a minor compaction will trigger for the table when at least 4 (and no more than 32) SSTables are found to be within a calculated threshold of the average SSTable file size.

- `LeveledCompactionStrategy`: The leveled compaction strategy builds out SSTable files as levels, where each level is 10 times the size of the previous level. In this way, a row can be guaranteed to be contained within a single SSTable file 90% of the time. A typical leveled `compaction` config looks like this:

```
compaction = {'class':
'org.apache.cassandra.db.compaction.LeveledCompactionStrategy',
 'sstable_size_in_mb': '160'}
```

Leveled `compaction` is a good idea for operational patterns where reads are twice (or more) as frequent as writes.

- `TimeWindowCompactionStrategy`: Time-window compaction builds SSTable files according to time-based buckets. Rows are then stored according to these (configurable) buckets. Configuration for time window `compaction` looks like this:

```
compaction = {'class':
'org.apache.cassandra.db.compaction.TimeWindowCompactionStrategy',
 'compaction_window_unit': 'hours', 'compaction_window_size': '24'}
```

This is especially useful for time-series data, as it allows data within the same time period to be stored together.

Time-window compaction can greatly improve query performance (over other strategies) for time-series data that uses **time to live** (TTL). This ensures that data within a bucket is tombstoned together, and therefore the TTL tombstones should not interfere with queries for newer data.

`TimeWindowCompactionStrategy` is new as of Apache Cassandra 3.0, and replaces `DateTieredCompactionStrategy`, which was shipped with Apache Cassandra 2.1 and 2.2.

```
compression = {'chunk_length_in_kb': '64', 'class':
'org.apache.cassandra.io.compress.LZ4Compressor'}
```

This property is another map structure that allows the compression settings for a table to be configured. Apache Cassandra ships with three compressor classes: `LZ4Compressor` (default), `SnappyCompressor`, and `DeflateCompressor`. Once the class has been specified, `chunk_length` can also be specified. By default, a table will use `LZ4Compressor`, and will be configured as shown here:

```
compression = {'class': 'org.apache.cassandra.io.compress.LZ4Compressor',
  'chunk_length_in_kb': '64'}
```

 To disable compression, specify `compression =` `{'sstable_compression': ''}`.

It should be noted that the default `chunk_length_in_kb` of `64` is intended for write-heavy workloads. Access patterns that are more evenly read and write, or read-heavy may see a performance benefit from bringing that value down to as low as four. As always, be sure to test significant changes, like this:

```
crc_check_chance = 1.0
```

With compression enabled, this property defines the probability that the CRC compression checksums will be verified on a read operation. The default value is `1.0`, or 100%:

```
dclocal_read_repair_chance = 0.1
```

This property specifies the probability that a read repair will be invoked on a read. The read repair will only be enforced within the same (local) data center:

```
default_time_to_live = 0
```

This allows all data entered into a table to be automatically deleted after a specified number of seconds. The default value is 0, which disables TTL by default. TTLs can also be set from the application side, which will override this setting. The maximum value is `630720000`, or 20 years.

 Don't forget that TTLs also create tombstones. So, if your table employs a TTL, be sure to account for that in your overall data modeling approach.

```
gc_grace_seconds = 864000
```

This property specifies the amount of time (in seconds) that tombstones in the table will persist before they are eligible for collection via compaction. By default, this is set to `864000` seconds, or 10 days.

> Remember that the 10 day default exists to give your cluster a chance to run a repair. This is important, as all tombstones must be successfully propagated to avoid data ghosting its way back into a result set. If you plan to lower this value, make sure that you also increase the frequency by which the repair is run.

```
min_index_interval & max_index_interval
```

These properties work together to determine how many entries end up in the table's index summary (in RAM). The more entries in the partition index, the quicker a partition can be located during an operation. The trade-off, is that more entries equal more RAM consumed. The actual value used is determined by how often the table is accessed. Default values for these properties are set as follows:

```
max_index_interval = 2048
min_index_interval = 128
memtable_flush_period_in_ms = 0
```

The number of milliseconds before the table's memtables are flushed from RAM to disk. The default is zero, effectively leaving the triggering of memtable flushes up to the commit log and the defined value of `memtable_cleanup_threshold`:

```
read_repair_chance = 0.0
```

Similar to `dclocal_read_repair_chance`, this setting specifies the probability that a cross-data center read repair will be invoked. This defaults to zero (0.0), to ensure that read repairs are limited to a single data center at a time (and therefore less expensive):

```
speculative_retry = '99PERCENTILE';
```

This property configures rapid read protection, in that read requests are sent to other replicas despite their consistency requirements having been met. This property has four possible values:

- `ALWAYS`: Every ready sends additional read requests to other replicas.
- `XPERCENTILE`: Sends additional read requests only for requests that are determined to be in the slowest X percentile. The default value for this property is `99PERCENTILE`, which will trigger additional replica reads for request latencies in the 99th percentile, based on past performance of reads for that table.

- XMS: Sends additional replica reads for requests that do not complete within X milliseconds.
- NONE: Disables this functionality.

Data types

Apache Cassandra comes with many common types that can help you with efficient data storage and representation. As Cassandra is written in Java, the Cassandra data types correlate directly to Java data types:

CQL type	Java class	Description
ascii	String	US-ASCII (United States – American Standard Codes for Information Interchange) character string.
bigint	Long	64-bit signed long.
blob	java.nio.ByteBuffer	Supports storage of BLOBs (binary large objects).
date	java.time.LocalDate	32-bit integer denoting the number of days elapsed since January 1, 1970. Dates can also be specified in CQL queries as strings (such as July 22, 2018).
decimal	java.math.BigDecimal	Arbitrary precision floating-point numeric.
double	Double	64-bit floating-point numeric.
float	Float	32-bit floating-point numeric.
inet	java.net.InetAddress	String type for working with IP addresses. Supports both IPv4 and IPv4 addresses.
int	Integer	32-bit signed Integer.
list	java.util.List	A collection of ordered items of a specified type.
map	java.util.Map	A key/value collection that stores values by a unique key. Type can be specified for both key and value.

set	java.util.Set	A collection of unique items of a specified type.
smallint	Short	16-bit integer.
text	String	UTF-8 character string.
time	Long	The current time in milliseconds elapsed since midnight of the current day.
timestamp	java.util.Date	Date/time with milliseconds, can also be specified in CQL queries as strings (such as 2018-07-22 22:51:13.442).
timeuuid	java.util.UUID	Type 1 UUID (128-bit), used for storing times.
tinyint	Byte	8-bit integer.
tuple	com.datastax.driver.core.TupleValue	A tuple type, consisting of a collection of 2 to 3 values.
uuid	java.util.UUID	Type 4 (randomly-generated) UUID.
varchar	String	UTF-8 character string.
varint	java.math.BigInteger	Arbitrary precision integer.

Table 3.1: List of CQL data types with their Java equivalents and descriptions

Type conversion

One common point of consternation for many folks new to Cassandra is converting between types. This can be done either by altering the existing table, or coercing the results at query-time with CAST. While some of the types may seem interchangeable, issues can arise when converting between types where the target type cannot support the amount of precision required. The following type conversions can be done without issue:

Starting type	Compatible types
ascii	text, varchar
bigint	timestamp, varint
date	timestamp
int	bigint
text	varchar

time	bigint
timestamp	bigint, varint, date
timeuuid	UUID
varchar	text

Table 3.2: A list of valid CQL type conversions

Some notes about CQL data type conversion:

- `blob` is the only ubiquitous type to convert into. You can convert any column or column value into `blob`.
- `varint` successfully converts into the new `date` type in Apache Cassandra 2.2.0, but the table is not able to be queried after that. This was later identified as a bug (`https://issues.apache.org/jira/browse/CASSANDRA-10027`) and fixed in Apache Cassandra 2.2.4. If you are running on that version and have a `varint` column in a table, I do not recommend attempting to convert it to `date`.
- `varchar` and `text` are interchangeable. In fact, describing a table consisting of `varchar` columns displays them as text columns.
- `timeuuid` can be converted into `UUID`, but the opposite is not true. This is because, while all timeuuids are UUIDs, not all UUIDs are timeuuids (which is a type 1 UUID).
- Type conversions do not work for collections. A column cannot be changed into a `LIST` or `SET` of its current type, and a `LIST` cannot be converted into a `SET` (of the same type) and vice versa.

The primary key

The most important part of designing your data model is how you define the primary key of your tables. As mentioned previously in this chapter, primary keys are built at table-creation time, and have the following options:

```
PRIMARY KEY ((<partition_key>[,additional
<partition_key>])[,<clustering_keys])
```

Tables in Apache Cassandra may have (both) multiple partition and clustering keys. As previously mentioned, the partition keys determine which nodes are responsible for a row and its replicas. The clustering keys determine the on-disk sort order within a partition.

Designing a primary key

When designing a primary key, Cassandra modelers should have two main considerations:

- Does this primary key allow for even distribution, at scale?
- Does this primary key match the required query pattern(s), at scale?

Note that on the end of each statement is the phrase at scale. A model that writes all of its table's data into a single partition distributes evenly when you have a 3-node cluster. But it doesn't evenly distribute when you scale up to a 30-node cluster. Plus, that type of model puts your table in danger of approaching the limit of 2,000,000,000 cells per partition. Likewise, almost any model will support high-performing unbound queries (queries without a WHERE clause) when they have 10 rows across the (aforementioned) 3-node cluster. But increase that to 10,000,000,000 rows across 30 nodes, and watch the bad queries start to time out.

Apache Cassandra is a great tool for supporting large amounts of data at large scale. But simply using Cassandra for that task is not enough. Your tables must be designed to take advantage of Cassandra's storage and distribution model, or trouble will quickly ensue.

Selecting a good partition key

So, how do we pick a partition key that distributes well at scale? Minding your model's potential cardinality is the key. The cardinality of a partition key represents the number of possible values of the key, ranging from one to infinity.

Avoid extreme ends of cardinality. Boolean columns should not be used as a single partition key (results in only two partitions). Likewise, you may want to avoid UUIDs or any kind of unique identifier as a single partition key, as its high cardinality will limit potential query patterns.

A bad partition key is easy to spot, with proper knowledge of the business or use case. For instance, if I wanted to be able to query all products found in a particular store, store would seem like a good partition key. However, if a retailer has 1,000,000 products, all of which are sold in all 3 of their stores, that's obviously not going to distribute well.

Let's think about a time-series model. If I'm going to keep track of security logs for a company's employees (with multiple locations), I may think about building a model like this:

```
CREATE TABLE security_logs_by_location (
    employee_id TEXT,
    time_in TIMESTAMP,
    location_id TEXT,
    mailstop TEXT,
    PRIMARY KEY (location_id, time_in, employee_id));
```

This will store the times that each employee enters by location. And if I want to query by a specific location, this may work for query requirements. The problem is that, with each write, the `location_id` partition will get bigger and bigger. Eventually, too many employees will check in at a certain location, and the partition will get too big and become unable to be queried. This is a common Cassandra modeling anti-pattern, known as **unbound row growth**.

> Cardinality may also be an issue with `location_id`. If the company in question has 20-50 locations, this might not be so bad. But if it only has two, this model won't distribute well at all. That's where knowing and understanding the business requirements comes into play.

To fix unbound row growth, we can apply a technique called **bucketing**. Let's assume that we know that each building location will only have 300 employees enter each day. That means if we could partition our table by day, we would never have much more than 300 rows in each partition. We can do that by introducing a day bucket into the model, resulting in a composite partition key:

```
DROP TABLE security_logs_by_location;

CREATE TABLE security_logs_by_location (
  employee_id TEXT,
  time_in TIMESTAMP,
  location_id TEXT,
  day INT,
  mailstop TEXT,
  PRIMARY KEY ((location_id, day), time_in, employee_id));
```

Creating a compound partition key is as simple as specifying the comma-delimited partition keys inside parentheses.

Now when I insert into this table and query it, it looks something like this:

```
INSERT INTO security_logs_by_location
(location_id,day,time_in,employee_id,mailstop)
VALUES ('MPLS2',20180723,'2018-07-23 11:04:22.432','aaronp','M266');

SELECT * FROM security_logs_by_location ;

 location_id | day       | time_in                             | employee_id |
 mailstop
-------------+-----------+-------------------------------------+-------------+--
---------
      MPLS2  | 20180723  | 2018-07-23 12:04:22.432000+0000 |      aaronp |
 M266

(1 rows)
```

Now my application can write as many rows as it needs to, without worrying about running into too many cells per partition. The trade-off is that when I query this table, I'll need to specify the location and day. But business-reporting requirements typically (in this hypothetical use case) require querying data only for a specific day, so that will work.

Selecting a good clustering key

As mentioned previously, clustering determine the on-disk sort order for rows within a partition. But a good clustering key can also help to ensure uniqueness among the rows. Consider the table used in the preceding examples. This section will make more sense with more data, so let's start by adding a few more rows:

```
INSERT INTO security_logs_by_location
(location_id,day,time_in,employee_id,mailstop)
 VALUES ('MPLS2',20180723,'2018-07-23 9:04:59.377','tejam','M266');
INSERT INTO security_logs_by_location
(location_id,day,time_in,employee_id,mailstop)
 VALUES ('MPLS2',20180723,'2018-07-23 7:17:38.268','jeffb','M266');
INSERT INTO security_logs_by_location
(location_id,day,time_in,employee_id,mailstop)
 VALUES ('MPLS2',20180723,'2018-07-23 7:01:18.163','sandrak','M266');
INSERT INTO security_logs_by_location
(location_id,day,time_in,employee_id,mailstop)
 VALUES ('MPLS2',20180723,'2018-07-23 6:49:11.754','samb','M266');
```

```
INSERT INTO security_logs_by_location
(location_id,day,time_in,employee_id,mailstop)
 VALUES ('MPLS2',20180723,'2018-07-23 7:08:24.682','johno','M261');
INSERT INTO security_logs_by_location
(location_id,day,time_in,employee_id,mailstop)
 VALUES ('MPLS2',20180723,'2018-07-23 7:55:45.911','tedk','M266');
```

Now, I'll query the table for all employees entering the MPLS2 building between 6 AM and 10 AM, on July 23, 2018:

```
SELECT * FROM security_logs_by_location
WHERE location_id='MPLS2'
AND day=20180723 AND time_in > '2018-07-23 6:00'
AND time_in < '2018-07-23 10:00';
```

```
 location_id | day      | time_in                        | employee_id |
mailstop
-------------+----------+--------------------------------+-------------+--
--------
       MPLS2 | 20180723 | 2018-07-23 11:49:11.754000+0000 |        samb |
M266
       MPLS2 | 20180723 | 2018-07-23 12:01:18.163000+0000 |     sandrak |
M266
       MPLS2 | 20180723 | 2018-07-23 12:04:22.432000+0000 |      aaronp |
M266
       MPLS2 | 20180723 | 2018-07-23 12:08:24.682000+0000 |       johno |
M261
       MPLS2 | 20180723 | 2018-07-23 12:17:38.268000+0000 |       jeffb |
M266
       MPLS2 | 20180723 | 2018-07-23 12:55:45.911000+0000 |        tedk |
M266
       MPLS2 | 20180723 | 2018-07-23 14:04:59.377000+0000 |       tejam |
M266

(7 rows)
```

Here are some things to note about the preceding result set:

- As required by the table's PRIMARY KEY, I have filtered my WHERE clause on the complete partition key (location_id and day)
- I did not specify the complete PRIMARY KEY, choosing to omit employee_id
- The results are sorted by time_in, in ascending order; I did not specify ORDER BY

- I specified a range on `time_in`, mentioning it twice in the WHERE clause, instructing Cassandra to return a range of data
- While Cassandra is aware of my system's time zone, the `time_in` timestamp is shown in UTC time

As per my clustering key definition, my result set was sorted by the `time_in` column, with the oldest value at the top. This is because, while I did clearly specify my clustering keys, I did not specify the sort order. Therefore, it defaulted to ascending order.

Additionally, I omitted the `employee_id` key. I can do that because I specified the keys that preceded it. If I opted to skip `time_in` and specify `employee_id`, this query would fail. There's more on that later.

So why make `employee_id` part of PRIMARY KEY? It helps to ensure uniqueness. After all, if two employees came through security at the exact same time, their writes to the table would conflict. Although unlikely, designating `employee_id` as the last clustering key helps to ensure that a last-write-wins scenario does not occur.

Another good question to ask would be, if Cassandra requires specific keys, how can range query be made to work. Recall that Apache Cassandra is built on a log-based storage engine (LSM tree). This means that building a table to return data in the order in which it is written actually coincides with how Cassandra was designed to work. Cassandra has problems when it is made to serve random reads but sequential reads actually work quite well.

Now assume that the requirements change slightly, in that the result set needs to be in descending order. How can we solve for that? Well, we could specify an ORDER BY clause at query time, but flipping the sort direction of a large result set can be costly for performance. What is the best way to solve that? By creating a table designed to serve that query naturally, of course:

```
CREATE TABLE security_logs_by_location_desc (
    employee_id TEXT,
    time_in TIMESTAMP,
    location_id TEXT,
    day INT,
    mailstop TEXT,
    PRIMARY KEY ((location_id, day), time_in, employee_id))
WITH CLUSTERING ORDER BY (time_in DESC, employee_id ASC);
```

If I duplicate my data into this table as well, I can run that same query and get my result set in descending order:

```
INSERT INTO security_logs_by_location_desc
(location_id,day,time_in,employee_id,mailstop)
 VALUES ('MPLS2',20180723,'2018-07-23 9:04:59.377','tejam','M266');
INSERT INTO security_logs_by_location_desc
(location_id,day,time_in,employee_id,mailstop)
 VALUES ('MPLS2',20180723,'2018-07-23 7:17:38.268','jeffb','M266');
INSERT INTO security_logs_by_location_desc
(location_id,day,time_in,employee_id,mailstop)
 VALUES ('MPLS2',20180723,'2018-07-23 7:01:18.163','sandrak','M266');
INSERT INTO security_logs_by_location_desc
(location_id,day,time_in,employee_id,mailstop)
 VALUES ('MPLS2',20180723,'2018-07-23 6:49:11.754','samb','M266');
INSERT INTO security_logs_by_location_desc
(location_id,day,time_in,employee_id,mailstop)
 VALUES ('MPLS2',20180723,'2018-07-23 7:08:24.682','johno','M261');
INSERT INTO security_logs_by_location_desc
(location_id,day,time_in,employee_id,mailstop)
 VALUES ('MPLS2',20180723,'2018-07-23 7:55:45.911','tedk','M266');

SELECT * FROM security_logs_by_location_desc
WHERE location_id='MPLS2'
AND day=20180723
AND time_in > '2018-07-23 6:00' AND time_in < '2018-07-23 10:00';

 location_id | day        | time_in                         | employee_id |
mailstop
-------------+------------+---------------------------------+-------------+--
--------
       MPLS2 | 20180723 | 2018-07-23 14:04:59.377000+0000 |        tejam |
M266
       MPLS2 | 20180723 | 2018-07-23 12:55:45.911000+0000 |         tedk |
M266
       MPLS2 | 20180723 | 2018-07-23 12:17:38.268000+0000 |        jeffb |
M266
       MPLS2 | 20180723 | 2018-07-23 12:08:24.682000+0000 |        johno |
M261
       MPLS2 | 20180723 | 2018-07-23 12:04:22.432000+0000 |       aaronp |
M266
       MPLS2 | 20180723 | 2018-07-23 12:01:18.163000+0000 |      sandrak |
M266
       MPLS2 | 20180723 | 2018-07-23 11:49:11.754000+0000 |         samb |
M266

 (7 rows)
```

In this way, it is clear how picking the right clustering keys (and sort direction) also plays a part in designing tables that will perform well at scale.

Querying data

While Apache Cassandra is known for its restrictive query model (design your tables to suit your queries), the previous content has shown that CQL can still be quite powerful. Consider the following table:

```
CREATE TABLE query_test (
 pk1 TEXT,
 pk2 TEXT,
 ck3 TEXT,
 ck4 TEXT,
 c5 TEXT,
 PRIMARY KEY ((pk1,pk2), ck3, ck4))
WITH CLUSTERING ORDER BY (ck3 DESC, ck4 ASC);

INSERT INTO query_test (pk1,pk2,ck3,ck4,c5) VALUES
('a','b','c1','d1','e1');
INSERT INTO query_test (pk1,pk2,ck3,ck4,c5) VALUES
('a','b','c2','d2','e2');
INSERT INTO query_test (pk1,pk2,ck3,ck4,c5) VALUES
('a','b','c2','d3','e3');
INSERT INTO query_test (pk1,pk2,ck3,ck4,c5) VALUES
('a','b','c2','d4','e4');
INSERT INTO query_test (pk1,pk2,ck3,ck4,c5) VALUES
('a','b','c3','d5','e5');
INSERT INTO query_test (pk1,pk2,ck3,ck4,c5) VALUES
('f','b','c3','d5','e5');
```

Let's start by querying everything for `pk1`:

```
SELECT * FROM query_test WHERE pk1='a';

InvalidRequest: Error from server: code=2200 [Invalid query]
message="Cannot execute this query as it might involve data filtering and
thus may have unpredictable performance. If you want to execute this query
despite the performance unpredictability, use ALLOW FILTERING"
```

So what happened here? Cassandra is essentially informing us that it cannot ensure that this query will be served by a single node. This is because we have defined pk1 and pk2 as a composite partition key. Without both pk1 and pk2 specified, a single node containing the requested data cannot be ascertained. However, it does say the following:

```
If you want to execute this query despite the performance unpredictability,
use ALLOW FILTERING
```

So let's give that a try:

```
SELECT * FROM query_test
WHERE pk1='a' ALLOW FILTERING;

pk1 | pk2 | ck3 | ck4 | c5
-----+-----+-----+-----+----
  a  |  b  |  c3 |  d5 | e5
  a  |  b  |  c2 |  d2 | e2
  a  |  b  |  c2 |  d3 | e3
  a  |  b  |  c2 |  d4 | e4
  a  |  b  |  c1 |  d1 | e1

(5 rows)
```

That worked. But the bigger question is why? The ALLOW FILTERING directive tells Cassandra that it should perform an exhaustive seek of all partitions, looking for data that might match. With a total of six rows in the table, served by a single node cluster, that will still run fast. But in a multi-node cluster, with millions of other rows, that query will likely time out.

So, let's try that query again, and this time we'll specify the complete partition key, as well as the first clustering key:

```
SELECT * FROM query_test
WHERE pk1='a' AND pk2='b' AND ck3='c2';

pk1 | pk2 | ck3 | ck4 | c5
-----+-----+-----+-----+----
  a  |  b  |  c2 |  d2 | e2
  a  |  b  |  c2 |  d3 | e3
  a  |  b  |  c2 |  d4 | e4

(3 rows)
```

That works. So what if we just want to query for a specific ck4, but we don't know which ck3 it's under? Let's try skipping ck3:

```
SELECT * FROM query_test
WHERE pk1='a' AND pk2='b' AND ck4='d2';

InvalidRequest: Error from server: code=2200 [Invalid query]
message="PRIMARY KEY column "ck4" cannot be restricted as preceding column
"ck3" is not restricted"
```

Remember, components of the PRIMARY KEY definition can be omitted, as long as (some of) the preceding keys are specified. But they can only be omitted in order. You can't pick and choose which ones to leave out.

So how do we solve this issue? Let's use ALLOW FILTERING:

```
SELECT * FROM query_test
WHERE pk1='a' AND pk2='b' AND ck4='d2' ALLOW FILTERING;

 pk1 | pk2 | ck3 | ck4 | c5
-----+-----+-----+-----+----
   a |   b |  c2 |  d2 | e2

(1 rows)
```

That works. But given what we know about the ALLOW FILTERING directive, is this OK to do? The answer to this question lies in the fact that we have indeed specified the complete partition key. By doing that, Cassandra knows which node can serve the query. While this may not follow the advice of *build your tables to support your queries*, it may actually perform well (depending on the size of the result set).

Avoid using ALLOW FILTERING. It might make certain ad-hoc queries work, but improper use of it may cause your nodes to work too hard, and whichever is chosen as the coordinator may crash. Definitely do not deploy any production code that regularly uses CQL queries containing the ALLOW FILTERING directive.

For a quick detour, what if I wanted to know what time it was on my Apache Cassandra cluster? I could query my table using the `now()` function:

```
SELECT now() FROM query_test;

 system.now()
---------------------------------------
 f83015b0-8fba-11e8-91d4-a7c67cc60e89
 f83015b1-8fba-11e8-91d4-a7c67cc60e89
 f83015b2-8fba-11e8-91d4-a7c67cc60e89
 f83015b3-8fba-11e8-91d4-a7c67cc60e89
 f83015b4-8fba-11e8-91d4-a7c67cc60e89
 f83015b5-8fba-11e8-91d4-a7c67cc60e89

(6 rows)
```

What happened here? The `now()` function was invoked for each row in the table. First of all, this is an unbound query and will hit multiple nodes for data that it's not even using. Secondly, we just need one result. And third, returning the current time as `TIMEUUID` isn't very easy to read.

Let's solve problems one and two by changing the table we're querying. Let's try that on the `system.local` table:

```
SELECT now() FROM system.local ;

 system.now()
--------------------------------------
 94a88ad0-8fbb-11e8-91d4-a7c67cc60e89

(1 rows)
```

The `system.local` table is unique to each node in a Cassandra cluster. Also, it only ever has one row in it. So, this query will be served by one node, and there will only be one row returned. But how can we make that more easier to read? We can use the `dateof()` function for this:

```
SELECT dateof(now()) FROM system.local;

 system.dateof(system.now())
---------------------------------
 2018-07-25 03:37:08.045000+0000

(1 rows)
```

Cassandra has other built-in functions that can help to solve other problems. We will cover those later.

> You can execute `SELECT CAST(now() as TIMESTAMP) FROM system.local;` to achieve the same result.

The IN operator

So we've seen that CQL has an `AND` keyword for specifying multiple filters in the `WHERE` clause. Does it also have an `OR` keyword, like SQL?

No, it does not. This is because Apache Cassandra is designed to serve sequential reads, not random reads. It works best when its queries give it a clear, precise path to the requested data. Allowing filters in the `WHERE` clause to be specified on an `OR` basis would force Cassandra to perform random reads, which really works against how it was built.

However, queries can be made to perform similarly to `OR`, via the `IN` operator:

```
SELECT * FROM query_test WHERE pk1='a' AND pk2 IN ('b','c');
```

While this query technically will work, its use is considered to be an anti-pattern in Cassandra. This is because it is a multi-key query, meaning the primary key filters are filtering on more than one key value. In this case, Cassandra cannot figure out which node the requested data is on. We are only giving it one part of the partition key. This means that it will have to designate one node as a coordinator node, and then scan each node to build the result set:

```
SELECT * FROM query_test WHERE pk1='a' AND  pk2='b' AND ck3 IN ('c1','c3');
```

This query is also a multi-key query. But, this query will perform better, because we are at least specifying a complete partition key. This way, a token-aware application will not require a coordinator node, and will be able to go directly to the one node that can serve this request.

Do note that, if you use `IN`, the same restrictions apply as for other operators. You cannot skip primary keys, and if you use `IN` on a key, you must do the following:

- Specify all of the keys prior to it
- Use `IN` only on the last key specified in the query

Like its ALLOW FILTERING counterpart, IN queries can still be served by one node if the complete partition key is specified. However, it's a good idea to limit the number of values specified with the IN operator to less than 10.

Writing data

Given the ways in which Apache Cassandra has been shown to handle things such as INSERT, UPDATE, and DELETE, it is important to discuss what they have in common. They all result in writes to the database. Let's take a look at how each one behaves in certain scenarios. Assume that we need to keep track of statuses for orders from an e-commerce website. Consider the following table:

```
CREATE TABLE order_status (
  status TEXT,
  order_id UUID,
  shipping_weight_kg DECIMAL,
  total DECIMAL,
  PRIMARY KEY (status,order_id))
WITH CLUSTERING ORDER BY (order_id DESC);
```

The order_status table is for example purposes only, and is intended to be used to show how writes work in Apache Cassandra. I do not recommend building an order-status-tracking system this way.

Inserting data

Let's write some data to that table. To do this, we'll use the INSERT statement. With an INSERT statement, all PRIMARY KEY components must be specified; we will specify status and order_id. Additionally, every column that you wish to provide a value for must be specified in a parenthesis list, followed by the VALUES in their own parenthesis list:

```
INSERT INTO order_status (status,order_id,total) VALUES
('PENDING',UUID(),114.22);
INSERT INTO order_status (status,order_id,total) VALUES
('PENDING',UUID(),33.12);
INSERT INTO order_status (status,order_id,total) VALUES
('PENDING',UUID(),86.63);
INSERT INTO order_status (status,order_id,total,shipping_weight_kg)
   VALUES ('PICKED',UUID(),303.11,2);
INSERT INTO order_status (status,order_id,total,shipping_weight_kg)
```

```
  VALUES ('SHIPPED',UUID(),218.99,1.05);
INSERT INTO order_status (status,order_id,total,shipping_weight_kg)
  VALUES ('SHIPPED',UUID(),177.08,1.2);
```

TIP

If you're going to need a unique identifier for things such as IDs, the UUID() and TIMEUUID() functions can be invoked in-line as a part of INSERT.

As you can see, not all columns need to be specified. In our business case, assume that we do not know the shipping weight until the order has been PICKED. If I query for all orders currently in a PENDING status, it shows shipping_weight_kg as null:

```
SELECT * FROM order_status WHERE status='PENDING';

 status  | order_id                              | shipping_weight_kg |
 total
---------+---------------------------------------+--------------------+------
---
 PENDING | fcb15fc2-feaa-4ba9-a3c6-899d1107cce9 |                null |
114.22
 PENDING | ede8af04-cc66-4b3a-a672-ab1abed64c21 |                null |
86.63
 PENDING | 1da6aef1-bd1e-4222-af01-19d2ab0d8151 |                null |
33.12

(3 rows)
```

Remember, Apache Cassandra does not use null in the same way that other databases may. In the case of Cassandra, null simply means that the currently-requested column does not contain a value.

TIP

Do not literally INSERT a null value into a table. Cassandra treats this as a DELETE, and writes a tombstone. It's also important to make sure that your application code is also not writing nulls for column values that are not set.

Updating data

So now let's update one of our PENDING orders to a status of PICKED, and give it a value for shipping weight. We can start by updating our shipping_weight_kg for order fcb15fc2-feaa-4ba9-a3c6-899d1107cce9, and we'll assume that it is 1.4 kilograms. This can be done in two different ways. Updates and inserts are treated the same in Cassandra, so we could actually update our row with the INSERT statement:

```
INSERT INTO order_status (status,order_id,shipping_weight_kg)
   VALUES ('PENDING',fcb15fc2-feaa-4ba9-a3c6-899d1107cce9,1.4);
```

Or, we can also use the UPDATE statement that we know from SQL:

```
UPDATE order_status SET shipping_weight_kg=1.4
WHERE status='PENDING'
AND order_id=fcb15fc2-feaa-4ba9-a3c6-899d1107cce9;
```

Either way, we can then query our row and see this result:

```
SELECT * FROM order_status
WHERE status='PENDING'
AND order_id=fcb15fc2-feaa-4ba9-a3c6-899d1107cce9;

 status  | order_id                              | shipping_weight_kg |
total
---------+---------------------------------------+--------------------+------
---
 PENDING | fcb15fc2-feaa-4ba9-a3c6-899d1107cce9 |                1.4 |
114.22

(1 rows)
```

Ok, so now how do we set the PENDING status to PICKED? Let's start by trying to UPDATE it, as we would in SQL:

```
UPDATE order_status SET status='PICKED'
WHERE order_id='fcb15fc2-feaa-4ba9-a3c6-899d1107cce9';

InvalidRequest: Error from server: code=2200 [Invalid query]
message="PRIMARY KEY part status found in SET part"
```

With the UPDATE statement in CQL, all the PRIMARY KEY components are required to be specified in the WHERE clause. So how about we try specifying both PRIMARY KEY components in WHERE, and both columns with values in SET:

```
UPDATE order_status SET shipping_weight_kg=1.4,total=114.22
WHERE status='PICKED'
AND order_id=fcb15fc2-feaa-4ba9-a3c6-899d1107cce9;
```

So that doesn't error out, but did it work? To figure that out, let's run a (bad) query using ALLOW FILTERING:

```
SELECT * FROM order_status WHERE order_id=fcb15fc2-feaa-4ba9-
a3c6-899d1107cce9 ALLOW FILTERING;

 status  | order_id                             | shipping_weight_kg |
 total
---------+--------------------------------------+--------------------+-----
---
 PENDING | fcb15fc2-feaa-4ba9-a3c6-899d1107cce9 |                1.4 |
 114.22
  PICKED | fcb15fc2-feaa-4ba9-a3c6-899d1107cce9 |                1.4 |
 114.22

(2 rows)
```

So for this order ID, there are now two rows present in our table; not at all what we really wanted to do. Sure, we now have our order in a PICKED state, but our PENDING row is still out there. Why did this happen?

First of all, with both INSERT and UPDATE you must specify all of the PRIMARY KEY components or the operation will fail. Secondly, primary keys are unique in Cassandra. When used together, they essentially point to the column values we want. But that also means they cannot be updated. The only way to update a PRIMARY KEY component is to delete and then rewrite it.

> To Cassandra, INSERT and UPDATE are synonymous. They behave the same, and can mostly be used interchangeably. They both write column values to a specific set of unique keys in the table. You can insert new rows with UPDATE and you can update existing rows with INSERT.

Deleting data

While deleting data and its associated implications have been discussed, there are times when rows or individual column values may need to be deleted. In our use case, we discussed the difficulties of trying to work with the primary key on something that needs to be dynamic, such as `status`. In our case, we have an extra row for our order that we need to delete:

```
DELETE FROM order_status
WHERE status='PENDING'
AND order_id=fcb15fc2-feaa-4ba9-a3c6-899d1107cce9;
```

As mentioned previously, `DELETE` can also enforce the removal of individual column values:

```
DELETE shipping_weight_kg FROM order_status
WHERE status='PICKED'
AND order_id=99886f63-f271-459d-b0b1-218c09cd05a2;
```

Again, take care when using `DELETE`. Deleting creates tombstones, which can be problematic to both data consistency and query performance.

Similar to the previous write operations, `DELETE` requires a complete primary key. But unlike the other write operations, you do not need to provide all of the clustering keys. In this way, multiple rows in a partition can be deleted with a single command.

Lightweight transactions

One difference between the CQL `INSERT` and `UPDATE` statements is in how they handle lightweight transactions. Lightweight transactions are essentially a way for Apache Cassandra to enforce a sequence of read-and-then-write operations to apply conditional writes.

Lightweight transactions are invokable at query time. Apache Cassandra implements the paxos (consensus algorithm) to enforce concurrent lightweight transactions on the same sets of data.

A lightweight transaction in flight will block other lightweight transactions, but will not stop normal reads and writes from querying or mutating the same data.

In any case, an INSERT statement can only check whether a row does not already exist for the specified the PRIMARY KEY components. If we consider our attempts to insert a new row to set our order status to PENDING, this could have been used:

```
INSERT INTO order_status (status,order_id,shipping_weight_kg
VALUES ('PENDING',fcb15fc2-feaa-4ba9-a3c6-899d1107cce9,1.4)
IF NOT EXISTS;
```

Essentially what is happening here is that Cassandra is performing a read to verify the existence of a row with the specified keys. If that row exists, the operation does not proceed, and a response consisting of applied with a value of false (along with the column values which failed to write) is returned. If it succeeds, an applied value of true is returned.

On the other hand, UPDATE allows for more granular control in terms of lightweight transactions. It allows for the use of both IF EXISTS and IF NOT EXISTS. Additionally, it can determine whether a write should occur based on arbitrary column values. In our previous example, we could make our update to shipping_weight_kg and order total based on a threshold for shipping_weight_kg:

```
UPDATE order_status SET shipping_weight_kg=1.4,total=114.22
WHERE status='PICKED' AND order_id=fcb15fc2-feaa-4ba9-a3c6-899d1107cce9
IF shipping_weight_kg > 1.0;
```

Deletes can also make use of lightweight transactions, much in the same way that updates do:

```
DELETE FROM order_status
WHERE status='PENDING'
AND order_id=fcb15fc2-feaa-4ba9-a3c6-899d1107cce9
IF EXISTS;
```

Lightweight transactions do incur a performance penalty, so use them sparingly. However using them with DELETE is probably the best use case, as the performance hit is preferable to generating many needless tombstones.

Executing a BATCH statement

One of the more controversial features of CQL is the `BATCH` statement. Essentially, this allows for write operations to be grouped together and applied at once, automatically. Therefore, if one of the statements should fail, they are all rolled back. A common application of this is for developers to write the same data to multiple query tables, keeping them in sync. `BATCH` statements in CQL can be applied as such:

```
BEGIN BATCH
 INSERT INTO security_logs_by_location
(location_id,day,time_in,employee_id,mailstop)
 VALUES ('MPLS2',20180726,'2018-07-26 11:45:22.004','robp','M266');
 INSERT INTO security_logs_by_location_desc
(location_id,day,time_in,employee_id,mailstop)
 VALUES ('MPLS2',20180726,'2018-07-26 11:45:22.004','robp','M266');
APPLY BATCH;
```

Note that statements in `BATCH` are not guaranteed to be executed in any particular order. All statements within a batch are assumed to have been applied at the same time, and so will bear the same write timestamps.

What makes this functionality controversial is that it bears a resemblance to a keyword in the RDBMS world, which behaves very differently. RDBMS developers are encouraged to apply several (sometimes thousands) of writes in a batch, to apply them all in one network trip, and gain some performance. With Cassandra, this approach is dangerous, because batching too many writes together can exacerbate a coordinator node and potentially cause it to crash.

> `BATCH` was just not designed to apply several updates to the same table. It was designed to apply one update to several (such as five or six) tables. This fundamental misunderstanding of the purpose of `BATCH` can potentially affect cluster availability.

The expiring cell

Apache Cassandra allows for data in cells to be expired. This is called setting a TTL. TTLs can be applied at write-time, or they can be enforced at the table level with a default value. To set a TTL on a row at write time, utilize the `USING TTL` clause:

```
INSERT INTO query_test (pk1,pk2,ck3,ck4,c5)
VALUES ('f','g','c4','d6','e7')
USING TTL 86400;
```

Likewise, TTLs can also be applied with the UPDATE statement:

```
UPDATE query_test
USING TTL 86400
SET c5='e7'
WHERE pk1='f' AND pk2='g' AND ck3='c4' AND ck4='d6';
```

TTLs represent the number of seconds elapsed since write-time.

One day is 86,400 seconds.

Altering a keyspace

Changing a keyspace to use a different RF or strategy is a simple matter of using the ALTER KEYSPACE command. Let's assume that we have created a keyspace called packt_test:

```
CREATE KEYSPACE packt_test WITH replication = {
  'class': 'SimpleStrategy', 'replication_factor': '1'}
AND durable_writes = true;
```

As it is preferable to use NetworkTopologyStrategy, we can alter that easily:

```
ALTER KEYSPACE packt_test  WITH replication = {
'class':'NetworkTopologyStrategy',
  'datacenter1': '1'};
```

If, at some point, we want to add our second data center, that command would look like this:

```
ALTER KEYSPACE packt_test  WITH replication = { 'class':
'NetworkTopologyStrategy',
  'datacenter1': '1', 'datacenter2': '1'};
```

If we added more nodes to both data centers, and needed to increase the RF in each, we can simply run this:

```
ALTER KEYSPACE packt_test  WITH replication = {'class':
'NetworkTopologyStrategy',
  'datacenter1': '3', 'datacenter2': '3'};
```

Updating an RF on a keyspace does not automatically move data around. The data will need to be streamed via repair, rebuild, or bootstrap.

Dropping a keyspace

Removing a keyspace is a simple matter of using the DROP KEYSPACE command:

```
DROP KEYSPACE packt_test;
```

 Dropping a keyspace does not actually remove the data from disk.

Altering a table

Tables can be changed with the ALTER statement, using it to add a column:

```
ALTER TABLE query_test ADD c6 TEXT;
```

Or to remove a column:

```
ALTER TABLE query_test DROP c5;
```

 Primary key definitions cannot be changed on a table. To accomplish this, the table must be recreated.

Table options can also be set or changed with the ALTER statement. For example, this statement updates the default TTL on a table to one day (in seconds):

```
ALTER TABLE query_test WITH default_time_to_live = 86400;
```

Truncating a table

To remove all data from a table, you can use the TRUNCATE TABLE command:

```
TRUNCATE TABLE query_test;
```

Dropping a table

Removing a table is a simple matter of using the DROP TABLE command:

```
DROP TABLE query_test;
```

 Try to avoid frequent drops or creates of a table with the same name. This process has proven to be problematic with Apache Cassandra in the past. If you need to recreate a table, it's always a good idea to TRUNCATE it before dropping it. It may be helpful to create a table with a version number on the end of it (query_test_v2) to prevent this problem from occurring.

Truncate versus drop

It's important to note that dropping a table is different from truncating it. A drop will remove the table from the schema definition, but the data will remain on-disk. With truncate, the data is removed, but the schema remains. Truncate is also the only way to clear all data from a table in a single command, as a CQL delete requires key parameters.

Creating an index

Cassandra comes with the ability to apply distributed, secondary indexes on arbitrary columns in a table. For an application of this, let's look at a different solution for our order_status table. For starters, we'll add the date/time of the order as a clustering column. Next, we'll store the total as a BIGINT representing the number of cents (instead of DECIMAL for dollars), to ensure that we maintain our precision accuracy. But the biggest difference is that, in talking with our business resources, we will discover that bucketing by week will give us a partition of manageable size:

```
CREATE TABLE order_status_by_week (
    week_bucket bigint,
    order_datetime timestamp,
    order_id uuid,
    shipping_weight_kg decimal,
    status text,
    total bigint,
    PRIMARY KEY (week_bucket, order_datetime, order_id)
) WITH CLUSTERING ORDER BY (order_datetime DESC, order_id ASC)
```

Next, we will add similar rows into this table:

```
INSERT INTO order_status_by_week
(status,order_id,total,week_bucket,order_datetime)
VALUES ('PENDING',UUID(),11422,20180704,'2018-07-25 15:22:28');
INSERT INTO order_status_by_week
(status,order_id,total,week_bucket,order_datetime)
VALUES ('PENDING',UUID(),3312,20180704,'2018-07-27 09:44:18');
INSERT INTO order_status_by_week
(status,order_id,total,week_bucket,order_datetime)
VALUES ('PENDING',UUID(),8663,20180704,'2018-07-27 11:33:01');
INSERT INTO order_status_by_week
(status,order_id,total,shipping_weight_kg,week_bucket,order_datetime)
VALUES ('PICKED',UUID(),30311,2,20180704,'2018-07-24 16:02:47');
INSERT INTO order_status_by_week
(status,order_id,total,shipping_weight_kg,week_bucket,order_datetime)
VALUES ('SHIPPED',UUID(),21899,1.05,20180704,'2018-07-24 13:28:54');
INSERT INTO order_status_by_week
(status,order_id,total,shipping_weight_kg,week_bucket,order_datetime)
VALUES ('SHIPPED',UUID(),17708,1.2,20180704,'2018-07-25 08:02:29');
```

Now I can query for orders placed during the fourth week of July, 2018:

```
SELECT * FROM order_status_by_week WHERE week_bucket=20180704;

week_bucket | order_datetime                  | order_id |
shipping_weight_kg | status  | total
------------+--------------------------------+-------------------------
-----------+----------------------+---------+------
   20180704 | 2018-07-27 16:33:01.000000+0000 | 02d3af90-f315-41d9-
ab59-4c69884925b9 |                 null | PENDING | 8663
   20180704 | 2018-07-27 14:44:18.000000+0000 | cb210378-752f-4a6b-
bd2c-6d41afd4e614 |                 null | PENDING | 3312
   20180704 | 2018-07-25 20:22:28.000000+0000 | 59cf4afa-742c-4448-
bd99-45c61660aa64 |                 null | PENDING | 11422
   20180704 | 2018-07-25 13:02:29.000000+0000 | c5d111b9-d048-4829-
a998-1ca51c107a8e |                  1.2 | SHIPPED | 17708
   20180704 | 2018-07-24 21:02:47.000000+0000 | b111d1d3-9e54-481e-858e-
b56e38a14b57 |                    2 | PICKED  | 30311
   20180704 | 2018-07-24 18:28:54.000000+0000 |
c8b3101b-7804-444f-9c4f-65c17ff201f2 |                 1.05 | SHIPPED | 21899

(6 rows)
```

This works, but without status as a part of the primary key definition, how can we query for PENDING orders? Here is where we will add a secondary index to handle this scenario:

```
CREATE INDEX [index_name] ON [keyspace_name.]<table_name>(<column_name>);
```

You can create an index without a name. Its name will then default to
`[table_name]_[column_name]_idx`.

In the following code block, we will create an index, and then show how it is used:

```
CREATE INDEX order_status_idx ON order_status_by_week(status);

SELECT week_bucket,order_datetime,order_id,status,total FROM
order_status_by_week
 WHERE week_bucket=20180704 AND status='PENDING';

 week_bucket | order_datetime        | order_id                             |
status  | total
-------------+-----------------------+--------------------------------------
+------------------
    20180704 | 2018-07-27 16:33:01 | 02d3af90-f315-41d9-ab59-4c69884925b9 |
PENDING |  8663
    20180704 | 2018-07-27 14:44:18 | cb210378-752f-4a6b-bd2c-6d41afd4e614 |
PENDING |  3312
    20180704 | 2018-07-25 20:22:28 | 59cf4afa-742c-4448-bd99-45c61660aa64 |
PENDING | 11422

(3 rows)
```

In this way, we can query on a column that has a more dynamic value. The status of the
order can effectively be updated, without having to delete the entire prior row.

Caution with implementing secondary indexes

While secondary indexes seem like a simple solution to add a dynamic querying capability
to a Cassandra model, caution needs to be given when addressing their use. Effective, high-
performing, distributed database-indexing is a computing problem that has yet to be
solved. Proper, well-defined queries based on primary key definitions are high-performing
within Apache Cassandra, because they take the underlying storage model into
consideration. Secondary indexing actually works against this principle.

Secondary indexes in Apache Cassandra store data in a hidden table (behind the scenes)
that only contains lookups for data contained on the current node. Essentially, a secondary
index query (which is not also filtered by a partition key) will need to confer with every
node in the cluster. This can be problematic with large clusters and potentially lead to
query timeouts.

Our preceding example using a secondary index gets around this problem, because our query is also filtering by its partition key. This forces the query to limit itself to a single node.

Cardinality is another problem to consider when building a secondary index in Apache Cassandra. Let's say we created a secondary index on `order_id`, so that we can pull up an individual order if we had to. In that scenario, the high cardinality of `order_id` would essentially mean that we would query every node in the cluster, just to end up reading one partition from one node.

Author (and DataStax Cassandra MVP) Richard Low accurately explains this in his article *The Sweet Spot for Cassandra Secondary Indexing*, when he describes creating an index on a high-cardinality column such as an email address:

> *This means only one node (plus replicas) store data for a given email address but all nodes are queried for each lookup. This is wasteful—every node has potentially done a disk seek but we've only got back one partition.*

On the flip-side of that coin, consider a secondary index on a low-cardinality column, such as a Boolean. Now consider that the table in question has 20,000,000 rows. With an even distribution, both index entries will each point to 10,000,000 rows. That is far too many to be querying at once.

We have established that querying with a secondary index in conjunction with a partition key can perform well. But is there a time when querying only by a secondary index could be efficient? Once again, Low's article concludes the following:

> *...the best use case for Cassandra's secondary indexes is when p is approximately n; i.e. the number of partitions is about equal to the number of nodes. Any fewer partitions and your n index lookups are wasted; many more partitions and each node is doing many seeks. In practice, this means indexing is most useful for returning tens, maybe hundreds of results.*

In conclusion, secondary indexing can help with large solutions at scale under certain conditions. But when used alone, the trade-off is usually one of giving up performance in exchange for convenience. The number of nodes in the cluster, total partition keys, and cardinality of the column in question must all be taken into consideration.

Dropping an index

Dropping a secondary index on a table is a simple task:

```
DROP INDEX [index_name]
```

If you do not know the name of the index (or created it without a name), you can describe the table to find it. Indexes on a table will appear at the bottom of the definition. Then you can DROP it:

```
CREATE INDEX ON query_test(c5);
DESC TABLE query_test ;

CREATE TABLE packt_ch3.query_test (
    pk1 text,
    pk2 text,
    ck3 text,
    ck4 text,
    c5 text,
    PRIMARY KEY ((pk1, pk2), ck3, ck4)
) WITH CLUSTERING ORDER BY (ck3 DESC, ck4 ASC)
...
    AND speculative_retry = '99PERCENTILE';
CREATE INDEX query_test_c5_idx ON packt_ch3.query_test (c5);

DROP INDEX query_test_c5_idx ;
```

Creating a custom data type

Apache Cassandra allows for the creation of custom **user-defined types** (**UDTs**). UDTs allow for further denormalization of data within a row. A good example of this is a mailing address for customers. Assume a simple table:

```
CREATE TABLE customer (
 last_name TEXT,
 first_name TEXT,
 company TEXT,
 PRIMARY KEY (last_name, first_name));
```

Now, our customers have mailing addresses. Corporate customers usually have addresses for multiple things, including billing, shipping, headquarters, distribution centers, store locations, and data centers. So how do we track multiple addresses for a single customer? One way to accomplish this would be to create a collection of a UDT:

```
CREATE TYPE customer_address (
 type TEXT,
 street TEXT,
 city TEXT,
 state TEXT,
 postal_code TEXT,
 country TEXT);
```

Now, let's add the `customer_address` UDT to the table as a list. This way, a customer can have multiple addresses:

```
ALTER TABLE customer ADD addresses LIST<FROZEN <customer_address>>;
```

The `FROZEN` types are those that are immutable. They are written once and cannot be changed, short of rewriting all underlying properties.

With that in place, let's add a few rows to the table:

```
INSERT INTO customer (last_name,first_name,company,addresses) VALUES
('Washburne','Hoban','Serenity',[{type:'SHIPPING',street:'9843 32nd
Place',city:'Charlotte',state:'NC',postal_code:'05601',country:'USA'}]);
INSERT INTO customer (last_name,first_name,company,addresses) VALUES
('Washburne','Zoey','Serenity',[{type:'SHIPPING',street:'9843 32nd
Place',city:'Charlotte',state:'NC',postal_code:'05601',country:'USA'},{type
:'BILL TO',street:'9800 32nd
Place',city:'Charlotte',state:'NC',postal_code:'05601',country:'USA'}]);
INSERT INTO customer (last_name,first_name,company,addresses) VALUES
('Tam','Simon','Persephone General Hospital',[{type:'BILL TO',street:'83595
25th
Boulevard',city:'Lawrence',state:'KS',postal_code:'66044',country:'USA'}]);
```

Querying it for Zoey Washburne shows that her company has two addresses:

```
SELECT last_name,first_name,company,addresses FROM customer
WHERE last_name='Washburne' AND first_name='Zoey';

last_name | first_name |   company | addresses
------------+------------+-------------------------------------------------------
---------------------------------------------------------------------------------
---------------------------------------------------------------------------------
-----------------------------------------------------------------+---------
-
Washburne |        Zoey | Serenity |[{type: 'SHIPPING', street: '9843 32nd
Place', city: 'Charlotte', state: 'NC', postal_code: '05601', country:
'USA', street2: null}, {type: 'BILL TO', street: '9800 32nd Place', city:
'Charlotte', state: 'NC', postal_code: '05601', country: 'USA', street2:
null}]

(1 rows)
```

Altering a custom type

UDTs can have columns added to them. For instance, some addresses have two lines, so we can add an address2 column:

```
ALTER TYPE customer_address ADD address2 TEXT;
```

UDT columns can also be renamed with the ALTER command:

```
ALTER TYPE customer_address RENAME address2 TO street2;
```

 Columns within a UDT cannot be removed or dropped, only added or renamed.

Dropping a custom type

UDTs can be dropped very easily, just by issuing the DROP command. If we create a simple UDT:

```
CREATE TYPE test_type (value TEXT);
```

It can be dropped like this:

```
DROP TYPE test_type;
```

User management

As of Apache Cassandra 2.2, Cassandra uses a role-based permission system. CQL can be utilized by a superuser to create and manage roles within Apache Cassandra. Roles can be general permission designations assigned to users or they can be users themselves.

 The syntax provided will be for the role security of Apache Cassandra 2.2 and up. The syntax for managing users in prior versions is different. Thus, these commands will not work. For information on managing security in earlier versions, please consult the documentation for the appropriate version.

Creating a user and role

This creates a new role called `cassdba` (as seen in `Chapter 1`, *Quick Start*) and gives it a password and the ability to log in and makes it a superuser:

```
CREATE ROLE cassdba WITH PASSWORD='flynnLives' AND LOGIN=true and
SUPERUSER=true;
```

We can also create simple roles:

```
CREATE ROLE data_reader;
CREATE ROLE data_test;
```

Creating non-superuser roles looks something like this:

```
CREATE ROLE kyle WITH PASSWORD='bacon' AND LOGIN=true;
CREATE ROLE nate WITH PASSWORD='canada' AND LOGIN=true;
```

Altering a user and role

By far, the most common reason for modifying a role is to change the password. This was also demonstrated in `Chapter 1`, *Quick Start*, in showing how to change the default `cassandra` password:

```
ALTER ROLE cassandra WITH
PASSWORD=dsfawesomethingdfhdfshdlongandindecipherabledfhdfh';
```

Dropping a user and role

Removing a user or role is done like this:

```
DROP ROLE data_test;
```

Granting permissions

Once created, permissions can be granted to roles:

```
GRANT SELECT ON KEYSPACE packt_test TO data_reader;
GRANT MODIFY ON KEYSPACE packt_test TO data_reader;
```

Roles can also be granted to other roles:

```
GRANT data_reader TO kyle;
```

More liberal permissions can also be granted:

```
GRANT ALL PERMISSIONS ON KEYSPACE packt_test TO kyle;
```

Revoking permissions

Sometimes a permission granted to a role will need to be removed. This can be done with the REVOKE command:

```
REVOKE MODIFY ON KEYSPACE packt_test FROM data_reader;
```

Other CQL commands

CQL has some additional commands and constructs that provide additional functionality. A few of them bear a resemblance to their similarly-named SQL counterparts, but may behave differently.

COUNT

CQL allows you to return a count of the number of rows in the result set. Its syntax is quite similar to that of the COUNT aggregate function in SQL. This query will return the number of rows in the customer table with the last name Washburne:

```
SELECT COUNT(*) FROM packt_ch3.customer WHERE last_name='Washburne';

 count
-------
     2
(1 rows)
```

The most common usage of this function in SQL was to count the number of rows in a table with an unbound query. Apache Cassandra allows you to attempt this, but it does warn you:

```
SELECT COUNT(*) FROM packt_ch3.customer;

 count
-------
     3
(1 rows)
Warnings :
Aggregation query used without partition key
```

This warning is Cassandra's way of informing you that the query was not very efficient. As described earlier, unbound queries (queries without WHERE clauses) must communicate with every node in the cluster. COUNT queries are no different, and so these queries should be avoided.

cqlsh has a hard limit of 10,000 rows per query, so COUNT queries run from cqlsh on large tables will max out at that number.

DISTINCT

CQL has a construct that intrinsically removes duplicate partition key entries from a result set, using the DISTINCT keyword. It works in much the same way as its SQL counterpart:

```
SELECT DISTINCT last_name FROM customer;

 last_name
-----------
       Tam
 Washburne
(2 rows)
```

The main difference of DISTINCT in CQL is that it only operates on partition keys and static columns.

> The only time in which DISTINCT is useful is when running an unbound query. This can appear to run efficiently in small numbers (fewer than 100). Do remember that it still has to reach out to all the nodes in the cluster.

LIMIT

CQL allows the use of the LIMIT construct, which enforces a maximum number of rows for the query to return. This is done by adding the LIMIT keyword on the end of a query, followed by an integer representing the number of rows to be returned:

```
SELECT * FROM security_logs_by_location LIMIT 1;

 location_id | day      | time_in             | employee_id | mailstop
-------------+----------+---------------------+-------------+----------
       MPLS2 | 20180723 | 2018-07-23 11:49:11 |        samb | M266
(1 rows)
```

STATIC

Static columns are data that is more dependent on the partition keys than on the clustering keys. Specifying a column as STATIC ensures that its values are only stored once (with its partition keys) and not needlessly repeated in storage with the row data.

A new table can be created with a `STATIC` column like this:

```
CREATE TABLE packt_ch3.fighter_jets (
  type TEXT PRIMARY KEY,
  nickname TEXT STATIC,
  serial_number BIGINT);
```

Likewise, an existing table can be altered to contain a `STATIC` column:

```
ALTER TABLE packt_ch3.users_by_dept ADD department_head TEXT STATIC;
```

Now, we can update data in that column:

```
INSERT INTO packt_ch3.users_by_dept (department,department_head) VALUES
('Engineering','Richard');
INSERT INTO packt_ch3.users_by_dept (department,department_head) VALUES
('Marketing','Erlich');
INSERT INTO packt_ch3.users_by_dept (department,department_head) VALUES
('Finance/HR','Jared');

SELECT department,username,department_head,title FROM
packt_ch3.users_by_dept ;
```

department	username	department_head	title
Engineering	Dinesh	Richard	Dev Lead
Engineering	Gilfoyle	Richard	Sys Admin/DBA
Engineering	Richard	Richard	CEO
Marketing	Erlich	Erlich	CMO
Finance/HR	Jared	Jared	COO

```
(5 rows)
```

As shown, `department_head` only changes as per `department`. This is because `department_head` is now stored with the partition key.

User-defined functions

As of version 3.0, Apache Cassandra allows users to create **user-defined functions** (**UDFs**). As CQL does not supply much in the way of extra tools and string utilities found in SQL, some of that function can be recreated with a UDF. Let's say that we want to query the current year from a `date` column. The `date` column will return the complete year, month, and day:

```
SELECT todate(now()) FROM system.local;

system.todate(system.now())
```

```
------------------------------
               2018-08-03
(1 rows)
```

To just get the year back, we could handle that in the application code, or, after enabling user-defined functions in the `cassandra.yaml` file, we could write a small UDF using the Java language:

```
CREATE OR REPLACE FUNCTION year (input DATE)
  RETURNS NULL ON NULL INPUT RETURNS TEXT
  LANGUAGE java AS 'return input.toString().substring(0,4);';
```

Now, re-running the preceding query with `todate(now())` nested inside my new `year()` UDF returns this result:

```
SELECT packt_ch3.year(todate(now())) FROM system.local;

packt_ch3.year(system.todate(system.now()))
---------------------------------------------
                                         2018
(1 rows)
```

 To prevent injection of malicious code, UDFs are disabled by default. To enable their use, set `enable_user_defined_functions: true` in `cassandra.yaml`. Remember that changes to that file require the node to be restarted before they take effect.

cqlsh commands

It's important to note that the commands described in this section are part of cqlsh only. They are not part of CQL. Attempts to run these commands from within the application code will not succeed.

CONSISTENCY

By default, cqlsh is set to a consistency level of ONE. But it also allows you to specify a custom consistency level, depending on what you are trying to do. These different levels can be set with the CONSISTENCY command:

```
CONSISTENCY LOCAL_QUORUM;

SELECT last_name,first_name FROM customer ;
```

```
last_name | first_name
-----------+------------
      Tam |      Simon
Washburne |      Hoban
Washburne |       Zoey

(3 rows)
```

On a related note, queries at CONSISTENCY ALL force a read repair to occur. If you find yourself troubleshooting a consistency issue on a small to mid-sized table (fewer than 20,000 rows), you can quickly repair it by setting the consistency level to ALL and querying the affected rows.

> Querying at consistency ALL and forcing a read repair comes in handy when facing replication errors on something such as the system_auth tables.

```
CONSISTENCY ALL;
Consistency level set to ALL.

SELECT COUNT(*) FROM system_auth.roles;

 count
-------
     4
(1 rows)

Warnings :
Aggregation query used without partition key
```

COPY

The COPY command delivered with cqlsh is a powerful tool that allows you to quickly export and import data. Let's assume that I wanted to duplicate my customer table data into another query table. I'll start by creating the new table:

```
CREATE TABLE customer_by_company ( last_name text,
   first_name text,
   addresses list<frozen<customer_address>>,
   company text,
   PRIMARY KEY (company, last_name, first_name));
```

Next, I will export the contents of my `customer` table using the `COPY TO` command:

```
COPY customer (company,last_name,first_name,addresses) TO
'/home/aploetz/Documents/Packt/customer.txt' WITH DELIMITER= '|' AND
HEADER=true;
Reading options from the command line: {'header': 'true', 'delimiter': '|'}
Using 3 child processes

Starting copy of packt_ch3.customer with columns [company, last_name,
first_name, addresses].
Processed: 3 rows; Rate: 28 rows/s; Avg. rate: 7 rows/s
3 rows exported to 1 files in 0.410 seconds.
```

And finally, I will import that file into a new table using the `COPY FROM` command:

```
COPY customer_by_company (company,last_name,first_name,addresses) FROM
'/home/aploetz/Documents/Packt/customer.txt' WITH HEADER=true and
DELIMITER='|';
Reading options from the command line: {'header': 'true', 'delimiter': '|'}
Using 3 child processes

Starting copy of packt_ch3.customer_by_company with columns [company,
last_name, first_name, addresses].
Processed: 3 rows; Rate: 5 rows/s; Avg. rate: 7 rows/s
3 rows imported from 1 files in 0.413 seconds (0 skipped).
```

Sometimes exporting larger tables will require additional options to be set, in order to eliminate timeouts and errors. For instance, the `COPY TO` options of `PAGESIZE` and `PAGETIMEOUT` control how many rows are read for export at once and how long each read has before it times out. These options can help to effectively break up the export operation into smaller chunks, which may be necessary based on the size and topology of the cluster.

> `COPY` has a bit of a bad reputation, as early versions were subject to timeouts when exporting large tables. Remember that the `COPY` tool itself is also subject to the constraints applied by the Apache Cassandra storage model. This means that exporting a large table is an expensive operation. That being said, I have managed to leverage the `PAGESIZE` and `PAGETIMEOUT` options to successfully export 350,000,000 rows from a 40-node cluster without timeouts or errors.

DESCRIBE

DESCRIBE is a command that can be used to show the definition(s) for a particular object. Its command structure looks like this:

```
DESC[RIBE] (KEYSPACE|TABLE|TYPE|INDEX) <object_name>;
```

In putting it to use, you can quickly see that it can be used to view things such as full table options, keyspace replication, and index definitions.

The DESCRIBE command can be shortened to DESC.

Here, we will demonstrate using the DESC command on a table:

```
DESC TYPE customer_address;

CREATE TYPE packt_ch3.customer_address (
  type text,
  street text,
  city text,
  state text,
  postal_code text,
  country text,
  street2 text
);
```

Likewise, the DESC command can be used to describe an INDEX:

```
DESC INDEX order_status_idx;

CREATE INDEX order_status_idx ON packt_ch3.order_status_by_week (status);
```

TRACING

The TRACING command is a toggle that allows the tracing functionality to be turned on:

```
TRACING ON
Now Tracing is enabled

TRACING
Tracing is currently enabled. Use TRACING OFF to disable
```

Tracing is useful in that it can show why particular queries may be running slowly. A tracing report allows you to view things about a query, such as the following:

- Nodes contacted
- Number of SSTables read
- Number of tombstones encountered
- How long the query took to run

Tracing will be covered in more detail in Chapter 5, *Performance Tuning*.

Summary

Our goals for this chapter included discussing the details behind CQL. This includes its syntax and usage and evolution as a language and comparing some of its capabilities to the well-known SQL of the relational database world. In addition, I have included tips and notes regarding the application of the functionalities covered, as well as how they can be leveraged in certain situations.

One point that should be abundantly clear is that building a good data model is a key part of the foundation to any high-performing, scalable application. The main component of which is the primary key definition. Building your primary keys properly, while taking into account data distribution and appropriate query flexibility, is without a doubt the most important lesson in this chapter, and arguably in this book.

While the next chapters will include more information about performance-tuning Apache Cassandra nodes, clusters, and networks, remember that the main point for tuning is the data model itself. There is no amount of tuning that can mediate a bad data model. Do your best to start with a data model that takes Cassandra's storage architecture *and* your application's query requirements into account, and the amount of further tuning required should be minimal. It is my sincere hope that the examples covered in this chapter help you to leverage the power of CQL and Apache Cassandra to build successful applications.

4
Configuring a Cluster

This chapter will cover planning, configuring, and deploying an Apache Cassandra cluster. By the end of this chapter, you will understand the decisions behind provisioning resources, installing Cassandra, and getting nodes to behave properly while working together to serve large-scale datasets. When appropriate, considerations for cloud deployments will be interjected.

Specifically, this chapter will cover the following topics:

- Sizing hardware and computer resources for Cassandra deployments
- Operating system optimizations
- Tips and suggestions on orchestration
- Configuring the JVM
- Configuring Cassandra

At the end of this chapter, you should be able to make good decisions about architecting an Apache Cassandra cluster. You should have an understanding of the target instances and providers to deploy on, and be able to articulate the pros/cons of deploying to different types of infrastructure.

Additionally, you will have found ways to configure Cassandra to work under various conditions and use cases.

Evaluating instance requirements

Knowing how to appropriately size hardware for a new Cassandra cluster is a vital step to helping your application team succeed. Instances running Apache Cassandra must have sufficient resources available to be able to support the required operational workload.

One important note about the hardware/instance requirements for Cassandra is that it was designed to run on commodity-level hardware. While some enterprise RDBMS suppliers recommend copious amounts of RAM and several dozen CPU cores on a proprietary chassis, Cassandra can run on much, much less. In fact, Cassandra can be made to run on small to mid-sized cloud instances, or even something as meager as a Raspberry Pi. However, as with most databases, Cassandra will obviously perform better with more resource.

 The word instance was chosen here instead of hardware or machine. This is because many large-scale Cassandra deployments are now fully running in public clouds. Compare this with the situation as little as 5 years ago, when most deployments were made on dedicated, on-premises hardware.

RAM

Cassandra runs on a JVM, and therefore needs to have a sufficient amount of RAM available. The JVM heap size will be the primary consideration, as most of the memory that Cassandra will use will be on-heap. The off-heap activity will be largely driven by how much is configured for off-heap memtables (see the following section on configuring Cassandra). And of course, the operating system needs to have its share of RAM as well.

Most Cassandra production deployments should have between 32 GB and 64 GB per instance. Cloud instances with as little as 16 GB of RAM can be effective as well. While Cassandra can be made to work on less, great care should be taken if a production cluster is built on instances with a smaller amount of RAM. Compare this to many relational databases, which typically recommend system RAM be in the 64 GB to 256 GB range.

CPU

The CPU is still the heart of the instance, and today most have multiple CPU cores. While CPU is not typically a bottleneck with Cassandra, having more available processing power can give a boost to heavy operational workloads.

One way in which modern CPUs get more processing power is by provisioning a single CPU core into two virtual CPUs. This is known as **Hyper-Threading**. Hyper-Threading allows a single CPU core to handle multiple tasks in parallel, essentially functioning as if it were two cores. Author and engineer Amy Tobey provides some insight here in her "Amy's Cassandra 2.1 tuning guide," indicating that although many databases (Tobey, 2015) recommend disabling Hyper-Threading, Cassandra has shown to benefit from it.

A production instance running Cassandra should have between eight and 24 CPU cores at its disposal, with Hyper-Threading enabled. Instances can be built with less than that, but try not to go lower than four. Also make sure that the CPU has an adequate amount of cache at its disposal (16 MB to 32 MB).

In the multi-core CPU world, reading from RAM takes about 100 nanoseconds (Bonér, 2012). CPU cache reads happen in single-digit ns (Bonér, 2012). The more CPU cache available, the less frequently RAM needs to be read from (Tobey, 2015).

Disk

This is the one resource that probably has the most room for variance. Several factors can help to determine the optimal disk size:

- Anticipated size of a single copy of the dataset
- **Replication Factor (RF)**
- Operational throughput requirements
- Cost of cloud volumes (usually per hour)
- Compaction strategy used on the larger tables
- Whether the size of the dataset will be static, or grow over time
- Whether the application team has an archival strategy

I have built production Cassandra instances on as much as 1 TB, and as little as 40 GB. Typically, nodes with larger amounts of data also need to have more compute resource available to them.

Let's walk through a little exercise here.

Assume that we need to build a cluster for an application team that needs to store 100 GB of data. The dataset is largely static, and is not expected to grow significantly. We'll go with an RF of three, so the cluster will hold three copies of the data, or 300 GB in total.

We work with the application team, and help them come up with an efficient data model. 100 GB of data isn't too much, so we start with three-nodes. Their largest table is a mix of read and write activity, so we leave the compaction strategy at the default setting of `SizeTieredCompactionStrategy`.

But we also know that `SizeTieredCompactionStrategy` can sometimes double the size of the dataset's largest table during the compaction process. Based on the available data, we need to support 300 GB of data, plus another 300 GB just in case compaction needs it.

That's 600 GB of total disk space required. So, if you guessed that we would need to build our three-nodes with 200 GB of storage, you were correct.

As the application team begins to load their cluster with data and run performance testing, the three-node cluster seems to be topping out at a maximum of 3,000 operations per second. They are concerned that it will not be able to support the 5,000 operations per second that they are anticipating during the holiday season.

Fortunately, we also know that Apache Cassandra scales linearly. That is, if the application team is seeing 3,000 operations per second with three-nodes. We can build two more nodes (making a total of five) to put them at 5,000 operations per second. In fact, we'll build three more (making a total of six), so they should be able to support 6,000 operations per second.

But what does that do for our anticipated disk storage? Keeping our RF the same (three), but doubling the number of nodes from three to six, makes each node responsible for less data. When we started with a three-node cluster with *RF=3*, each node was responsible for 100% of a single copy of the data (100 GB). When we grow to a six-node cluster with *RF=3*, each node is now only responsible for 50% of a single copy of the data, or 50 GB.

That changes things. Assuming that we still use `SizeTieredCompactionStrategy` on the largest table, we should still have 50% of the disk available, just in case. While our total disk space required for the entire cluster remains the same, it reduces the amount of disk space we need for each node. In this way, we can build our nodes with as little as 100 GB and they'll probably be fine.

In the following sections, we'll quickly discuss types of storage and how they should be used with Apache Cassandra.

Solid state drives

Disk I/O tends to be the main bottleneck with Cassandra. Therefore, if money isn't a barrier, you should always use **solid state drives** (**SSDs**). Cassandra has configuration properties that can help to take advantage of the increased read times that SSDs can offer.

On the other hand, there are times when it makes economic sense to go with spinning disks instead. In this case, you'll want to employ some other optimizations, such as procuring a CPU with a larger amount of cache and defining your `commitlog` to be on a different mount point.

Cloud storage offerings

If you are deploying in a public cloud, you should ask your provider if they have SSD-backed storage options available. They can be pricey, but for clusters that are sensitive to read latency they are worth it.

SAN and NAS

One of the most widely-known **Cassandra anti-patterns** is backing your instances with storage from **network attached storage** (**NAS**) or **storage area networks** (**SANs**). While reads from disk may be slow, reads from the network are typically slower.

Furthermore, using a SAN or NAS turns all of your disk I/O into network I/O. This can be especially painful when your cluster is deployed over a large geographic region.

Network

Another possible pain point (if done incorrectly) is network I/O. Make sure your instance has a high-performance NIC, and that your network hardware is solid. A poorly configured or inconsistent network can lead to problems. After all, a distributed database depends on network uptime to be able to adequately communicate with all nodes.

Here, we will outline two networking aspects to be examined prior to a production deployment.

Public cloud networks

As deployments in public clouds have become more prevalent, the uptime of the network connections becomes more important. This can become even more problematic when a single cluster is distributed into data centers across multiple providers.

When working with your cloud providers, the best (and most expensive) option is to go with a direct connection or pipe to their data centers. If that's not possible, a **virtual private network (VPN)** connection can link the provider with your enterprise network. For best results, that connection should be able to support between 1 GB and 10 GB per second.

> I have worked through issues with problematic VPN connections with multiple major cloud providers. Many of the issues stemmed from improper VPN configuration. Be sure to consult with your cloud provider about proper configuration recommendations, and then follow through on them.

Firewall considerations

Once the network is properly configured, it is possible that you may have to open firewall rules to allow traffic between Cassandra nodes and clients. Remember that Cassandra requires the following ports to be opened for TCP traffic:

- 9042 native binary client protocol
- 7199 JMX
- 7000 internode communication
- 7001 internode communication via SSL

> If you are using Cassandra 2.0 or an earlier version, some tools like cqlsh will still connect over port 9160 (Thrift protocol). Use of the Thrift protocol was reduced with Cassandra 2.2, and disabled by default as of Cassandra 3.0. With these newer versions, port 9160 is no longer required to be opened.

Depending on your cloud provider, you may or may not have cross-region communications (such as east to west, and vice versa). To account for this, you may need to set up appropriate security groups for your cloud instances.

Specifically, they will want to allow TCP ingress traffic (for the ports specified previously) for a specified range of IPs, nodes, or tags.

See your cloud provider's documentation on inter-region communication and security.

Strategy for many small instances versus few large instances

One aspect to consider when planning Cassandra node instances is to take the approach of many, smaller instances versus fewer, larger instances. Each approach has its share of advantages and shortcomings.

Larger nodes, consisting of 24+ core CPUs, 64 GB of RAM or more, and disk space consisting of more than a TB, can offer the benefit of concentrating resources onto a smaller number of nodes. Depending on the resource parameters chosen, they can also cost less in the cloud.

But larger nodes can sometimes be difficult to manage in terms of streaming operations, such as repairs or joining new nodes or data centers. Larger nodes also typically means larger JVM heaps, which (prior to the acceptance of the **Garbage First Garbage Collector (G1GC)**) have been pain points for Cassandra, historically.

Smaller nodes, in the neighborhood of four to eight core CPUs, 16 GB of RAM, and disk space of around 100 GB, offer the benefit of distributing data over several smaller containers. This helps for a wider distribution of data, and an increase of overall throughput. Streaming operations tend to be faster, as there is less data to stream and more places to stream it from.

But, with more nodes comes the possibility of more points of failure. In a use case requiring queries at quorum, this may be problematic if multiple nodes happen to fail.

 For the larger node approach, you may find that **ScyllaDB** better suits your needs. ScyllaDB is a drop-in replacement for Cassandra, and is designed for low latency under large node conditions. Visit `https://www.scylladb.com/` for more information.

Operating system optimizations

Apache Cassandra has a long-standing presence on Linux-based operating systems (OS), and will run just fine on many flavors of Linux (both RHEL and Debian-based), UNIX, and BSD. As of Apache Cassandra 2.2, Windows is now supported as a host operating system.

For production clusters, Apache Cassandra should be deployed on the most recent, **Long Term Support (LTS)** release of a Debian or RHEL based Linux.

Cassandra on Windows is still a very new development. If you want to ensure that your cluster is high-performing and problem-free, run it on Linux. The majority of the material in this book assumes that Cassandra is being deployed on Linux.

This book will describe installation variants for Ubuntu 16.04 LTS (Debian), and CentOS 7.4 (RHEL) Linux.

Disable swap

Using swap space with Cassandra is bad for performance. Remember that swap space is essentially disk space used to extend RAM. The big difference is that reading references from RAM can be done in 100 nanoseconds, while disk seeks alone take about 20 milliseconds (Bonér, 2012). The bottom line is that it's better to have less memory than to have lots of slow memory.

Disabling swap is fairly simple, and can be done with this command:

```
sudo swapoff --all
```

Persisting this change after a reboot is done by editing /etc/fstab and removing the swap entries.

XFS

Volumes serving Cassandra data should be formatted with the XFS filesystem. If you are not able to use XFS, then the EXT4 filesystem is a good alternative. ZFS also has a good following in the Cassandra community, but it is currently not supported by most enterprise Linux vendors.

BTRFS should be used with caution (Apache, 2016), and EXT3 is too slow to warrant consideration.

Limits

Here are the additional resource limits and Linux kernel parameters that should be set to ensure maximum performance.

limits.conf

Adjustments to the `/etc/security/limits.conf` file will need to be made for the user that Apache Cassandra will be running as.

It is not recommended to have Cassandra running as the root user. Part of the deployment process should be to create a `cassandra` user, which Cassandra should be made to run as. These entries should be made to the file:

```
cassandra - memlock unlimited
cassandra - nofile 100000
cassandra - nproc 32768
cassandra - as unlimited
```

If there is another user that Cassandra runs as, simply change the `cassandra` username listed in the preceding four entries, and replace it with the other username.

sysctl.conf

The following adjustments to `/etc/sysctl.conf` are recommended. For starters, the default kernel value on max map counts will be too low, so adjust that to the following value:

```
vm.max_map_count = 1048575
```

If any of your firewalls or other network devices are configured to terminate long-lived, idle connections, you should adjust the TCP `keepalive` settings. These keep connections between nodes, data centers, and client apps from being forcibly disconnected:

```
net.ipv4.tcp_keepalive_time=60
net.ipv4.tcp_keepalive_probes=3
net.ipv4.tcp_keepalive_intvl=10
```

Additionally, adjusting the following settings allows the instance to be better equipped to handle the multitude of concurrent connections required by Cassandra (DataStax, 2018):

```
net.core.rmem_max=16777216
net.core.wmem_max=16777216
net.core.rmem_default= 6777216
net.core.wmem_default=16777216
net.core.optmem_max=40960
net.ipv4.tcp_rmem=4096 87380 16777216
net.ipv4.tcp_wmem= 096 65536 16777216
```

I have dealt with issues concerning network configurations with private, internal clouds, resulting in Cassandra connections being terminated prematurely. Be sure to work with your cloud engineering team to ensure that intrinsic or default network settings are not interfering with Cassandra internode or client connections.

Restart the instance to make sure these changes are active, or execute the following command:

```
sudo sysctl -p
```

Time synchronization

As Cassandra's log-based storage is timestamp-driven, it is absolutely critical that all nodes in a cluster have synchronized clocks. To this end, instances running Cassandra should be using NTPD or another time synchronization application to keep all system clocks in a cluster in sync.

Issues related to time synchronization discrepancies can manifest themselves as obsolete data or deleted data ghosting itself.

Consider the following current times from instances in a three-node cluster:

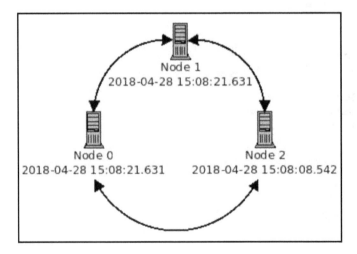

Figure 4.1: A three-node cluster, where one node is behind by about 13 seconds

Let's say I run the following CQL to create a simple table:

```
cassdba@cqlsh:packt> CREATE TABLE keyvalue (key TEXT PRIMARY KEY, value
TEXT);
cassdba@cqlsh:packt> INSERT INTO keyvalue(key,value)
VALUES('timetest','blue');
```

These requests are handled by **Node 1**, and, with an RF of three, replicate out to **Node 0** and **Node 2**. Selecting the key, value, and writetime of that value returns this result:

```
cassdba@cqlsh:packt> SELECT key,value,writetime(value) FROM keyvalue WHERE
key='timetest';

 key       | value | writetime(value)
-----------+-------+--------------------
  timetest |  blue | 1524929184866290
```

So far, so good. Now, let's say about 5 seconds later, I run another INSERT request:

```
cassdba@cqlsh:packt> INSERT INTO keyvalue(key,value)
VALUES('timetest','green');
```

Let's say that this request is handled by **Node 2**, which is behind the other two by 13.009 seconds. The new value of green is persisted on **Node 2**, and the snitch ensures that the other two replicas get written to **Node 0** and **Node 1**.

Let's see what happens when we re-run our SELECT query:

```
cassdba@cqlsh:packt> SELECT key,value,writetime(value) FROM keyvalue WHERE
key='timetest';

 key       | value | writetime(value)
-----------+-------+--------------------
  timetest |  blue | 1524929184866290
```

Wait a minute, shouldn't value be green? What happened was that, as the request was handled by **Node 2**, the value of green was persisted with a writetime of 1524929178272916.

As you can see, this is about 6.6 seconds before the writetime for blue of 1524929184866290.

Essentially, this means that as far as Cassandra is concerned, the most recent write to that data was already present. Hopefully, this demonstrates why it is so important to have your instance clocks synchronized with Cassandra.

Configuring the JVM

Apache Cassandra was written in Java, and therefore requires a JVM to run. Make sure to download a **Java Runtime Environment** (**JRE**) or **Java Development Kit** (**JDK**) to include as a part of your Cassandra installation. Unless otherwise noted, the latest patch of version 8 of the Oracle JDK or OpenJDK should be used.

 At the time of writing, Apache Cassandra is not currently compatible with Java 9 or higher.

Adjustments to the JVM settings used by Cassandra can be made in the `jvm.options` configuration file. Many of those settings deal with the configuration and tuning of the garbage collector.

Garbage collection

Probably the most noticeable aspect of the JVM is how it manages garbage collection. There are two main garbage collectors used: **Concurrent Mark Sweep** (**CMS**) and the G1GC. Both have their strengths and weaknesses, and both can be made to perform well with Cassandra.

 There is so much information available on JVM garbage collection configuration that an entire book could be written on the subject. As this is out of scope for this book, JVM garbage collection settings will be discussed within the parameters of what works best with Cassandra.

CMS

The CMS garbage collector is the default garbage collector that is used with Apache Cassandra. CMS is known as a **generational** garbage collector. It works by dividing the Java heap into contiguous ranges of memory. Each range of memory or generation is responsible for holding objects that are created (and eventually discarded) by a Java application.

When certain conditions arise, the garbage collector runs and reclaims heap space by collecting unused objects, and promoting the remaining objects (survivors) to a different generation:

Eden	Survivor Space		Tenured Space	Permanent Space
	S0	S1	Tenured Space	Permanent Space
Young Gen			Old Gen	Permanent Gen

Figure 4.2: A representation showing the different sections of the JVM heap when using the CMS garbage collector

All objects are created in the `Eden` space of the `Young Gen` (DataStax, 2018). When the `Eden` space is full, unused objects are collected. Those still referenced are moved to a `Survivor Space`.

When these spaces are full (or other thresholds are met), the survivors are then promoted to `Tenured Space`. When this type of collection runs to clean up the `Young Gen`, it is known as a **Minor GC**.

When the space of the `Old Gen` reaches 92% full (Eichwald, 2016), the collection process runs on it as well.

Collections run on the `Old Gen` are not necessarily bad. But, sometimes, a collection can be triggered on both generations concurrently. This process, known as a **Full GC** or a **stop-the-world GC**, is what you want to avoid. It is single threaded (DataStax, 2018), and can be very slow (with Cassandra, stop-the-world pauses as long as 10 seconds are not unheard of).

 The promotion of objects between generations is very expensive, and can happen in both minor and full collections.

Let's examine a graph which exhibits a common, healthy heap usage pattern with the CMS garbage collector:

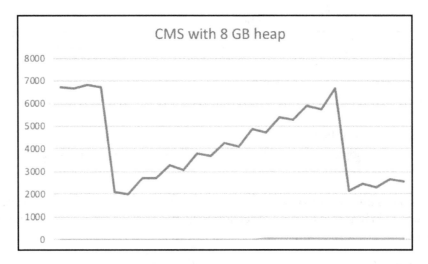

Figure 4.3: A representation of the typical sawtooth garbage collection activity using CMS

The preceding diagram provides a visual representation of the heap memory reclamation pattern typically seen with the CMS garbage collector. Sometimes known as a **sawtooth pattern**, the small changes in heap memory usage represent minor collections, while the big drops (from 6.9 GB down to 2.1 GB) are full collections.

 It is a good idea to graph-out your heap usage, so that you can map and compare it to other graphs, such as read or write latencies. This (combined with the garbage collection logs) can help you to see if you have an issue with garbage collection consuming too much resource.

Here are some helpful settings for using the CMS garbage collector with Apache Cassandra. In fact, if you look in the `jvm.options` file (`cassandra-env.sh` for version <= 2.2), you should see the following JVM properties:

- `-XX:+UseParNewGC`: This indicates that a parallel collector should be used for the new generation, in conjunction with the CMS garbage collector.
- `-XX:+UseConcMarkSweepGC`: This indicates that the CMS collector should be used for the `Old Gen`.
- `-XX:+CMSParallelRemarkEnabled`: This indicates that the remarking cycle is done in parallel. Recommended for many-core instances.

- -XX:SurvivorRatio: This defaults to eight, meaning that each Survivor Space (S0, S1) is one-eighth of the total Young Gen size.
- -XX:MaxTenuringThreshold: This indicates the number of times an object can be copied between Young Gen spaces (Eden and each Survivor Space). Once an object has been copied this many times, it is promoted to the Old Gen. While it is typically defaulted to 1 in the Cassandra configs, increasing it is usually a good idea.
- -XX:+CMSClassUnloadingEnabled: This tells the JVM to unload classes that are no longer needed.
- -Xms: This indicates the initial size of the JVM heap.
- -Xmx: This indicates the maximum size of the JVM heap.
- -Xmn: This indicates the new and Young Gen size (aka the heap new size).

When configuring a CMS heap for use with Apache Cassandra, the cassandra-env.sh file will compute the default size of your heap. First, the maximum heap size is calculated, based on the following formula:

$$Max\ Heap\ Size = max((\tfrac{1}{2}\ RAM, max\ of\ 1024\ MB), (\tfrac{1}{4}\ RAM, max\ of\ 8192\ MB))$$

Similarly, the size of the Young Gen is computed with this formula:

$$Heap\ New\ Size = min((\tfrac{1}{4}\ Max\ Heap\ Size), (cpu\ cores * 100\ MB))$$

The default calculations will probably be fine on a local instance, or maybe even a development environment. But for a stage/test or production environment, the initial, maximum, and new heap sizes should be overridden.

Also by default, the initial heap size and max heap size are set to the same value. This prevents possible latency due to heap sizing.

The default calculation for the maximum heap size is meant to prevent new users from setting their heap sizes too big. Typically, max heap sizes greater than 8 GB are not encouraged with CMS garbage collection. The idea is that (with the current heap new size default formula), increasing the heap simply increases the size of the Old Gen and Permanent Gen, leading to longer pauses during full garbage collections.

In addition to the default calculation, some older documentation on Apache Cassandra also recommends setting the heap new size (the -Xmn parameter) to 100 MB per CPU core. For instances with fewer resources, this is often not sufficient, and can cause the JVM to have to work too hard/often to run collection and promotion on the Eden space and each Survivor Space. A better plan (Tobey, 2015) is to size the new generation to 25% of the maximum heap size (-Xmx).

Some additional recommendations come from the official Apache Cassandra Jira issues project (CASSANDRA-8150). This Jira ticket (Apache, 2016) was opened in late 2014, as an attempt to revisit and update some of the default CMS garbage collection settings. At the time of writing (2018), it remains unresolved.

Despite this, it did spark some good discussion on acceptable CMS settings, based on results observed on clusters backing large-scale social media sites.

According to Haddad, 2018, some of the suggestions are:

- Increasing the max heap size to 20 GB.
- Increasing the size of the new generation between 25% and 50% of max heap size.
- Increasing MaxTenuringThreshold to a value of around six or eight. This allows surviving objects to remain in the Young Gen longer, thus avoiding costly promotions.
- Setting parallel and concurrent garbage collections threads to the minimum value of 20 or more number of cores. The idea here is to find a happy point where the collector can use enough threads to run efficiently, without choking the system of resources.

While CASSANDRA-8150 can help to provide a great deal of information as to how the CMS garbage collector works with Cassandra, do not simply mix and match settings. Please read through the ticket, and only implement settings once you understand what they do. It is also a good idea to implement GC settings in a test or stage environment first (sometimes on a single node for comparison), before trying them in production.

G1GC

A newer garbage collector innovated in the last few years is the G1GC. The G1GC organizes its heap memory differently to the contiguous memory diagram previously seen, used for parallel collectors, such as CMS.

The G1 heap is targeted as a matrix of 2,048 small regions. Each region is between 1 MB and 32 MB, and can be either `Eden` space, `Survivor Space`, or (tenured) `Old Gen` space (Eichwald, 2016). This is demonstrated in the following diagram:

	E	O		O
O		S	S	
O			O	E
S		E	O	O
	O		O	

Figure 4.4: A representation of the different sections of the G1GC heap (25 regions shown for brevity)

In the preceding diagram, the **E** represent the `Eden` space, the **S** represent `Survivor Space`, and the **O** represent `Old Gen`.

The primary setting for G1GC is `MaxGCPauseMillis`. This is a target time for how long a pause will be incurred by the collector. This comes into play as the collector will analyze a sampling of the regions in the heap, and determine which regions it can run on within its target time (DataStax, 2018). The collection of other regions are then delayed until later:

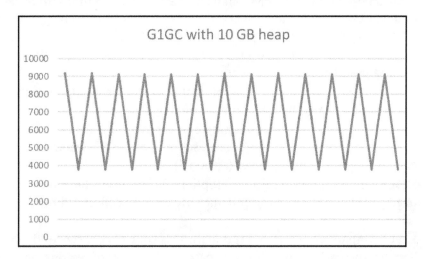

Figure 4.5: A representation of garbage collection activity using G1GC

One easily noticeable difference between the CMS and G1 garbage collectors is that the pattern of heap memory usage graphs quite differently. While CMS heap usage/activity typically resembles the sawtooth pattern, G1 does not.

The G1 collector sees a much larger deviation in heap usage over a short period of time. This rapid reclamation of heap is observed because G1 is designed to make intelligent decisions about which regions to collect and promote.

Another difference is that G1 almost always performs better with larger heap sizes. With heap sizing for G1, the general idea is to estimate how much data will be on-heap at a time and then double it. Ideally, G1 will run with half its space free, allowing it more freedom with region allocation and `Young Gen` sizing.

While a CMS heap shouldn't typically exceed 8 GB, a G1 heap can easily be sized (instance resources permitting) between 20 GB and 26 GB.

Here are some helpful settings for using the G1 garbage collector with Apache Cassandra. As with the CMS settings, the `jvm.options` file (`cassandra-env.sh` for version<=2.2) contains a list of default and optional settings:

- `-XX:+UseG1GC`: This indicates that the JVM should use G1GC.
- `-XX:+G1RSetUpdatingPauseTimePercent=5`: This instructs the JVM to do less remembered set work during stop-the-world pauses.
- `-XX:MaxGCPauseMillis=500`: As mentioned earlier, this is the most impactful setting for tuning G1GC. 500 milliseconds is a good starting point. Note that this is only a target time; the JVM will try to keep collection times under/at this number, but will not always succeed. Increase this value to help with throughput issues; lower it to reduce stop-the-world pauses.
- `-XX:InitiatingHeapOccupancyPercent=70` (optional): This delays region scanning until the heap is 70% full.
- `-XX:ParallelGCThreads=16` (optional): For systems with more than eight CPU cores, the default is 5/8 of the number of logical cores.
- `-XX:ConcGCThreads=16` (optional): The default value is one-quarter of `ParallelGCThreads`. In some cases, setting both to the same value may decrease stop-the-world pauses (optional).
- `-XX:G1MixedGCCountTarget=8` (optional): This indicates the target number of mixed garbage collections after a marking cycle to collect old regions. The default is 8.
- `-XX:G1HeapRegionSize=n` (optional): This controls the size of the heap regions. Note that increasing this value decreases the number of regions, and vice versa. Not setting this property lets the G1 collector compute it (recommended).

- -Xms: This indicates the initial heap size.
- -Xmx: This indicates the maximum heap size.

You should notice the absence of the heap new size parameter (-Xmn) for the size of the Young Gen. G1GC computes the size of the Young Gen on its own, and adjusts it adaptively to help the collector complete within the specified target time (MaxGCPauseMillis). You'll find that G1 will compute this and many other values on its own.

As with the CMS garbage collector, max heap size and initial heap size should be set to the same value.

Just in case the previous paragraph was not completely clear, do not set a value for the heap new size parameter (-Xmn) when using G1GC. Simply comment-out that line in the cassandra-env.sh or jvm.options file.

Newer versions of Apache Cassandra require JDK version 1.8., patch level 40. You can use G1GC with older versions of Cassandra (2.0, 2.1, and 2.2), but it is not advisable to use G1GC with JDK version 1.7. If you are stuck running on a pre-1.8 JDK, you should opt for the CMS garbage collector.

Initially, with Apache Cassandra 3.0, the G1 collector was intended to be the new default. However, this soon was discovered to be problematic. Smaller, local development instances of Cassandra became subject to garbage collection latencies. The default cassandra-env.sh calculation of heap sizes made it difficult for the G1 collector to adequately adapt to its available resources on most developers' laptops. Thus, the CMS collector remains the default garbage collector for Apache Cassandra, for now.

Despite these problems with development instances, the G1 collector should be the go-to garbage collector for production Cassandra instances. Although CMS is still relevant, and quite capable of achieving minimal interference from garbage collection, it typically requires more configuration and a thorough understanding of the JVM to utilize it properly.

My team supports dozens of clusters across hundreds of production nodes, and we've used G1GC exclusively for the last 2 years.

Garbage collection with Cassandra

High throughput use cases will almost always generate garbage collection. Even clusters with access patterns that tend to be mostly read-serving can see heavy collection activity when their batch loaders run. For a cluster that backs something customer-facing, minimizing garbage collection pause times is imperative.

In the pre-G1GC days, stop-the-world garbage collections were a common pain point for many production clusters. Successfully tuning the CMS (and other collectors) takes a great deal of skill, time for testing, and knowledge of the JVM and its behaviors. The inherent efficiency tuning intrinsic to G1GC tends to simplify the process greatly, which is one of the reasons its use is recommended for Apache Cassandra.

Installation of JVM

Installation of the JVM is quite simple. Download the most recent patch version of the JDK, and distribute it to the node(s) you are building via `scp`, `wget`, `curl`, or another method of orchestration.

Remember, Cassandra 3.x should use Java 8.

With the JDK downloaded, untar it, and move it to a location other than your home directory. For the purposes of this example, we'll put it in `/usr/local/`:

```
sudo tar -zxvf jdk-8u171-linux-x64.tar.gz
sudo mv jdk1.8.0_171 /usr/local
sudo alternatives --install /usr/bin/java java
/usr/local/jdk1.8.0_171/bin/java 1
sudo alternatives --set java /usr/local/jdk1.8.0_171/bin/java
```

Alternatively, you can install the JDK via your Linux package management system. For Debian Linux, try:

```
sudo apt-get install openjdk-8-jdk
```

Or for Red Hat Linux:

```
sudo yum install java-1.8.0-openjdk
```

Now test your JDK by executing `java -version`:

```
java -version

openjdk version "1.8.0_171"
OpenJDK Runtime Environment (build 1.8.0_171-b11)
OpenJDK 64-Bit Server VM (build 25.171-b11, mixed mode)
```

It's recommended to install the JDK, as it has extra tools that can help you configure and troubleshoot issues with your JVM. I've never installed the JDK and wished that I had only used the JRE instead. But I have been in a position where I needed something in the JDK, only to find out that I only had a JRE at my disposal.

JCE

If you plan on using node-to-node or client-to-node SSL, you may be required to download the **Java Cryptography Extensions** (**JCE**). The JCE exists as a separate download, and is not packaged with the JRE or JDK. This is due to legal issues surrounding export restrictions to certain countries from the United States.

Downloading and installing the JCE enables certain additional cipher suites to be used with Apache Cassandra.

With Ubuntu or another Debian Linux flavor, installing the JCE is as simple as this:

```
sudo apt-get install oracle-java8-unlimited-jce-policy
```

It can also be downloaded from Oracle and installed via the command line. Visit http://www.oracle.com/technetwork/java/javase/downloads/jce8-download-2133166.html and download jce_policy-8.zip:

```
unzip jce_policy-8.zip

Archive:  jce_policy-8.zip
   creating: UnlimitedJCEPolicyJDK8/
  inflating: UnlimitedJCEPolicyJDK8/local_policy.jar
  inflating: UnlimitedJCEPolicyJDK8/README.txt
  inflating: UnlimitedJCEPolicyJDK8/US_export_policy.jar
```

Once the file is unzipped, move the policy files to the `jre/lib/security` directory of your JDK (`$JAVA_HOME`):

```
cd /usr/local/jdk1.8.0_171/jre/lib/security/
sudo cp ~/UnlimitedJCEPolicyJDK8/US_export_policy.jar .
sudo cp ~/UnlimitedJCEPolicyJDK8/local_export_policy.jar .
```

Configuring Cassandra

Configuring a single node for Apache Cassandra is done in a few files located in the `conf` directory of the instance's Cassandra installation. Modification of many of these files can be optional for local instance, development deployments (the defaults should suffice). But for production deployments, most of these files should be adjusted.

cassandra.yaml

The `cassandra.yaml` file is the main configuration file for each node in a Cassandra cluster. Many of the behaviors of a node can be controlled or influenced from this file.

While the settings in `cassandra.yaml` are specific to the node on which the file resides, some settings do need to be the same throughout the cluster (these will be noted). Failure to do this may cause the node to fail to start, join, or cause unpredictable behavior.

This file is in the **yet another markup language (YAML)** format, so be aware that proper spacing and formatting are important. The `cassandra.yaml` properties are listed here in the order which they appear in the file:

- `cluster_name`: This is the name of the cluster, and it is case sensitive. New nodes joining an existing cluster must have a matching `cluster_name`.
- `auto_bootstrap`: This is a Boolean property, no longer present in the `cassandra.yaml` file, that controls whether or not the node streams data when joining a cluster. It is set to true by default. If you want to disable this behavior, simply add it to the file with a value of false.
- `num_tokens`: This is an integer, representative of the number of token ranges this node should be responsible for. Setting this property to a value greater than one invokes vnodes. This value defaults to 256, as this setting came about with the old storage engine and allocation algorithms. With Apache Cassandra 3.0 and up, most production installations should be fine running on a value between 12 and 32.

- `allocate_tokens_for_keyspace`: This designates the name of a single keyspace to optimize token allocation for the node. This option is only valid when using the `Murmur3Partitioner`. The `allocate_tokens_for_keyspace` parameter essentially helps Apache Cassandra figure out the optimal token distribution based on the RF of the specified keyspace.
- `initial_token`: This allows for manual specification of token ranges. When used with vnodes, it expects a comma-separated list of token start values.
- `hinted_handoff_enabled`: This is a Boolean value, indicating whether or not this node will participate in hinted handoffs.
- `hinted_handoff_disabled_datacenters`: When hinted handoff is enabled, this allows the specification of data centers that will be excluded from participation.
- `max_hint_window_in_ms`: When hinted handoff is enabled, this determines how long hints are stored for an unresponsive node. The default is 10,800,000 milliseconds (3 hours).
- `hinted_handoff_throttle_in_kb`: This allows hinted handoff activity to be tuned, so as to not consume too much resource. Note that this throttle rating represents a per-thread value of throughput to be shared by the entire cluster. For example, with a default value of 1024 Kbps, a five-node cluster will divide that value evenly by four (256 Kbps), with one node assumed to be receiving the hint traffic.
- `max_hints_delivery_threads`: This designates the number of threads to be used by the node to deliver hints to other nodes. It defaults to a value of two.
- `hints_directory`: New to Apache Cassandra 3.0, this specifies a location on-disk to store any hints to be delivered to other nodes. If not set, the default is `$CASSANDRA_HOME/data/hints`.
- `hints_flush_period_in_ms`: This determines how often hints should be flushed to disk. The default is 10,000 (10 seconds).
- `max_hints_file_size_in_mb`: This controls the size of the hints files on-disk. When this limit is reached, a new file is written.

- `hints_compression`: This indicates the compression class and options to be used for on-disk hint storage. The default is none, which means hints will be written uncompressed. The available compression classes are `LZ4Compressor`, `SnappyCompressor`, and `DeflateCompressor`. Additional properties can also be added, as follows:

```
hints_compression:
    - class_name: LZ4Compressor
      parameters:
          - chunk_length_kb: 64
          - crc_check_chance: 1.0
```

- `batchlog_replay_throttle_in_kb`: This indicates the overall maximum throttle for hint replay. As with `hinted_handoff_throttle_in_kb`, this represents a total value of throughput to be shared by the entire cluster. The default value is `1024`.

- `authenticator`: This controls how users are authenticated when connecting to this Cassandra node. By default, it is set to a value of `AllowAllAuthenticator`, which does not require a valid username and password combination to connect. The other delivered authentication class is `PasswordAuthenticator`. This should be used for production systems, and creates the `system_auth` keyspace with the default `cassandra/cassandra` username and password combination.

- `authorizer`: This controls which users have access to certain keyspaces or tables, as well as the permissions available to them. `AllowAllAuthorizer` is the default, and allows all users the ability to perform any action. When using `PasswordAuthenticator`, it is a good idea to also enable `CassandraAuthorizer` to enforce access and permission assignment.

- `role_manager`: This allows for the implementation of role-based security, in which roles can be assigned permissions, and users can be assigned to roles. The default value is `CassandraRoleManager`, which is sufficient for most deployments.

- `role_validity_in_ms`: As pulling back roles can be somewhat expensive, user roles granted are cached and reloaded asynchronously after this time period elapses. The default is 2000 (2 seconds). It has a corresponding setting known as `roles_update_interval_in_ms` that defaults to the same value, but can be set to update the role cache at a different interval.

- `permissions_validity_in_ms`: Similar to `role_validity_in_ms`, this represents the amount of time for which the permissions cache is valid. The default is 2000 (2 seconds). It has a corresponding setting known as `permissions_update_interval_in_ms` that defaults to the same value, but can be set to update the permissions cache at a different interval.
- `partitioner`: This configures which `partitioner` will be used for this node/cluster. Once one is chosen, it cannot be changed without deleting and reloading all data. The default `Murmur3Partitioner` should not be changed for new deployments.
- `data_file_directories`: This specifies where on-disk the data for the node's keyspaces and tables should be stored. The default location is `$CASSANDRA_HOME/data/data`. If multiple directories are specified, the data will be spread across them evenly; for example:

```
data_file_directories:
    - /cass_ssd_data0
    - /cass_ssd_data1
    - /cass_ssd_data2
```

- `commitlog_directory`: This specifies the location where the `commitlog` files should be stored. If the instance is using spinning disk drives, this should be a different physical disk to the data drive(s). The default location is `$CASSANDRA_HOME/data/commitlog`.

> Any changes to the `cassandra.yaml` file must be followed by a restart of the Cassandra process in order for them to take effect.

- `cdc_enabled`: This is a Boolean value indicating whether or not **Change Data Capture (CDC)** is enabled.
- `cdc_raw_directory`: This specifies the on-disk location where the CDC data is stored. The default value is `$CASSANDRA_HOME/data/cdc_raw`.
- `disk_failure_policy`: This setting determines the node behavior if a disk should fail. The default value is `stop`. Possible other values are as follows:
  - `die`: Stops the node for any type of filesystem errors or SSTable errors
  - `stop_paranoid`: Stops the node for single SSTable errors
  - `stop`: Stops gossip and client availability, but can still be reached via JMX

- **best_effort**: Node remains running, but it stops trying to use the affected disk and completes incoming requests using the remaining available resources
- **ignore**: Node remains running and allows requests to fail

- **commit_failure_policy**: This setting determines the node behavior if a write to the **commitlog** should fail. The default value is **stop**. Possible other values are as follows:
  - **die**: Stops the node
  - **stop**: Stops gossip and client availability, but can still be reached via JMX
  - **stop_commit**: Essentially disables the **commitlog**, allowing the node to continue to service reads
  - **ignore**: Node remains running and allows **commitlog** batches to fail

- **prepared_statements_cache_size_mb**: This setting determines how much of the JVM heap to use for caching prepared statements. The default value is either 10 MB or 1/256 of the heap, whichever is the larger.

> If you notice errors in the log about discarding prepared statements because the limit has been reached, resist the urge to increase this value without further investigation. You should first reach out to the application team, and make sure that they are not creating prepared statements inside a loop construct.

- **key_cache_size_in_mb**: This sets the amount of memory on-heap to use for the key cache. It defaults to either 100 MB or 5% of the heap, whichever is the lesser. Setting it to zero will disable key caching.
- **key_cache_save_period**: This determines how long to keep keys in the key cache. The default is 14,400 seconds (4 hours).
- **key_cache_keys_to_save**: This determines how many keys to save in the cache. By default, there is no limit and all keys are saved for the duration specified by **key_cache_save_period**.

- `row_cache_class_name`: This specifies which row caching mechanism to use. While it is disabled by default, there are two possible implementations:
  - `SerializingCacheProvider`: The original off-heap row cache implementation
  - `OHCProvider`: A newer implementation; this also stores the row cache in off-heap memory, but faster than `SerializingCacheProvider`

- `row_cache_size_in_mb`: This sets the amount of memory to use for the row cache. As row caching can use a significant amount of memory, this is disabled by default (set to zero) as a precaution.
- `row_cache_save_period`: This indicates the number of seconds that a row should be cached for. The default is zero to disable row caching.
- `row_cache_keys_to_save`: This determines the maximum number of rows to save in the cache.
- `counter_cache_size_in_mb`: This sets the amount of memory on-heap to use for the counter cache, which can help reduce problems with counter lock contention. By default, it is sized at either 2.5% of the heap or 50 MB, whichever is the lesser. It can be disabled by setting it to zero.
- `counter_cache_save_period`: This determines how long to keep entries in the counter cache. The default is 7200 seconds (2 hours).
- `counter_cache_keys_to_save`: This determines the maximum number of entries to save in the counter cache.
- `saved_caches_directory`: This specifies the on-disk location of the saved caches. It defaults to `$CASSANDRA_HOME/data/saved_caches`.
- `commitlog_sync`: This determines the behavior around how often `fsync` is invoked to persist the `commitlog` to disk. Available options are as follows:
  - `batch`: The node does not acknowledge writes until `fsync` has completed on the `commitlog`, waiting `commitlog_sync_batch_window_in_ms` time between `fsync` calls
  - `periodic`: The node acknowledges writes immediately, but `fsync` may not be called on the `commitlog` until the next `commitlog_sync_period_in_ms` interval

Just because `fsync` has been called, that does not necessarily mean that the data has been fully-persisted, as it could be in the disk cache.

- `commitlog_segment_size_in_mb`: This determines the size of the `commitlog` files. Note that this setting works in tandem with the settings from the `commitlog_archiving.properties` file. You can use them together to accurately set/estimate the disk footprint of your `commitlog`.
- `max_mutation_size_in_kb`: This forces an upper limit on the size of a mutation in KB. If this setting is used, `commitlog_segment_size_in_mb` should be set to twice its value (times 1024).
- `commitlog_compression`: The `commitlog` can be compressed by specifying the compression class and options to be used. The default is none, which means the `commitlog` will be uncompressed. Available compression classes are `LZ4Compressor`, `SnappyCompressor`, and `DeflateCompressor`, as follows:

```
commitlog_compression:
  - class_name: LZ4Compressor
    parameters:
       - chunk_length_kb: 64
       - crc_check_chance: 1.0
```

- `seed_provider`: Apache Cassandra delivers with one seed provider: the `SimpleSeedProvider`. Most users will never need to alter this.

Like many classes in Apache Cassandra, this setting is pluggable, allowing you to use third-party or custom seed providers. You can write your own, as long as it implements the `SeedProvider` interface.

- `seeds`: A parameter of `SimpleSeedProvider`, this is where you specify your list of seed nodes (in double quotes, comma-delimited). The default value is `127.0.0.1`, which is always wrong in a plural node configuration, for example:

```
seeds: "192.168.0.101,192.168.0.102,192.168.1.21,192.168.1.22"
```

Remember, specifying a node as a seed node does not differentiate it from its peers in any way. All seed nodes really do is provide a way for a new node to figure out the cluster topology. Any existing node can be a seed node for a new node. Nodes that specify themselves as seed nodes will not bootstrap (stream data upon joining).

- `concurrent_reads`: This compute `concurrent_reads` as the number of hard drives x 16. The default value of 32 should work for most implementations. Note that Cassandra will fail to start if this value is less than 1.
- `concurrent_writes`: As writes tend to be more dependent on CPU cores than they are on-disk I/O, `concurrent_writes` can be computed as CPU cores x eight. The default value of 32 should work for most implementations.
- `concurrent_counter_writes`: The `concurrent_counter_writes` property should be computed in the same way as `concurrent_reads`. This is because counter updates perform a read before they write, and will be bottlenecked more by their read time than their write time. It also defaults to 32.
- `concurrent_materialized_view_writes`: This also performs a read, so it should be set under similar conditions to `concurrent_counter_writes`. It also defaults to 32.
- `file_cache_size_in_mb`: This sets the maximum amount of off-heap RAM to be used for SSTable chunk cache and buffer pooling. The default is either 512 MB or one-quarter of the maximum heap size, whichever is the lesser.
- `disk_optimization_strategy`: Cassandra can make small optimizations to help reads perform better. There are two possible options:
    - `ssd`: The default setting, for use if the instance is backed by SSDs
    - `spinning`: To be used if the instance is backed by platter and spindle-based storage

- `memtable_heap_space_in_mb`: This indicates the maximum amount of RAM to use for on-heap memtables. The default value is one-quarter of the maximum heap size.
- `memtable_offheap_space_in_mb`: This indicates the maximum amount of RAM to use for off-heap memtables. The default value is one-quarter of the maximum heap size.
- `memtable_allocation_type`: This property is new as of Cassandra 2.1, and allows you to direct Cassandra to move some of its memtable processing off the JVM heap. On machines with smaller heaps, this can help to alleviate some of the heap pressure. The following options are available for configuration:
    - `heap_buffers`: This is the default setting, and keeps memtable objects on the JVM heap
    - `offheap_buffers`: This moves cell names and values to buffer objects off-heap (Ellis, 2014)
    - `offheap_objects`: This moves the whole cell off-heap, leaving only a reference on the heap (Ellis, 2014), pointing to the off-heap cells

- `commitlog_total_space_in_mb`: This indicates the maximum amount of on-disk space to use for the `commitlog`. When the active `commitlog` file exceeds this value, the tables in the oldest segment are flushed to disk. The default size is either one-quarter of the max heap or 8 GB, whichever is the lesser.
- `memtable_flush_writers`: This property indicates how many threads should be used to flush memtables to disk. The default value is calculated at two threads per data directory.
- `cdc_total_space_in_mb`: If CDC is enabled for a table, this sets the maximum amount of disk space to use for CDC logs. The default is either 4 GB or one-eighth of the available disk, whichever is the lesser.
- `cdc_free_space_check_interval_ms`: This property indicates how much time Cassandra waits before checking if more CDC space is available on-disk. The default value is 250 milliseconds.
- `index_summary_capacity_in_mb`: This indicates the amount of RAM allocated for SSTable index summaries. The default value is 5% of the maximum heap size.
- `index_summary_resize_interval_in_minutes`: This is the duration in minutes after which the index summaries are resampled. The default value is 60 minutes.
- `trickle_fsync: false`: This enables calling `fsync` during sequential writes, which instructs the OS to flush the output buffers to disk. Without this setting, the OS decides when to flush the buffers, which can impact read performance. It is set to false by default, but should be enabled when Cassandra is backed by SSDs.
- `trickle_fsync_interval_in_kb`: This sets a threshold in KB for when to force `fsync` call, if `trickle_fsync` is enabled.
- `storage_port`: This indicates the port that Apache Cassandra uses for internode communication, via TCP. It defaults to `7000`.
- `ssl_storage_port`: When node-to-node SSL encryption is enabled, Apache Cassandra uses this port for internode communication, via TCP. It defaults to `7001`.
- `listen_address`: This indicates the address of the instance to bind to and advertise to other Cassandra nodes. If the instance has both internal and external IP addresses, this should be set to the internal IP address. It defaults to `localhost`, which is always wrong in a plural node configuration.
- `listen_interface_prefer_ipv6`: This is a Boolean property that is useful if the instance has both IPv4 and IPv6 addresses, and instructs Cassandra to prefer one over the other when binding the `listen_address`. The default value is false.

- `listen_interface_`: This indicates the network interface to listen on. This can be specified instead of `listen_address`, but do not specify both.
- `broadcast_address`: This indicates the address of the instance to broadcast to the other nodes in the cluster. If the instance has both internal and external IP addresses, this should be set to the external IP address. It defaults to the value specified for `listen_address`.
- `start_native_transport`: This is a Boolean property that specifies whether or not Apache Cassandra should start its native transport server process. The default value is true.

> The native binary protocol is the new **de facto standard** for handling client connections to Cassandra. It should always be set to true, as the delivered `cqlsh` tool connects using this protocol.

- `native_transport_port`: This property specifies the port on which to listen for native binary protocol client traffic (TCP). The default value is 9042.
- `start_rpc`: This is a Boolean property indicating whether or not Apache Cassandra should start the Thrift RPC server process. The default value is false.

> Cassandra's Thrift RPC server has been deprecated since Cassandra 2.2, and will be removed with Apache Cassandra version 4.0. As the Hector project (Cassandra's early Thrift-based client library) has been marked as inactive, and `cqlsh` no longer uses Thrift, there should not be any reason to enable this setting.

- `rpc_address`: This indicates the address of the instance to bind to and advertise for client connections, for both native binary and Thrift. If the instance has both internal and external IP addresses, this should be set to the internal IP address. It defaults to `localhost`, which is always wrong in a plural node configuration.
- `rpc_interface_prefer_ipv6`: This is a Boolean property that is useful if the instance has both IPv4 and IPv6 addresses, and instructs Cassandra to prefer one over the other for client connections. The default value is false.
- `rpc_interface`: This indicates the network interface to listen for client connections on. It can be specified instead of `rpc_address`, but do not specify both.
- `rpc_port`: This property specifies the port on which to listen for Thrift traffic (TCP). The default value is 9160.

- `broadcast_rpc_address`: This indicates the address of the instance to broadcast to client connections, for both native binary and Thrift. If the instance has both internal and external IP addresses, this should be set to the external IP address. It defaults to the value specified for `rpc_address`.
- `rpc_keepalive`: This is a Boolean property that indicates whether or not a keepalive should be used with client connections. The default value is true.
- `rpc_server_type`: This property specifies how client connections are managed. In addition to the possibility of writing a custom class to handle this, there are two options provided:
  - `sync`: This indicates the default value, which indicates one thread per client connection
  - `hsha`: Half synchronous, half asynchronous handles client connections asynchronously with a small number of threads. Actual requests made by clients are still synchronous.

- `rpc_max_threads`: This sets the maximum limit as to how many client requests can be handled concurrently. If setting the `rpc_server_type` to sync, this also limits the number of client connections. This setting is used as a way to protect the node(s) from being overloaded by client requests. It is commented-out by default, providing no limit to the number of threads for client requests.
- `incremental_backups`: This is a Boolean property that indicates whether or not incremental backups are enabled. This creates a hard link to the SSTable files in the `backups` directory of each table. The default value is false, as this does tend to consume disk space.
- `snapshot_before_compaction`: This is a Boolean property that indicates whether or not to take a snapshot of each table before compaction runs on it. The default value is false, as this does tend to consume disk space.
- `auto_snapshot`: This is a Boolean property that indicates whether or not to take a snapshot of a table before applying a TRUNCATE command or dropping the table. The default value is false, as this does tend to consume disk space.
- `column_index_size_in_kb`: This indicates the space to use for the index of rows in a partition, in KB. The default value is 64, but should be increased for data models that have a high number of rows per partition. This setting also has a direct impact on how much data is stored in the key cache.
- `column_index_cache_size_in_kb`: This indicates the space to use for the serialized index per SSTable. The default value is two.

- `concurrent_compactors`: This indicates the number of concurrent compactions to allow on the node. If your storage is SSD-based, this can be set to the number of CPU cores. Setting it too high can increase GC activity, so a good strategy to use for this value (Apache, 2016) is to set it to four (with SSDs). Then test your system watching for resource consumption, and adjust from there.

- `compaction_throughput_mb_per_sec`: This setting assigns a value of throughput in Mbps (megabits per second) to help control how much available computing resources should be used for compaction. This defaults to 16, but resources should be monitored and it should be adjusted as needed. If this setting is too high, the node may use too much resource to compaction, affecting its ability to serve requests. If the setting is too low, then compactions may not happen frequently enough to keep up, resulting in pending compactions building up and queries getting slower due to row fragmentation across SSTable files.

Setting `compaction_throughput_mb_per_sec` to zero effectively disables throttling, essentially removing a limit as to how much resource compaction can consume.

This setting is your main control to throttle compaction up or down, as the need arises. While adjusting the property in the `cassandra.yaml` file is the only way to make a value permanent (requiring a restart), this setting can be adjusted at any time using the nodetool utility.

- `stream_throughput_outbound_megabits_per_sec`: This setting allows for throttling the amount of data streamed to other nodes, such as during a repair or bootstrapping process. The default is 200 Mbps (megabits per second).

- `inter_dc_stream_throughput_outbound_megabits_per_sec`: This setting allows for throttling the amount of data streamed to nodes in other data centers, which can happen when running a rebuild. This is useful if there are bandwidth constraints between different physical data centers or cloud providers. The default is 200 Mbps (megabits per second).

- `*_request_timeout_in_ms`: There are several settings that govern different types of request timeouts. These timeouts exist to protect the node from devoting too much resource to a single request. They are listed as follows, along with their default values:
    - `read_request_timeout_in_ms`: 5000
    - `range_request_timeout_in_ms`: 10000
    - `write_request_timeout_in_ms`: 2000

- `counter_write_request_timeout_in_ms`: 5000
- `cas_contention_timeout_in_ms`: 1000
- `truncate_request_timeout_in_ms`: 60000
- `request_timeout_in_ms`: 10000

> You should never need to adjust the request timeouts. They exist to protect the node, and ultimately the cluster. If a developer tells you that their queries are getting rejected because of these timeout values, have a look at their data model and the queries it is trying to serve. It is the responsibility of the developer to build well-performing queries for their data model. It is not a Cassandra DBA's responsibility to adjust settings to accommodate poor queries or bad data models.

- `slow_query_log_timeout_in_ms`: Queries that take longer than this value will be logged. The default value is 500 milliseconds. Setting this value to zero will disable the logging of slow queries.
- `cross_node_timeout`: This is a Boolean property that allows for sharing of request information between nodes. This can help increase the accuracy of request timeouts, and prevent wasting resources on requests that have already timed out. The default value is false, because this setting can be problematic if the clocks are not synced accurately across all nodes.
- `phi_convict_threshold`: Apache Cassandra uses the Phi Failure Accrual algorithm to determine the health of another node in gossip. A higher value increases the accuracy of the node-to-node health check, but can take longer to determine an answer. For a cluster built on-premises with a consistent network, the default value of 8 should suffice. However, if the cluster spans multiple data centers across different providers, or if network connection consistency is a problem, then a higher value of 10 or 12 should help prevent false positives.
- `endpoint_snitch`: This determines which `snitch` class to use. There are several to choose from:
    - `SimpleSnitch`: The default snitch, which treats every node in the cluster as though it is in the same data center and rack. This is only suitable for single node, local deployments.
    - `GossipingPropertyFileSnitch`: The best choice for production. The data center and rack are configured on each node (`cassandra-rackdc.properties`).

- `PropertyFileSnitch`: This was a common choice for production prior to the existence of `GossipingPropertyFileSnitch`. Each node has a list of all the other nodes in the cluster (along with their rack and data center), defined in the `cassandra-topology.properties` file.

- `Ec2Snitch`: This is intended to be used with **Amazon Web Services** (**AWS**) EC2 deployments to a single region, designating the region as a data center and the availability zone as the rack. This snitch only uses private IP addresses, so it will fail if used with a cluster deployed across multiple regions.

- `Ec2MultiRegionSnitch`: This is intended to be used with AWS EC2 deployments for clusters deployed across multiple regions. It uses public IP addresses (`broadcast_address`) to communicate with nodes in another region, and private IP addresses are used among nodes within the same region.

- `RackInferringSnitch`: Each node's data center is inferred by the second octet in the node's IP address. Likewise, each node's rack is inferred by the third octet in the node's IP address. If your network topology is not built to match that, then it is best not to use this snitch.

- `GoogleCloudSnitch`: This is intended to be used with nodes deployed on the **Google Cloud Platform** (**GCP**). The region is used as the node's data center, and the zone is used as the rack.

When in doubt, use `GossipingPropertyFileSnitch` for production deployments. It can be made to work with all cloud providers. Do not mix endpoint snitches in a cluster. Each node should be configured to use the same snitch, regardless of data center or provider.

- `dynamic_snitch`: This is a Boolean property that determines if the dynamic snitch is enabled. If not set, the default value is true.

Jon Haddad (*Principal Engineer for The Last Pickle*) recently mentioned (Haddad, 2018) that disabling dynamic snitching often increases read performance.

- `dynamic_snitch_update_interval_in_ms`: The amount of time in milliseconds that determines how frequently to calculate host scores (expensive). The default is 100 milliseconds.

- `dynamic_snitch_reset_interval_in_ms`: The amount of time in milliseconds that determines how frequently the host scores are reset. The default is 600,000 milliseconds, or 10 minutes.
- `dynamic_snitch_badness_threshold`: This is a decimal representing a percentage of how much faster a competing node must be to be a preferred target for a specific replica.
- `request_scheduler`: This is a request scheduling class to be used for client requests. By default, the `NoScheduler` class is used. The `RoundRobin` class can also be used to adjust request throttling and per-keyspace weighting, which can be useful in multi-tenant clusters.
- `server_encryption_options`: This is a set of properties that configures node-to-node **secure socket layer** (**SSL**). Available properties are as follows:
    - `Internode_encryption`:
        - `none`: Node-to-node SSL is disabled
        - `all`: All communication between nodes in the cluster is encrypted
        - `dc`: Communication is encrypted between logical data centers
        - `rack`: Communication is encrypted between logical racks
    - `keystore`: The on-disk location of the Java KeyStore file
    - `keystore_password`: The password of the Java KeyStore
    - `truststore`: The on-disk location of the Java TrustStore file
    - `truststore_password`: The password of the Java TrustStore
    - `require_client_auth`: Sets whether or not certificate authentication is enabled (two-way SSL)
    - `require_endpoint_verification`: Sets whether or not hostname verification is enabled

- `client_encryption_options`: This is a set of properties that configures client-to-node SSL. Available properties are as follows:
    - `enabled`: A Boolean value indicating whether or not client-to-node SSL is enabled
    - `keystore`: The on-disk location of the Java KeyStore file
    - `keystore_password`: The password of the Java KeyStore
    - `truststore`: The on-disk location of the Java TrustStore file
    - `truststore_password`: The password of the Java TrustStore

- `require_client_auth`: Sets whether or not certificate authentication is enabled (two-way SSL)
- `require_endpoint_verification`: Sets whether or not hostname verification is enabled

> When installing and configuring a Java KeyStore with Apache Cassandra, remember to set the key with the same password as the KeyStore itself.

- `internode_compression`: This determines whether communication between nodes is sent in a compressed format. Possible values are as follows:
    - `all`: All communication is compressed
    - `dc`: Communication between data centers is compressed
    - `none`: Internode compression is disabled
- `inter_dc_tcp_nodelay`: This allows for some adjustment of internode network communication. When disabled, larger but fewer network packets are sent, which can help in reducing TCP overhead.
- `enable_user_defined_functions`: This experimental feature allows the DBA to restrict UDFs.
- `enable_scripted_user_defined_functions`: This experimental feature allows for the use of languages other than Java to write UDFs. This setting becomes moot if `enable_user_defined_functions` is false.
- `enable_materialized_views`: This experimental feature allows the DBA to restrict the usage of materialized views.
- `transparent_data_encryption_options`: This is a set of properties that configures `commitlog` and hint file encryption on-disk. Available properties are as follows:
    - `enabled`: A Boolean value indicating whether or not **Transparent Data Encryption** (TDE) is enabled
    - `chunk_length_in_kb`: Size of the encrypted chunk length
    - `cipher`: Cipher standards to use with TDE
    - `key_alias`: Alias of the specific key inside the KeyStore to use
    - `keystore`: The on-disk location of the Java KeyStore file
    - `keystore_password`: The password of the Java KeyStore

- `store_type`: Standard used by the KeyStore file
- `key_password`: The password of the specific key inside the KeyStore

- `tombstone_warn_threshold`: This indicates the number of tombstones that can be scanned in a partition or query before a warning message will be issued. The default value is 1,000 tombstones.
- `tombstone_failure_threshold`: This indicates the number of tombstones that can be scanned in a partition or query before the query will fail. The default value is 100,000 tombstones.

> Tombstone management is a part of the data modeling process, not operation or configuration. Data models should be built in such a way that minimizes obsoleted and tombstoned data. These properties exist to protect the cluster from spending too much resource managing tombstones. If you're looking at these properties as a way to solve a production problem, it's already too late.

- `batch_size_warn_threshold_in_kb`: This indicates the size of a multi-partition batch statement that will trigger a warning. The default is 5 KB.
- `batch_size_fail_threshold_in_kb`: This indicates the size of a multi-partition batch statement that will cause the batch statement to fail. The default is 50 KB.
- `unlogged_batch_across_partitions_warn_threshold`: This indicates the number of partitions that a batch statement can span before triggering a warning. The default is ten.

> Like the tombstone-specific properties mentioned, the batch threshold properties also exist to protect your cluster. I have seen coordinator nodes crash while processing large batch statements. If development teams report seeing this error, the most likely reason is that they are misusing the CQL batch functionality. The responsibility to fix it is on the development side.

- `compaction_large_partition_warning_threshold_mb`: This indicates the size of a partition in megabytes that will trigger a warning during the compaction process. The default is 100 MB.

- gc_warn_threshold_in_ms: This indicates the length of time in milliseconds after which a garbage collection process will trigger a warning. The default is 1000 milliseconds, or 1 second.
- back_pressure_enabled: This Boolean property allows a back-pressure strategy to be enabled on coordinator nodes. This is an effort to prevent a client connection from pushing through too much write traffic, overloading and possibly crashing a Cassandra node.
- back_pressure_strategy: This section provides access to a list of properties that configures the specific back-pressure strategy.
- class_name: This indicates the name of the back-pressure strategy class to use, which can be a delivered class or a custom written class. Apache Cassandra delivers with the default org.apache.cassandra.net.RateBasedBackPressure strategy, which accepts three parameters, as follows:
  - high_ratio: This represents a target ratio of mutation responses to mutation requests. The default value is 0.90.
  - factor: If the ratio of responses to requests exceeds the value specified for high_ratio, then the rate limiting of the requests is increased by the specified value. The default value for the factor increase is five, and is recommended to be set between one and ten.
  - flow: This property has two possible values, FAST or SLOW. It controls how the rate limiting of mutations is applied, setting it to the speed of the fastest data replica or the slowest, respectively. The default value is FAST.

cassandra-env.sh

The cassandra-env.sh file is where much of the JVM configuration used to happen, before it was moved to the jvm.options file (to be explained in a following section). Currently, it is invoked when the node is started to ensure that Cassandra has the environment variables it needs.

Upon starting, it polls available system resources, and uses that data to calculate an acceptable heap size. It also applies some additional checks for specific versions of the JVM. Here are some additional, common settings that can be applied in the `cassandra-env.sh` file:

- `JMX_PORT`: This specifies which port should be used for **Java Management Extensions (JMX)** communications. It is passed to the JVM as – `Dcassandra.jmx.remote.port`.

- `LOCAL_JMX`: This defaults to yes, which means that JMX-based commands for a particular node can only be issued from that node itself.

- `-Dcom.sun.management.jmxremote.authenticate`: This is a Boolean parameter that determines whether JMX commands should require a valid username and password combination to run. It defaults to false, because `LOCAL_JMX` defaults to yes.

- `-Dcom.sun.management.jmxremote.rmi.port`: This specifies which port should be used for **Remote Method Invocation (RMI)** traffic. It can be set to the same port as JMX (default).

- `-Dcom.sun.management.jmxremote.password.file`: This specifies the location of the password file to use when JMX authentication is activated. By default, it is set to `/etc/cassandra/jmxremote.password`. Here is an example of a JMX password file:

  ```
  cassdba      flynnLives
  aploetz      cOrr3ctH0rs3B@tt3rySt@pl3
  ```

- `-Dcassandra.replace_address`: This is an optional parameter that allows a new node to join the cluster and assume the token ranges of a removed node. This becomes useful when a node experiences a hardware failure, and must be re-bootstrapped after maintenance. Without this parameter, starting an empty node with an IP address that is already in gossip will fail.

cassandra-rackdc.properties

In a vast improvement over the previously required `cassandra-topology.properties` file, the `cassandra-rackdc.properties` file makes configuring a multi data center deployment much easier. Remember that all data center, rack, and suffix names are case sensitive. This file is utilized only when the node is configured to use one of the following snitches:

- `Ec2Snitch`
- `Ec2MultiRegionSnitch`
- `GoogleCloudSnitch`
- `GossipingPropertyFileSnitch`

Four properties can be set inside this file: `dc`, `rack`, `dc_suffix`, and `prefer_local`.

dc

This property sets the logical data center for the current node. Data center names need to match up with the data center names used to define RFs at keyspace creation time. Good `dc` names can represent physical locations or a cloud region.

For example:

```
dc=US_Central
```

rack

This property sets the logical `rack` for the current node. These are used by the snitch to help distribute data in ways that support high availability. As with `dc`, good `rack` names may be physical racks on the data center floor, or they may be representative of availability zones in a public cloud.

For example:

```
rack=Central_2A
```

Public cloud availability zones can and do go down. Therefore, it is a good idea to make sure to take availability zones into account during deployment. This will help to ensure both even data distribution and maximum availability.

dc_suffix

This optional property sets a suffix to be added to the dc name for the current node.

For example:

```
dc_suffix=_externalFacing
```

This property is ignored unless using a snitch that is specific to a public cloud provider (GoogleCloudSnitch, Ec2Snitch, or Ec2MultiRegionSnitch).

prefer_local

In the event that nodes in a cluster are configured with both internal and external IP addresses, this optional property instructs the snitch to prefer local, internal IP addresses when possible.

For example:

```
prefer_local=true
```

cassandra-topology.properties

The cassandra-topology.properties file is used with the PropertyFileSnitch. It is also used as a backup to GossipingPropertyFileSnitch. It contains a hard-coded list of every node in the cluster, including its IP address, data center, and rack definition.

For example:

```
# datacenter US Central
  10.9.9.12=US-Central:central_13
  10.9.19.22=US-Central:central_16
  10.9.29.32=US-Central:central_19
  # datacenter US West
  10.4.4.16=US-West:west_14
```

```
10.4.14.26=US-West:west_2
10.4.24.36=US-West:west_27
```

Whenever a new node is added, it must be added to this file on every single node. In larger environments, this quickly becomes untenable. It can be especially tedious when employed in a frequently-scaling cloud environment.

> While this file can serve as a backup to the `cassandra-rackdc.properties` file when using `GossipingPropertyFileSnitch`, it is really only meant to be used that way for migration purposes. Old `cassandra-topology.properties` files have been known to cause gossip issues when using `GossipingPropertyFileSnitch`. Thus, that file should be renamed or deleted once migration is completed.

jvm.options

The `jvm.options` file is intended to apply custom, JVM-specific settings to a Cassandra node. The most common configurations applied in this file are those of heap sizing and garbage collection, as covered earlier in this chapter.

> `jvm.options` is a new configuration file added as of Cassandra 3.0. If you are using an older version of Cassandra, these properties should be set inside the `cassandra-env.sh` file instead.

Here is a list of commonly adjusted properties in `jvm.options`:

- `-Dcassandra.load_ring_state`: This property takes a Boolean value, and determines whether locally-stored gossip information should be used or wiped out at start time.
- `-Dcassandra.replace_address`: If you are replacing a dead node with a new node, this allows you to set the new node to have the old node's token ranges. Note that the data directories of the new node must be empty.
- `-Dcassandra.ring_delay_ms`: This allows specification of a custom time to wait before joining the cluster. The default value is 30,000 milliseconds, or 30 seconds.
- `-Dcassandra.triggers_dir`: This property overrides the default location in which Cassandra will look for custom trigger JAR files. The default is the `$CASSANDRA_HOME/conf/triggers` directory.

- `-Xss`: This indicates the per-thread stack size. This setting was commonly adjusted in older versions of Cassandra when upgrading the JVM to a newer version (thus requiring a larger stack size). The default value of 256 should be sufficient.
- `-Dcassandra.expiration_date_overflow_policy`: This defines how to handle mutations with TTLs exceeding the 20 years maximum. Possible values are as follows:
    - `REJECT`: TTLs exceeding 20 years from the current date will be rejected (default)
    - `CAP`: TTLs exceeding 20 years will be capped at 20 years, and a warning will be given
    - `CAP_NOWARD`: TTLs exceeding 20 years will be capped at 20 years, and a warning will not be given
- `-XX:+PrintGCDetails`: This enables GC logging, with more available details than `-XX:+PrintGC`.
- `-XX:+PrintGCDateStamps`: This adds an absolute date and time to each line of the GC log.
- `-XX:+PrintGCTimeStamps`: This adds a time to each line of the GC log, representing the number of seconds since the start of the JVM.
- `-XX:+PrintHeapAtGC`: This outputs the contents of the heap (at collection time) to the GC log.
- `-XX:+PrintTenuringDistribution`: This displays information about objects on the heap, including how old they are and how soon they may be collected. It can be useful when investigating long-lived objects on the heap.
- `-XX:+PrintGCApplicationStoppedTime`: This gives an approximation of how much time the application has waited for GC pauses.
- `-XX:+PrintPromotionFailure`: This displays information about objects that have failed promotion between generations.
- `-xloggc:/var/log/cassandra/gc.log`: This sets the directory location for the GC logs.
- `-XX:+UseGCLogFileRotation`: This prevents the JVM continually taking up disk space with GC logs, by only keeping the most-recent files used.
- `-XX:NumberOfGCLogFiles`: This allows you to set the maximum number of GC log files to be on-disk at any time.
- `-XX:GCLogFileSize`: This allows you to configure the size of each GC log file.

GC logging is now enabled by default (as of Apache Cassandra versions 2.2.5, 3.0.3, and 3.3). In the more recent versions of the JVM, it has been found not to slow things down, and its disk usage can be contained.

logback.xml

The `logback.xml` file allows for configuration of (some of) Cassandra's logging outputs. One of the main sections of this file is the system log appender, as follows:

```
<appender name="SYSTEMLOG"
class="ch.qos.logback.core.rolling.RollingFileAppender">
    <filter class="ch.qos.logback.classic.filter.ThresholdFilter">
      <level>INFO</level>
    </filter>
    <file>${cassandra.logdir}/system.log</file>
    <rollingPolicy
class="ch.qos.logback.core.rolling.FixedWindowRollingPolicy">
<fileNamePattern>${cassandra.logdir}/system.log.%i.zip</fileNamePattern>
      <minIndex>1</minIndex>
      <maxIndex>20</maxIndex>
    </rollingPolicy>
    <triggeringPolicy
class="ch.qos.logback.core.rolling.SizeBasedTriggeringPolicy">
      <maxFileSize>20MB</maxFileSize>
    </triggeringPolicy>
    <encoder>
      <pattern>%-5level [%thread] %date{ISO8601} %F:%L - %msg%n</pattern>
    </encoder>
  </appender>
```

The name and format of the log files and their archives can be adjusted in this file. Log file size and archival and retention specifications can be configured here as well.

By default, `system.log` will archive when it reaches a size of 20 MB. At this point, the log file will be compressed and numbered with the next available index between one and twenty. A new `system.log` file will then be created and appended to. Once the number of archived log files exceeds its configured maximum, the oldest file is deleted.

Most logs allow for the adjustment of the logging level. The default logging level for `system.log` is INFO, which is sufficient for production use. The complete list of logging levels is shown here, sorted in descending order of verbosity:

- ALL
- TRACE
- DEBUG
- INFO
- WARN
- ERROR
- OFF

When using a logging level higher than DEBUG, keep an eye on the disk space used by your logs.

The location for the logs is controlled by the `${cassandra.logdir}` variable. By default, this is set to the `$CASSANDRA_HOME/log` directory. It can be altered by adding the following line to your `cassandra-env.sh` file:

```
JVM_OPTS="$JVM_OPTS -Dcassandra.logdir=/var/cassandra/log"
```

Setting `cassandra.logdir` as a JVM option has been reported to be problematic with some versions of Apache Cassandra. If you have problems enforcing a new log location, you can always adjust the `logback.xml` file manually or with a regular expression via `sed`:

```
sed -i "s/\${cassandra\.logdir}/\/var\/log\/cassandra/g" logback.xml
```

Managing a deployment pipeline

When you start working with large, production-level clusters, having a good orchestration tool can save you a lot of work. After all, building and configuring a three-node cluster is one thing, but building and maintaining a 300 node cluster requires a different approach.

This comes into play when cluster-wide changes must be applied, such as a new SSL certificate or an upgrade to a new patch level. Manual methods, which are fine for the three-node cluster, quickly become untenable at a large scale.

For some Cassandra teams, a collection of Python or shell scripts will suffice for running some of the repeatable parts of their deployment process. But as scale increases and configurations change, this approach relies on the team to adjust the scripts so that they continue to work with changing requirements.

As the problems of maintaining a distributed database at a large scale begin to manifest themselves, forward-thinking teams begin to look at implementing and augmenting pre-built tools to do some of the heavy lifting.

There are two types of tools that can aid in solving this problem: orchestration tools, and configuration management tools.

Orchestration tools

Orchestration tools (Birkman, 2016) are designed to deploy instances. Popular choices for orchestration tools are **Terraform**, **Spinnaker**, and **CloudFormation**. These types of tools are useful with large-scale Cassandra deployments, as they can allow for quick remediation of availability issues, through the approach of immutable deployments (Birkman 2016).

Additionally, these tools allow DBAs the ability to scale up quickly, as well as providing intrinsic management of availability zones. With these tools, adding a new node to a cluster can be as simple as clicking a button.

Configuration management tools

Configuration management tools (Birkman, 2016) allow for the installation and management of software on existing instances. These configuration changes happen in a mutable fashion.

Essentially, changes are implemented as code, and existing instances are modified in place. Examples of tools that work in this manner are **Chef** and **Ansible**.

Recommended approach

While some configuration management tools offer some degree of deployment management, some orchestration tools also allow a degree of configuration management. But the approach is vastly different. While tools like Chef and Ansible alter existing instances, orchestration tools make similar changes by destroying and recreating instances.

As they both have their strengths, you may find that building an environment that utilizes both an orchestration tool and a configuration management tool helps lay the best course on the road to success.

Local repository for downloadable files

One thing to consider when deploying to a larger scale is where to put the components of your build process. You could be relying on one or more websites for the JDK, or even Cassandra itself. How do you deploy a new node if those sites go down, and you can't reach a suitable mirror?

The solution is to construct a repository of all your build's components, which prevents you from having to download everything for each deploy. The build process should use something like a network storage drive, or even a tool like **JFrog Artifactory**.

Remember that relying on connectivity to multiple, remote internet locations simply adds more points of failure to your deployment or build process.

Summary

There certainly is a lot to consider when planning and building a new Apache Cassandra cluster, and this chapter has put forth a great deal of information. We have considered details regarding compute resources, networking, and sizing strategies. Linux operating system adjustments to help optimize Apache Cassandra have also been discussed.

As Cassandra runs on a JVM, we have analyzed approaches to sizing and configuring the Java heap. After that, we examined Apache Cassandra configuration files. Detailed explanations for various properties were put forth, as well as the benefits (and possible drawbacks) that each can provide. Finally, some brief recommendations on deployment strategy were put forward, comparing the difference between configuration management and orchestration.

One last piece of advice, is to test thoroughly. Start the cluster, examine its performance, make an adjustment, and test again. Rinse and repeat. There absolutely is no substitute for it.

One can only theorize about the performance capabilities of a cluster when the different possible combinations of resource sizing, OS config, and node configuration are all taken into account. Even the most well-thought out approaches to cluster deployment and management can fall victim to performance bottlenecks, because of one overlooked aspect of configuration.

In the next chapter, we will discuss some of the finer points of configuring a cluster for optimal performance.

Performance Tuning

5

As an author, I have some reservations about discussing performance tuning for Apache Cassandra. Too often, application development teams will complain to their Cassandra DBA (database administrator) that their cluster is performing too slowly. The mere existence of a chapter entitled *Performance Tuning* in a Cassandra book implies that there must be some hidden gems of knowledge within these pages that will give a DBA the power to wave their magic wand and instantly cure slow queries. This could not be further from the truth.

In Chapter 3, *Effective CQL* we covered how to write good CQL, which relies on designing well-thought-out Cassandra data models. To be completely clear, building tables with primary keys designed to (both) distribute well and serve specific queries is the *best* way to achieve high performance with distributed databases, and that includes Apache Cassandra. There is no **magic bullet** to make overloaded clusters perform well. The data model is the magic bullet.

No amount of cluster-side tuning or configuration can make a bad data model perform well.

However, once the data model is already sound, there are some things that can be done to increase query speeds, lower latencies, and improve upon write throughput. These aspects will be the focus of this chapter:

- Using the Cassandra-Stress tool to discover opportunities for improvement
- Looking into situations to apply different table-compaction strategies
- Examining Apache Cassandra's cache and compression options
- Improving upon the efficiency of the JVM
- Optimizing network settings and configuration to avoid performance bottlenecks

At the end of this chapter, you will have an understanding of some of the finer points of configuring your cluster for optimal performance. You will have used the Cassandra-Stress tool, which will prove to be a valuable experience for assessing the performance of data models. Within those models, you should understand how certain options can improve read or write performance for different use cases. And you should have a thorough understanding of common anti-patterns that can cause problems for users of Apache Cassandra.

Cassandra-Stress

When examining the performance of your data model, firing up the Cassandra-Stress tool should be your first option. Cassandra-Stress comes built-in with Apache Cassandra, and allows you to benchmark your data model with predefined queries for reads, writes, and mixed operational loads. When running these queries, Cassandra-Stress will report figures on latency and operations per second. Its ultimate value lies in the information that it can provide about your data model, and its ability to perform at scale and under load.

The Cassandra-Stress YAML file

To start using the Cassandra-Stress tool, you must first construct a `stress.yaml` file. For this example, we will use the `security_logs_by_location_id_desc` table, which we created in `Chapter 3`, *Effective CQL*. First, let's create a new keyspace:

```
CREATE KEYSPACE IF NOT EXISTS packt_ch5
  WITH replication = {'class': 'NetworkTopologyStrategy',
'ClockworkAngels': '1'}
  AND durable_writes = true;

use packt_ch5;
```

Cassandra-Stress randomly generates column values for each row, so we want to ensure that its data doesn't become commingled with real data. To that end, let's recreate the `security_logs_by_location_id_desc` table with one small adjustment. We'll append a string of `_stress` to the end of the table's name. This way, the `_stress` tables should only contain randomly-generated stress data, and we ensure that we're keeping our real tables separate:

```
CREATE TABLE packt_ch5.security_logs_by_location_desc_stress (
    location_id text,
    day int,
    time_in timestamp,
```

```
    employee_id text,
    mailstop text,
    PRIMARY KEY ((location_id, day), time_in, employee_id)
) WITH CLUSTERING ORDER BY (time_in DESC, employee_id ASC);
```

With an understanding of what we are testing, let's create our new YAML file, and name it `security_logs_by_location_desc_stress.yaml`. Let's start by specifying our keyspace and table names:

```
#stress yaml for security_logs_by_location_desc_stress
#keyspace name
keyspace: packt_ch5
#table name
table: security_logs_by_location_desc_stress
```

Cassandra-Stress also allows you to specify your entire table definition inside of the `stress.yaml` file. But for our purposes, we'll ensure that everything is created ahead of time.

 The reason for creating our table and keyspace ahead of time is that earlier versions of Cassandra-Stress achieved table-creation with varying degrees of success. Defining them ourselves removes a possible point of failure.

Now, we can configure our column definitions and data distribution. This is done in the `columnspec` section of the `stress.yaml` file. Cassandra-Stress allows for constraints to be applied to the data that it randomly generates, as this helps to ensure that the tests are run with data of relative size and cardinality to the actual data. To this end, there are three distribution types that can be applied to the different properties:

- `UNIFORM`: Designates an even distribution of values
- `FIXED`: Designates a specific, static distribution of values
- `GAUSSIAN`: Designates a normal, bell-curve distribution, with more values centered around the middle of the range than the ends

Given each of these distribution levels, each column in your `stress.yaml` has four properties that can be defined: `name`, `size`, `population`, and `cluster`.

name

Each column defined in your `columnspec` section must contain a name that matches a corresponding column name in the table.

size

Defines the distribution off the size of each column value. If not specified, the size distribution will default to UNIFORM(4..8).

population

Defines the cardinality or distribution of unique values for this column. If not specified, the population distribution will default to UNIFORM(1..100B).

cluster

Only applies to clustering columns, and is used to control the number of rows underneath each partition. If not specified, the default cluster distribution will default to FIXED(1).

 Data will still be generated for columns that are omitted from the columnspec section. The preceding specified distribution defaults will be applied.

For reference, let's take a look at a similar table that we built in Chapter 3, *Effective CQL*:

```
SELECT * FROM packt_ch3.security_logs_by_location_desc LIMIT 6;

location_id | day      | time_in | employee_id | mailstop
------------+----------+---------------------+-------------+----------
      MPLS2 | 20180723 | 2018-07-23 14:04:59 |       tejam | M266
      MPLS2 | 20180723 | 2018-07-23 12:55:45 |        tedk | M266
      MPLS2 | 20180723 | 2018-07-23 12:17:38 |       jeffb | M266
      MPLS2 | 20180723 | 2018-07-23 12:08:24 |       johno | M261
      MPLS2 | 20180723 | 2018-07-23 12:01:18 |     sandrak | M266
      MPLS2 | 20180723 | 2018-07-23 11:49:11 |        samb | M266

(6 rows)
```

Based on this, we'll define a columnspec section as follows:

```
columnspec:
 -name: location_id
   size: FIXED(5)
   population: UNIFORM(1..1800)
 -name: day
   size: FIXED(8)
   population: UNIFORM(1..1000)
```

```
-name: time_in
  size: FIXED(5)
  population: UNIFORM(1..1000)
  cluster: UNIFORM(1..1000)
-name: employee_id
  size: GAUSSIAN(5..10)
 population: UNIFORM(1..1000)
cluster: UNIFORM(1..1000)
-name: mailstop
size: FIXED(4)
population: uniform(1..1800)
```

With our data distribution configured, we'll move on to the insert and query definition sections. We'll start by defining our insert behavior to write a single, fixed partition per batch, as well as only one row per partition per batch. Our batches will also be unlogged:

```
insert:
partitions: fixed(1)
batchtype: UNLOGGED
select: fixed(1)/10
```

Here, we will predefine the queries that Cassandra-Stress will run. This should be easy to do, as Cassandra tables are only defined to serve a small, finite numbers of queries. We will specify our cql query with question marks (?) for key values. We will designate that we want our key values to come from the same row (instead of getting location_id and day from multiple rows; combinations that may not exist):

```
queries:
  query1:
      cql: SELECT * FROM security_logs_by_location_desc WHERE location_id=?
AND day=?
      fields: samerow
```

Now that our security_logs_by_location_desc_stress.yaml file is complete, we can run our stress test. We can call cassandra-stress to invoke either a mixed load, write load, or read load. For now, we'll stick with separating reads and writes. This means we need to run our write load first, or else we won't have any data with which to test our reads. The following command will invoke our insert definition:

```
tools/bin/cassandra-stress user
profile=security_logs_by_location_desc_stress.yaml ops\(insert=1\) -node
192.168.0.101 -mode native cql3 user=cassdba password=flynnLives
```

Once that completes, we can re-run that command, but this time referencing our `query1` definition in the `ops` parameter:

```
tools/bin/cassandra-stress user
profile=security_logs_by_location_desc_stress.yaml ops\(query1=1\) -node
192.168.0.101 -mode native cql3 user=cassdba password=flynnLives
```

As we want to analyze the results, it is a good idea to send the output of `cassandra-stress` to a file. You can add the Linux `tee` command on the end of the statement to pipe the onscreen output for each operation to a file: `| tee stress_query1.log`.

All of these operations will iterate through a large volume of requests, and increase the operational thread count as they go. Cassandra-Stress keeps going until it determines that the cluster is being saturated and performance is not improving, or after it reaches a count of more than 900 threads.

Cassandra-Stress results

The results for both insert and query workloads will look very similar. Once each thread iteration is complete, it will display the progress in line with an increasing total operations count:

```
Running with 24 threadCount
Running [query1] with 24 threads until stderr of mean < 0.02
type    total ops,  op/s,  pk/s,   row/s,    mean,   med,    .95,    .99,   .999,     max,   time,  stderr, errors,  gc: #,  max ms,  sum ms,
total,      2342,  2342,     0,       0,     3.0,   0.5,    7.6,   94.2,  252.6,   253.2,   1.0,     NaN,      0,     0,      0,      0,
total,      4618,  2276,     0,       0,     3.9,   0.8,   16.3,   50.0,  149.6,   152.4,   2.0,     NaN,      0,     1,      7,      7,
total,      6868,  2250,     2, | 60211,    5.5,   0.6,   13.9,   86.0,  337.1,  1289.7,   3.0, -0.81650,     0,     1,      5,      5,
total,      8191,  1323,     1,   64980,    5.1,   0.6,   15.4,   70.1,  340.5,  1651.5,   4.0, -0.55833,     0,     2,      6,     12,
total,      8602,   411,     0,       0,     4.2,   0.4,   15.5,   92.9,  130.5,   130.5,   5.0, -0.60145,     0,     1,      6,      6,
total,      9332,   730,     1,   91065,   16.2,   0.6,   17.7,  144.0,  949.5,  2753.6,   6.0, -0.51513,     0,     1,      6,      6,
total,     10210,   878,     1,   43470,    5.4,   0.7,   21.1,   52.9,  341.0,   524.8,   7.0, -0.86659,     0,     3,      7,     19,
total,     10840,   630,     3,  307665,   22.3,   0.4,   13.9,   62.7, 4446.0,  7163.9,   8.0, -0.73133,     0,     2,      7,     13,
total,     11354,   514,     3,  523258,   33.7,   0.4,   16.4,  250.5, 7335.0,  7524.6,   9.0, -0.59181,     0,     2,      7,     13,
total,     11630,   276,     2,  263013,   35.6,   0.4,   11.6,   21.6, 7826.6,  7826.6,  10.0, -0.53973,     0,     1,      7,      7,
total,     11637,     7,     2,   60264,  747.0,  32.2, 2787.1, 2787.1, 2787.1,  2787.1,  11.0, -0.50144,     0,     0,      0,      0,
total,     12338,   701,     4,  747857,   47.7,   0.4,   13.7,   88.8,10687.1, 11232.3,  12.0, -0.43728,     0,     2,      7,     13,
total,     13158,   820,     2,  259744,   14.8,   0.4,   13.6,   79.5,  655.4,  8824.8,  13.0, -0.41260,     0,     3,      6,     18,
total,     13748,   590,     2,  473238,   42.0,   0.6,   19.6,   68.0,10729.0, 11240.7,  14.0, -0.38200,     0,     2,      7,     14,
total,     14458,   710,     3,  629654,   41.9,   0.7,   20.1,  125.1, 7608.5, 11366.6,  15.0, -0.34881,     0,     1,     13,     13,
total,     15653,  1195,     4,  534393,   23.4,   0.9,   12.9,   50.9, 9126.8, 13337.9,  16.0, -0.32804,     0,     1,     10,     10,
total,     15830,   177,     1,   85956,    8.8,   0.4,   11.2,   19.1, 1057.5,  1057.5,  17.0, -0.64198,     0,     1,      6,      6,
total,     16068,   238,     2,  292786,  101.4,   0.5,   51.2, 1750.1,17314.1, 17314.1,  18.0, -0.63871,     0,     0,      0,      0,
total,     17594,  1526,     5,  642187,   24.8,   0.4,   12.1,   64.4, 6828.3, 14931.7,  19.0, -0.62672,     0,     2,      8,     15,
total,     19524,  1930,     5,  547430,   16.9,   0.4,    8.2,  106.3,  673.7, 15208.5,  20.0, -0.61729,     0,     2,      6,     12,
total,     21171,  1647,     5,  786958,   27.3,   0.5,   12.7,   99.7, 8707.4, 16575.9,  21.0, -0.60476,     0,     1,      6,      6,
total,     22522,  1351,     2,   38512,    5.2,   0.6,   15.7,   97.1,  394.0,   766.5,  22.0, -0.66141,     0,     2,      8,     15,
total,     23755,  1233,     5,  626066,   24.0,   0.4,   10.6,   75.2, 9814.7, 11232.3,  23.0, -0.64382,     0,     1,      6,      6,
total,     25856,  2101,     6,  991906,   21.3,   0.6,   12.8,   68.3, 7851.7, 12239.0,  24.0, -0.61975,     0,     2,      6,     11,
```

Figure 5.1: A report for query1 with a thread count of 24

As you can see in preceding screenshot, the operations report shows many aspects of the workload. The following is a quick summary and explanation for each column of data:

- total ops: Total number of operations
- op/s: Operations per second
- pk/s: Primary keys processed per second
- rows: Rows processed per second
- mean: Mean latency of the operations
- med: Median latency of the operations
- .95: Latency for the 95th percentile of the operations (the worst 5%)
- .99: Latency for the 99th percentile of the operations (the worst 1%)
- .999: Latency for the 99.9th percentile of the operations (the worst 0.1%)
- max: Maximum latency of the operations
- time: Total time for the current thread count
- stderr: Standard error of the mean latency
- errors: Errors encountered
- gc: #: Number of times garbage collection was triggered
- max ms: Time of the longest garbage-collection pause
- sum ms: Total time of all garbage-collection pauses for the current operations
- sdv ms: Standard deviation of the garbage-collection times
- mb: Total size of the garbage collected in megabytes

 All the preceding times are in **milliseconds (ms)**.

Next, each iteration will also show a summary of the attempted operations. This is a report from a query load run with a thread count of 24:

```
Results:
Op rate                    : 912 op/s [query1: 912 op/s]
Partition rate             : 3 pk/s [query1: 3 pk/s]
Row rate                   : 367,939 row/s [query1: 367,939 row/s]
Latency mean               : 20.0 ms [query1: 20.0 ms]
Latency median             : 0.6 ms [query1: 0.6 ms]
Latency 95th percentile    : 14.5 ms [query1: 14.5 ms]
Latency 99th percentile    : 92.3 ms [query1: 92.3 ms]
Latency 99.9th percentile  : 7826.6 ms [query1: 7,826.6 ms]
```

```
Latency max              : 17314.1 ms [query1: 17,314.1 ms]
Total partitions         : 96 [query1: 96]
Total errors             : 0 [query1: 0]
Total GC count           : 51
Total GC memory          : 31.858 GiB
Total GC time            : 0.3 seconds
Avg GC time              : 6.6 ms
StdDev GC time           : 1.4 ms
Total operation time     : 00:00:37
```

At the end of the run, a total summary will be given, which will be used to gain insight as to which parts of your data model may need improving.

Write performance

Given its log-based storage model and memtable/commitlog design, Apache Cassandra usually does very well when it comes to high-performance data-ingestion. That being said, it is not uncommon to hear of application teams complaining about Cassandra nodes being saturated with load due to writes. Here is a short list of things to check when write performance suffers.

Commitlog mount point

One piece of advice, going back to the early days of Apache Cassandra, was to ensure that the commitlog was on a different physical mount point than the data drives. This is because disk I/O could become bottlenecked at the device level during periods of heavy writes. Putting the commitlog and data directories on separate mount points can alleviate this contention.

As **solid state drive** (**SSD**) technology evolved, it was discovered that this was less of an issue than it is with spinning disks. However, the era of cloud computing has significantly **muddied the waters** on this issue. For convenience and versatility, we have traded away specific knowledge of our backend. Even if you continue to separate them, it's still possible for your commitlog and data to end up on the same physical device. If disk I/O becomes an issue, you should speak to your cloud provider about appropriate storage types and provisioning strategies.

Scaling out

The obvious answer to solving write throughput issues is to scale horizontally by adding more nodes. Cassandra scales linearly. Assume that your application can write at 10,000 operations per second with 10 nodes without issue (assuming that the nodes are not becoming overwhelmed during periods of high-frequency writes). Therefore, if you want to be able to support writing at 20,000 operations per second, you could double the size of your cluster.

Scaling out a data center

It is common for enterprises to have a cluster spread across multiple data centers and infrastructure providers. A common pattern is for the application team to load data internally, and replicate it out to the cloud to be served by a customer-facing application. One solution, would be to create three logical data centers, as shown in the following table:

BigBoxCo Ecommerce cluster:

Data center name	RF	Nodes	Writes/ second	Reads/ second	CPUs	RAM (GB)
BBDC1	3	6	18,000	0	24	256
Cloud_East	3	18	0	36,000	16	64
Cloud_West	3	18	0	36,000	16	64

Table 5.1: An example 42-node cluster for an e-commerce implementation

Given the cluster setup in *Table 5.1*, over time, writes per second may begin to increase. If we start to notice that the CPU usage becomes maxed out and the application team starts to report write timeouts during the loading phase, we have a few options:

- Increase the number of nodes to accommodate the higher levels of write throughput.
- Adjust the backpressure strategy settings.

- Check the node(s) for issues with excessive resource consumption due to compaction or garbage collection.
- Build a throttling mechanism on the loading application, and lower the level of write throughput. This can be accomplished by limiting the number of asynchronous threads in flight at any given time.

As the nodes in this example are experiencing a significant amount of increased **writes per second** (**wps**), adjusting the backpressure settings will have little effect. Improperly-built applications can also cause nodes in a cluster to experience issues. Often this can be solved by limiting the write throughput at the application. We will cover how to accomplish this in the Chapter 8, *Application Development*.

> Be sure to check with your application team to ensure that they are not improperly using the BATCH functionality, as this has been known to cause similar problems.

In terms of scaling, the only viable option is the first. Given the data in *Table 5.1*, the BBDC1 data center (where the loading job runs) could previously support 18,000 wps with 6 nodes. This tells us that each node can handle 3,000 wps itself. If the cluster now has to support 30,000 wps, then adding another 4 nodes (for a total of 10) will allow the cluster to do this.

> While Apache Cassandra 3.0 and up has the ability to apply a backpressure strategy, this is only viable for small amounts of write backpressure. If a node is truly maxed out and trying to handle something in the realm of 2x normal throughput, no amount of backpressure configuration is going to help.

Read performance

If a cluster is exhibiting poor read performance, there are some obvious things to check on the application and data model (table definition) before adjusting any configuration settings. As previously mentioned, tables in Cassandra must be designed based on the queries that they are required to serve. If application teams are complaining about operation slowness for multi-key queries or queries that contact multiple nodes, there is little that can be done to improve the situation. On the other hand, if you are confident about the table design and are not violating any known **anti-patterns** (see the *Cassandra anti-patterns* section, under *Other performance considerations*), then configuration in some of these areas may be helpful.

Compaction strategy selection

Apache Cassandra 3.0 ships with three compaction strategies, which offer some control over the frequency and methods for managing the underlying files. These compaction strategy classes are `SizeTieredCompactionStrategy` (default), `LeveledCompactionStrategy`, and `TimeWindowCompactionStrategy`.

As previously mentioned, if not specified at table-creation time, a table will be built with with `SizeTieredCompactionStrategy`. While the size-tiered strategy does make for a good default, there are situations where performance can be improved by using a different strategy. One of Apache Cassandra's early main goals was the optimization of write throughput. Likewise, the size-tiered strategy is not necessarily the best option for read-heavy use cases.

Optimizing read throughput for time-series models

Since version 2.1, Apache Cassandra has delivered a compaction strategy that helps with optimizing file storage for time-series use cases.
Originally, `DateTieredCompactionStrategy` was delivered as a way to optimize data storage by time. With this strategy in place, SSTable files were sorted by relative time. This was efficient, as the idea with time-series models is that the application really only cares about specific date ranges of data. This allowed data for specific dates/times to be queried, while older, irrelevant data was ignored.

With Cassandra 3.10 came the advent of `TimeWindowCompactionStrategy`. This was an improvement over the date-tiered strategy in several areas (and was less buggy). But the general idea remains the same, where only data in a specific time window is queried. Again, data in different time windows does not interfere with requested data.

While only applicable to certain use cases, time-specific strategies are good at keeping data rows together, relative to the time they were written. This also results in a much lower possibility of a row having to be read from multiple SSTable files. As there are fewer (ideally one) SSTable files to have to look through, reads are faster.

Optimizing tables for read-heavy models

The original size-tiered strategy should work fine for use cases where the read/write ratio is less than 50:50, and thus is slanted more toward the write-heavy side. But if a table's use case calls for it to be read much more often than written to, `LeveledCompactionStrategy` should make for a good fit.

Using the leveled strategy helps read-heavy workloads perform better, as it significantly increases the chance of a row existing in a single SSTable file. Let's assume that I have a long-lived table that is updated on a semi-frequent basis, and that I want to query for a specific row:

```
SELECT * FROM users_by_dept
WHERE department='IT' AND username='tedk';
```

As this row (r) gets updated every time an employee's information needs to be updated, it is likely that it will span multiple SSTables under size-tiered compaction. A possible file layout for SSTable files behind the `users_by_dept` table is depicted here:

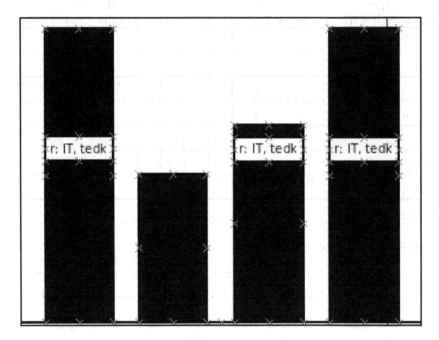

Figure 5.2: An example showing four SSTable files of different sizes, with three of them containing part of the row for IT and tedk

As shown in the preceding figure, the **tedk** user from the **IT** dept spans three SSTable files. When the preceding query is executed, each of those files will have to be read, and then the results of each will have to be compared and merged. From a time perspective, a disk seek takes 10 ms (Dean, Norvig 2012), and (with the preceding example) that will have to be done three times.

But with leveled compaction, each additional level is 10 times the size of the previous. Therefore, the mean chance (Hobbs 2012) that a row will be entirely contained within a single SSTable file is 90%:

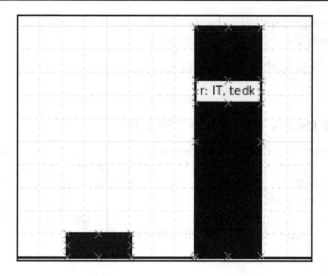

Figure 5.3: An example showing two levels of SSTable files, with one of them containing the row for IT and tedk

In this way, leveled compaction actually does a better job of mitigating issues that come from executing in-place updates (Hobbs 2012). Under these conditions, an Apache Cassandra node should only have to perform a single disk seek/read to return this row.

 Remember that leveled compaction does a better job of *mitigating* the effects of in-place updates. This does not make it a better compaction strategy for use cases with a higher ratio of writes to reads. This distinction is important to make.

Cache settings

Apache Cassandra has two mechanisms that can be used to cache table data: the key cache, and the row cache. As the name suggests, the key cache simply caches the location of the keys in RAM, providing a boost in efficiency to disk seeks for rows as well (Gilmore 2011). Similarly, enabling row-caching stores the entire row in cache. Hits on the row cache perform significantly better than reads from disk, as reads from RAM happen in a matter of nanoseconds (Dean, Norvig 2012).

Row-caching requires the size to be set in `cassandra.yaml` as well as the number of rows (per partition) to be set at the table level. Do note that row-caching is disabled by default, as its use is known to interfere with a node's ability to serve requests. However, key-caching helps in most use cases, so it is enabled by default (and also has a corresponding size setting in `cassandra.yaml`).

Size settings for both row and key caches represent a single amount of memory that is shared by all tables.

Appropriate uses for row-caching

As entire rows are stored in RAM with row-caching, it is important to note that some data models are intrinsically better for caching than others. Tables modeled with slim or narrow rows (Gilmore 2011) per partition are very efficiently cached. However, partitions with wide rows or rows with lots of data in collections are best left in tables with row-caching disabled. Row-caching also works best when applied to datasets with access patterns that follow a gaussian (normal) distribution (Gilmore 2011).

Compression

As discussed in prior chapters, table-level compression can also be specified. Apache Cassandra ships with both the LZ4 and snappy compressor classes, and the LZ4 compressor is used by default. Compression can also be disabled on a table, but this is not recommended. Compression of table data in Cassandra not only leads to a lighter disk footprint, but also to improved performance, due to a smaller amount of disk I/O at operation time.

Chunk size

By default, Apache Cassandra implements LZ4 compression with a `chunk_length_in_kb` size of 64. It's important to note that in read-heavy or mixed workloads, using a smaller chunk size can help to improve (reduce) our overall disk I/O usage. This is especially true if your data model is performing small, frequent reads. Jon Haddad of The Last Pickle put it best when he wrote the following:

> *Ultimately, we need to ensure we use a chunk length that allows us to minimize our I/O. Larger chunks can compress better, giving us a smaller disk footprint, but we end up needing more hardware, so the space savings becomes meaningless for certain workloads. There's no perfect setting that we can apply to every workload. Frequently, the most reads you do, the smaller the chunk size (Haddad 2018).*

When data is queried, it is read as chunks from an SSTable file. The chunks are of a fixed size, as we mentioned earlier, with a default value of `chunk_length_in_kb=64`. The problem though, is that Cassandra ends up having to read (and decompress) the entire 64 K chunk, instead of only the data that we actually need (Haddad 2018). By lowering the default size of the chunks, we can eliminate unnecessary disk I/O.

 In the article referenced in this section, Haddad lowers `chunk_length_in_kb` to `4`, and sees improvements along the lines of 50% additional ops and a 2x reduction in p99 latency (2018).

However, lowering the default chunk size for a table does not come without its trade-offs. The compression metadata is stored off-heap, and the size used is directly proportional to the number of chunks. A smaller default chunk size equals more chunks, which equals more off-heap memory used. Lowering the chunk size to 16 K (from 64 K) may help ops and latency, but it increases that table's off-heap compression metadata size usage by 4x.

Also, Haddad notes that there isn't a one-size-fits-all value for this setting. Like many settings in Cassandra, changes should be made incrementally, and then monitored to verify their impact. Additionally, he adds warnings at the end of his article:

> *I highly recommend taking the time to understand your workload and analyze your system resources to understand where your bottleneck is, as there is no absolute correct setting to use for every workload.*

He also cautions readers to consider the following:

> *When working with a memory constrained environment it may seem tempting to use 4 KB chunks everywhere, but it's important to understand that it'll use more memory.*

The bloom filter configuration

Another table setting that can help to tune performance is `bloom_filter_fp_chance`. Remember from earlier chapters that the bloom filter is a probabilistic data structure. Its job in the Cassandra read path is to provide guidance during query time. Specifically, the bloom filter is capable of indicating whether or not the requested data might be present in a particular SSTable file, or that it definitely is not. The **false-positive** (**fp**) chance is the main tunable property of the bloom filter. It defaults to a value of 0.01 (1%), unless the table is using Leveled compaction, and then it starts at 0.1 (10%).

Systems with SSDs can handle a higher value (of a false positive), as disk I/O is less of a bottleneck. Likewise, systems with slower (for example: spinning) disks will benefit from a smaller value. However, it is important to note that off-heap RAM usage increases dramatically with bloom filter accuracy. Setting a false-positive chance of 1% will use about 3x the memory that configuring a 10% chance will.

Read performance issues

As previously indicated, reads can be slow for other reasons:

- Too many tombstones
- Result set is too large
- Partitions are too large

Please note that none of the configuration settings mentioned in this section can solve these issues. They must be dealt with at the data-model/usage level. Chapter 3, *Effective CQL*, discusses strategies to help model around each of these performance issues.

Other performance considerations

In addition to the performance-tuning options mentioned in the preceding section, there are additional configuration settings that can be adjusted, depending on workload type. Also, it is important to understand that there are use cases for which Apache Cassandra is just not a good fit, and is not likely to perform well regardless of performance tuning. Similarly, there are some parts of the overall platform architecture that may have a direct impact on Apache Cassandra's performance, and little can be done to remedy this.

JVM configuration

In Chapter 4, *Configuring a Cluster*, configuration of the java virtual machine (specifically, garbage collection) was covered at length. While we won't waste time repeating the same information here, we'll add some quick guidelines that echo what was covered in Chapter 4, *Configuring a Cluster*:

- Be sure to monitor your nodes' garbage-collection logs. If your nodes are exhibiting long, **stop the world** (**STW**) pauses, there are adjustments that can be made to mitigate that.

- It's almost always a good idea to set the max heap size (-Xmx) and the initial heap size (-Xms) to be the same. This way, performance will not be impacted as the heap resizes itself.
- If you're not experienced with JVM tuning, configure your nodes to use G1GC (garbage-first garbage collector). G1GC takes a lot of the guesswork out of tuning, and does a good job of efficiently collecting garbage on its own. Just remember not to set a new generation size (-Xmn) with G1GC, as this can prevent it from allocating new generation spaces efficiently.
- With smaller instances (heap sizes of 8 GB or under) you may find more success using the CMS (concurrent mark and sweep) garbage collector. With CMS, you should specify the new generation size at 40-50% of the total JVM Heap. The idea here is that you want the young generation sized large enough that most objects are created, live, and die without being promoted. Intergenerational promotion often leads to performance issues.
- Remember that increasing the size of the JVM heap does not necessarily help with performance. Compute resources permitting, care should be taken when increasing a CMS heap above 8 GB or a G1 heap above 30 GB.
- The problem of smaller heaps in G1 is the reason that Apache Cassandra continues to default to the CMS collector, as laptop/dev environments would be negatively impacted.

Cassandra anti-patterns

With many distributed databases, there are known anti-patterns, or use cases, that they are just not good at. Apache Cassandra definitely has its share of these. Identifying them is important, as you will want to avoid heading down these paths at all costs.

 No amount of performance tuning can mitigate a bad use case or a known anti-pattern.

Building a queue

Using Apache Cassandra as a backend for a queue or queue-like structure is never going to end well. We have discussed at length that, due to Cassandra's log-based storage engine, inserts, updates, and deletes are all treated as writes. Well, what does a queue do? It does the following:

- Data gets written to a queue.
- Data gets updated while it's in the queue (example: status). Sometimes several times.
- When the data is no longer required, it gets deleted.

Given what we have covered about how Cassandra handles things, such as in-place updates (obsoleted data) and deletes (tombstones), it should be obvious that this is not a good idea. Remember, a data model built to accommodate a small amount of in-place updates or deletes is fine. A data model that relies on in-place updates and deletes isn't going to make anyone happy in the end.

Query flexibility

As with many distributed databases, the flexibility to work with dynamic query patterns is a key price to pay for not having all of your data in one place. While Apache Cassandra does have the ability to apply secondary indexing, they exist for convenience and not for performance. Despite new features added with the goal of removing some of the pain of distributed indexing (such as materialized views and SASI indexes), tables in Cassandra must still be built to suit a specific query pattern.

Querying an entire table

Almost as bad as building a table with multiple secondary indexes are use cases that require multi-key or unbound queries. Many developers just need to know exactly how many rows their 200 GB table contains, so they run an unbound query while selecting a count:

```
SELECT COUNT(*) FROM some_really_huge_table_that_will_timeout;
```

Cassandra is simply not designed to scan its entire contents and return them in a nicely-formatted report. Queries such as this on large tables will likely result in a timeout.

An application team may ask for the query request timeout to be relaxed to accommodate an occasional unbound query such as this. My advice, is to say NO. Writing queries within the constraints of the database is a responsibility that clearly falls to the developer! Do not put your entire cluster at risk for the sake of convenience.

Incorrect use of BATCH

As a Cassandra DBA, this is a common problem for which you will have to monitor your logs. All developers have been taught that batching-up tens of thousands of writes together helps performance; in the RDBMS world, it does. Inevitably, a developer will try this on one of your clusters, and could possibly cause the node to crash.

Remember, BATCH in Apache Cassandra is a misnomer. It should probably have been named ATOMIC, because it ensures that all writes within a batch are applied atomically. The idea is that four or five query tables can be kept in sync using BATCH, so that a failure of one write will cause all of the others to be rolled back. It really was not designed to help with performance; in fact, you take about a 30% performance hit just by using BATCH. It definitely was not designed to apply 60,000 writes to the same table.

Network

The network is one of those aspects of platform architecture over which Cassandra administrators have little control. Unfortunately, all theories of how distributed systems are supposed to work are premised on the fact that the network is an optimally-functioning constant. This could not be further from the truth, as real networks suffer from hardware and connection failures, brownouts (also know as **flapping**), noisy neighbors, bottlenecks, and poor connections between providers.

While not much can be done to maintain network connectivity, there are things (some proactive) that can be done to mitigate the effects of network failures:

- Follow vendor/provider network recommendations. Often, your provider will have configuration settings that they recommend you apply to maintain a solid connection. You should follow those, and ensure that your network team is doing so.
- Buy your network team a round of beers at the next company happy hour. When your on-premise nodes can't communicate with data centers in the cloud provider, you'll be glad that they know who you are.

- Try to limit the number of logical data centers in your cluster. If your application team needs four, that's fine. Moving past six introduces that many more points of failure for maintaining your replication factor.
- If your cluster is deployed across multiple providers, consider increasing `phi_convict` up to a value of 10 or 12. This will cause Cassandra to wait for a longer period of time before marking a node as down.

Summary

In this chapter, we covered a lot in terms of Apache Cassandra and its performance-tuning options. We started with Cassandra-Stress to establish a performance baseline for a specific data model. Then, we began to evaluate factors that can influence write performance. We spent a bit of time covering read performance, and the different configuration properties that can help Apache Cassandra perform well during read-heavy and mixed workloads. Finally, we examined and discussed other factors that may influence or affect cluster performance.

Here are some important takeaways from this chapter:

- There is no amount of tuning that can mitigate a poorly-designed data model.
- Cassandra-Stress is one of the most underrated, yet helpful, tools available for Apache Cassandra.
- Remember that Apache Cassandra was originally optimized for high-performance writes. If you plan on reading data (and most of us do), you'll want to look at some possible configuration changes to fit your use case.
- Selecting an appropriate compaction strategy is more about the ratio of reads to writes than the actual table or model. Remember that leveled is better-suited for handling a read-heavy model. Otherwise, the default (size-tiered) should be fine.
- When changing a configuration property, apply changes on a small and incremental basis.
- Don't forget to monitor your cluster, and check both the system and `gc` logs for issues.

In the next chapter, we'll discuss cluster management and how to handle day-to-day operations with your Apache Cassandra clusters.

Managing a Cluster

6

In this chapter, we will discuss several aspects related to maintaining and managing an Apache Cassandra cluster. First, we'll discuss the nodetool utility, and quickly move on to tasks associated with scaling your cluster up or down. From there, we'll talk a little about the backup functionality of Apache Cassandra. Finally, we'll present situations for maintenance on your cluster, and discuss routine tasks that can improve its ability to function properly. Topics discussed will include the following:

- Adding and removing nodes
- Working with logical data centers
- Backups
- Techniques for ensuring data consistency

At the conclusion of this chapter, you should have a thorough understanding of basic cluster operations. You will have discovered much of the functionality around nodetool, and will understand when to use certain of its functions. Additionally, you should understand how backups work with Apache Cassandra, as well as how to take a snapshot and how to restore from it. This chapter should serve as a good reference for future questions about operational tasks.

Revisiting nodetool

Much of this chapter will focus on using Apache Cassandra's nodetool utility. As mentioned previously, the nodetool utility installs with Cassandra, and is central to most aspects of cluster management. Before we get too far into discussing it, there are some important things to note about nodetool:

- It uses port `7199` for JMX.
- Remote JMX access must be explicitly enabled within each node's configuration.
- Without remote JMX, you will need to SSH into the node to utilize it in nodetool.
- Nodetool is separate from Apache Cassandra. Different versions of nodetool can communicate with different versions of Cassandra, so use it with caution.

A warning about using nodetool

As far as Apache Cassandra is concerned, nodetool is an admin-level management tool. Make sure that you know what you are doing prior to invoking nodetool commands. If care is not taken, serious damage can be done to a cluster with nodetool. If you're not sure how to put a command together, or what it will do, by all means look it up or ask someone! It's much better to be cautious now, rather than sorry later.

Scaling up

One common task for Apache Cassandra DBAs is to scale **horizontally** or scale up (that is, add more nodes to) a cluster. Usually, this is because the cluster needs to store additional data, or provide additional operational throughput. Oftentimes, large e-commerce retailers will scale up their clusters just prior to the holiday season, as a way to ensure their ability to remain highly available during periods of heavy traffic.

Adding nodes to a cluster

The basic task behind scaling up a cluster is adding a new node. To accomplish this, start with your newly provisioned instance. If you follow good DevOps practices, and can install Apache Cassandra simply by executing your deployment pipeline, then this should be very easy for you. If you are installing Apache Cassandra manually, remember that all of the Cassandra configuration files should be mostly the same as they are on the other nodes.

There will, of course, be some differences in the files. Listen and RPC address values (as well as the broadcast addresses) should be specific to the node you are on. You will want to update those in your `cassandra.yaml` file, and your `cassandra-env.sh` script if you have it configured there, too. The cluster name, seed list, and everything else should stay pretty much the same.

> Don't be afraid to use a different seed list for a new node, if you need to. Remember, the seed list designation isn't anything special. All that list does is provide the node with a list of endpoints from which to start gossiping. Give it a node or two that are known to be currently running, and it should work just fine.

> When adding a new node to your cluster, be sure that its clock is synchronized with the first node's clock. If possible, configure your instances to use a **Network Time Protocol** (**NTP**) server to eliminate time drift.

If you are adding new nodes to a single-node cluster, you may want to increase the replication factor of your keyspace before adding the new node. This will ensure that it gets all of the data that it should. This can be verified and altered by describing your keyspace using `cqlsh` to connect to the live node:

```
DESC KEYSPACE packt;

CREATE KEYSPACE packt WITH replication
  = {'class': 'NetworkTopologyStrategy', 'ClockworkAngels': '1'};
...

ALTER KEYSPACE packt WITH replication
  = {'class': 'NetworkTopologyStrategy', 'ClockworkAngels': '2'};
```

Once configuration is complete, start the new node. To accomplish this with service-based installations, run the following command:

```
sudo service cassandra start
```

Otherwise, you should have a script that runs the following command from the location where you installed Apache Cassandra:

```
bin/cassandra -p cassandra.pid
```

Depending on the size of your data, your new node may take a while to fully bootstrap. You can monitor the bootstrap process with the following command:

```
nodetool netstats | grep Already
Already received 35 files, 5085120999 bytes total
Already received 7 files. 8325238 bytes total
Already received 18 files. 3105392851 bytes total
```

While monitoring this process, you should see the `bytes total` numbers continuing to increase. If they appear to be stuck (that is, not moving), then you may need to stop Cassandra, wipe the data, and restart the process.

Some guidelines for adding a new node to a cluster are as follows:

- The `cassandra.yaml`, `cassandra-env.sh`, `jvm.options`, and `cassandra-rackdc.properties` files of the new node should be largely identical to their counterparts on the existing nodes. The exception to this rule is obviously the IP addresses.
- If you are adding a seed node, you will need to invoke either `nodetool repair` or `nodetool rebuild` afterward, as seed nodes do not bootstrap.
- You can only bootstrap one node to the cluster at a time.
- New nodes will fail to join if another node in the cluster is also currently joining.
- No matter how fast the nodes come up after joining, allow the cluster to stabilize (watch `system.log` for activity) before attempting to join another node. It's usually a good idea to wait a couple of minutes before proceeding.
- Allow the node to follow the bootstrap process, if possible. Bootstrapping, the node will have a status of `UJ`, meaning up and joining. This status prevents the node from being selected to handle requests.
- If the bootstrap process is failing, you can disable it by adding the setting of `auto_bootstrap: false` to `cassandra.yaml`. In this case, you'll have to run `nodetool repair` or `nodetool rebuild` from another data center to stream data to the node, and chances are good that it may be asked to serve requests while streaming.

During this time, `nodetool status` queries will show that the new node is UJ, for up and joining. In the example shown in the following snippet, `192.168.0.102` is shown joining the cluster:

```
nodetool status
Datacenter: ClockworkAngels
============================
Status=Up/Down
|/ State=Normal/Leaving/Joining/Moving
--  Address        Load      Tokens  Owns     Host ID       Rack
UN  192.168.0.101  114.26 GB  24     100.0%   0edb5efa...   R40
UJ  192.168.0.102  901.62 MB  24       ?       38782ca0...   R40
```

Cleaning up the original nodes

It is important to remember that, once you have completed adding all of the new nodes, the data streamed to them still resides on other nodes. The reason for this is that, as new nodes get added, the number of tokens that each node is responsible for becomes smaller. The original nodes will still have the data that they have streamed but are no longer responsible for. In larger clusters, this data can be sizable.

To ensure that a node only contains data for which it is responsible, you can invoke the `nodetool cleanup` command:

```
nodetool cleanup
```

Adding a new data center

Sometimes, there are reasons to add a new data center to a cluster. New data centers provide an easy means by which to migrate or expand your cluster to a new provider. Typically, development teams ask for their Cassandra cluster to be built on the same provider, region, or data center as their application runs in. This is known as building for **data locality**. The goal is to provide the shortest possible network trip from the application to the database, and back again.

Adjusting the cassandra-rackdc.properties file

The same steps must be taken as described in the preceding section. One addition to that list of steps is that an adjustment has to be made to the `cassandra-rackdc.properites` file. Recall how, in the first chapter, the file contained two important properties: `dc` and `rack`. To add a new data center, all of the new nodes will have to share the same `dc` property. An example from the `cassandra-rackdc.properties` file is shown as follows:

```
dc=ClockworkAngels
rack=R40
```

The `rack` property came about during the days when bare metal deployments were the norm. The idea was that the nodes in a cluster should be spread across multiple physical data centers, and mounted within each data center in multiple physical racks. When using a snitch designed to take advantage of multiple racks, the `rack` property will try to ensure that replicas are spread across the racks as evenly as possible. This way, if an entire rack should ever fail, the cluster should still have enough nodes and replicas available to still be able to serve requests.

For the new data center, I will specify the following for all nodes:

```
dc=VaporTrails
rack=R30
```

 This configuration is what helps Apache Cassandra to be aware of both `dc` and `rack`. Remember that this configuration is a logical definition, which may or may not correspond to actual physical data centers and racks.

Each node in the new data center should be started one at a time. As mentioned in the previous section on adding new nodes, you should wait for 2 minutes before starting another node. This will allow the node to join and gossip to settle. At the point of joining the cluster, the nodes will be empty.

A warning about SimpleStrategy

Do note that, if existing keyspaces are defined using `SimpleStrategy`, queries running at `LOCAL` consistency levels (mainly `LOCAL_QUORUM`) could begin to fail. The Simple replication strategy is not data center-aware, so queries could be directed to the new nodes before they have data. This behavior is the main failing of `SimpleStrategy`.

To get data to the nodes in the new data center, we'll need to first modify the keyspace(s) to allow replication to them, as follows:

```
ALTER KEYSPACE packt WITH replication = {'class':
'NetworkTopologyStrategy', 'ClockworkAngels': '3', 'VaporTrails': '3'};
```

 Remember, you will also need to adjust replication for the `system_auth`, `system_distributed`, and `system_traces` keyspaces as well.

At this point, applications or queries that do not define a local data center (discussed in a later chapter) could begin to exhibit failures. This is because incoming operations could query the new nodes (again) before they have data.

Streaming data

Streaming data to new nodes in a data center should be done with the `nodetool rebuild` command. This command takes an existing data center as a parameter, which it uses as a source. On each new node, run the following command:

```
nodetool rebuild -- ClockworkAngels
```

This could take a while, depending on how much data needs to be streamed.

 Streaming data to new nodes can consume resources on the existing nodes. It is recommended to use `notetool rebuild` on one node at a time, so as not to overwhelm the source data center.

Scaling down

Needing to scale down a cluster isn't a terribly common task. But sometimes a cluster uses more resources than it needs, due to application retirement or migration. This is especially true in the case of deploying into a public cloud, where extra compute comes with a price tag. In this case, being fiscally responsible with your company's money often translates into trimming down your cluster's resources for efficiency.

Removing nodes from a cluster

The most obvious way to trim resources is to remove nodes from the cluster. Sometimes, nodes may need to be removed after crashing on their own. In a cloud environment built with efficient DevOps processes, it is often much faster to re-provision a troublesome node than it is to spend time resurrecting it. There are two nodetool commands used to remove nodes from a cluster: `nodetool decommission` and `nodetool removenode`. These will be discussed based on their use cases (live node versus dead node) in the following section.

Removing a live node

Scaling down by removing a live node (that is, a node which is still functioning) can be accomplished using the `nodetool decommission` command. Decommissioning a live node begins by putting the node in a status of UL, for up and leaving. This prevents the node from being included in serving queries by a coordinator.

Additionally, the token range is adjusted for all nodes in the data center. Data on the node is then streamed to the nodes that will be responsible for the data. The command begins the decommissioning process on the node specified by the host (-h) parameter, or runs on the current node if none is specified:

```
nodetool decommission -h 192.168.0.101
```

Or we can use as follows:

```
nodetool decommission
```

Once the command is executed, the prompt waits while the decommission process begins. It runs in the background, so it is safe to break (using *Ctrl + C*) your way back to a Command Prompt.

When decommissioning nodes, it is always a good idea to be careful. I have found it easier to SSH to the target node, and run `nodetool decommission` (without any parameters). This eliminates the possibility of mistyping an IP or hostname.

If I wanted to remove `192.168.0.102`, I could do so with this command:

```
nodetool decommission -h 192.168.0.102
^C
nodetool status
Datacenter: ClockworkAngels
===========================
Status=Up/Down
|/ State=Normal/Leaving/Joining/Moving
-- Address Load Tokens Owns Host ID Rack
UN 192.168.0.101 114.26 GB 24 100.0% 0edb5efa... R40
UL 192.168.0.102 111.62 GB 24 100.0% 38782ca0... R40
UN 192.168.0.103 101.81 GB 24 100.0% e45b2ee0... R40
```

When the process completes, note the following:

- Any data owned by `192.168.0.102` will have been streamed to the nodes now responsible for its token ranges
- The `cassandra` process will still be running on `192.168.0.102`, but it will be out of the cluster
- At this point, the process can be killed or the instance can safely be shut down

Removing a dead node

Sometimes, a node may be down and unable to be restarted. Common scenarios involve the host experiencing a hardware failure, or a cloud instance being prematurely destroyed. In the case of `192.168.0.102` being unrecoverable, a cluster status would look like this:

```
nodetool status
Datacenter: ClockworkAngels
===========================
Status=Up/Down
|/ State=Normal/Leaving/Joining/Moving
--   Address        Load      Tokens  Owns    Host ID      Rack
UN   192.168.0.101  114.26 GB  24      100.0%  0edb5efa...  R40
DN   192.168.0.102  111.62 GB  24      100.0%  38782ca0...  R40
UN   192.168.0.103  101.81 GB  24      100.0%  e45b2ee0...  R40
```

As data cannot be streamed from a down node, `nodetool decommission` will not work. At this point, the best option for removing the node from the cluster will be to remove it. The `nodetool removenode` command exists for this scenario, and works by identifying the node by host ID:

```
nodetool removenode 38782ca0-5dee-4576-b0f9-5c54ab6fef6b
```

Similar to decommissioning, you can safely *Ctrl + C* back to a Command Prompt after invoking the `removenode` process. The process will continue to run in the background. During this time, data will be streamed to the new token ranges from other live replicas in the cluster. Once that completes, the node will be removed from gossip as well.

Other removenode options

Once you do that, you can query the current node for the `status` of the removal:

```
nodetool removenode status
RemovalStatus: Removing token (-7858886458974273909). Waiting for
replication confirmation from [/192.168.0.103].
```

Sometimes, the removal process may hang or become stuck. The chances of this happening have decreased with the newer and more stable versions of Apache Cassandra. If this should happen, you can invoke `force` from the node responsible for the removal as follows:

```
nodetool removenode force

nodetool removenode status
RemovalStatus: No token removals in process.
```

The removal process requires a current, live node to coordinate another node's removal. That node is considered responsible for the removal process. Attempts to query the status of a removal from a node that is *not* responsible for that process will yield the `No token removals in process` message, regardless of whether or not a removal may actually be in process.

Forcing the removal of a node may have some unintended consequences. Firstly, the data has probably not been replicated to the nodes newly responsible for the removed node's token ranges. Secondly, removal from gossip is also probably not completed. Applications still running with open connections to the cluster may experience warnings or failures associated with the removed node for several hours afterward.

It is a good idea to run a repair after forcing a node's removal.

When removenode doesn't work (nodetool assassinate)

Sometimes, despite our best efforts, even `nodetool removenode` fails to completely take a node out of the cluster. This can happen if the remove process hangs, or if another node crashes during this time. Whatever the cause, sometimes a node may appear to be removed to some nodes, but not to others. For edge cases like these, the `nodetool assassinate` command exists, and is used as follows:

```
nodetool assassinate 192.168.0.102
```

This command completely removes the node from the cluster, without streaming any data. It should only be used as a last resort, and only if either `decommission` or `removenode` fail to work.

If a node is particularly stubborn about leaving gossip, you may need to run `assassinate` several times. For more information, refer to Casares J(2018) *Assassinate - A Command of Last Resort within Apache Cassandra: The Last Pickle*, available at `http://thelastpickle.com/blog/2018/09/18/assassinate.html`. The idea here is to create enough messages to all nodes to influence them to forget about the node in question.

Assassinating a node on an older version

The `nodetool assassinate` command is new to Apache Cassandra as of version 2.2. Prior to Cassandra 2.2, this operation was still possible, but by invoking a command via JMX. For this to work, you will first need to download the **JMXTerm** JAR file from `http://wiki.cyclopsgroup.org/jmxterm/`.

Then, run the JAR file from the command line, connect to your node, and assassinate the endpoint:

```
$ java -jar ./jmxterm-1.0.0-uber.jar
Welcome to JMX terminal. Type "help" for available commands.

$>open 192.168.0.101:7199
#Connection to 192.168.0.101:7199 is opened

$>bean org.apache.cassandra.net:type=Gossiper
```

```
#bean is set to org.apache.cassandra.net:type=Gossiper

$>run unsafeAssassinateEndpoint 192.168.0.102
#calling operation unsafeAssassinateEndpoint of mbean
org.apache.cassandra.net:type=Gossiper
#operation returns: null

$>quit
```

Removing a data center

A good way to safely and seamlessly phase in new changes to your cluster is by adding a new data center. For instance, migrating between cloud providers can be easily accomplished with Apache Cassandra, simply by creating nodes within a new, logical data center on the new provider. However, improperly disabling or shutting down nodes, still hosted on the old provider, can introduce problems with gossip (as described previously). Therefore, knowing how to properly remove an existing data center is an important part of any Cassandra DBA's repertoire.

First of all, you should identify the name of the target data center and nodes to be removed. Consider the following cluster:

```
nodetool status
Datacenter: ClockworkAngels
===========================
Status=Up/Down
|/ State=Normal/Leaving/Joining/Moving
--  Address          Load        Tokens  Owns     Host ID       Rack
UN  192.168.0.101    114.26 GB   24      100.0%   0edb5efa...   R40
UN  192.168.0.102    111.62 GB   24      100.0%   38782ca0...   R40
UN  192.168.0.103    101.81 GB   24      100.0%   e45b2ee0...   R40
Datacenter: FlyByNight
===========================
Status=Up/Down
|/ State=Normal/Leaving/Joining/Moving
--  Address          Load        Tokens  Owns     Host ID       Rack
UN  192.168.17.91    104.22 GB   24      100.0%   17b833be...   ByTor
UN  192.168.17.92    101.77 GB   24      100.0%   84ceddbf...   ByTor
UN  192.168.17.93    105.29 GB   24      100.0%   10999a1c...   ByTor
```

In this scenario, we will remove the `FlyByNight` data center from our cluster. Let's `cqlsh` into one of our nodes, and take a look at our keyspace:

```
desc keyspace packt_chapter6 ;

CREATE KEYSPACE packt_chapter6 WITH replication = {'class':
'NetworkTopologyStrategy', 'ClockworkAngels': '3', 'FlyByNight': '3'} AND
durable_writes = true;
```

Let's start by changing our keyspace definition to no longer replicate to the `FlyByNight` data center. We can accomplish this with the `ALTER KEYSPACE` command:

```
ALTER KEYSPACE packt_chapter6 WITH replication = {'class':
'NetworkTopologyStrategy', 'ClockworkAngels': '3'};
```

 Be careful! Altering a keyspace to no longer replicate data does not actually remove the data, but it does prevent the nodes in that data center from serving requests for that data. Make sure that your application teams are no longer specifying the target data center as their local data center.

Run that command for any additional keyspaces that might be active in your cluster. This command also needs to be run for any system keyspaces that may share similar replication definitions. This includes the `system_auth,` `system_distributed`, and `system_traces` keyspaces.

 Do not alter or change replication for the `system` or `system_schema` keyspaces, as those use a different, local replication strategy.

With the keyspace replication of those nodes disabled for the target data center, you can now SSH to them and run `decommission` on each of them:

```
aploetz@skywalker:~/local/apache-cassandra-3.11.2$ ssh aaron@192.168.17.91
...
aaron@192.168.17.91: ~$ nodetool decommission
aaron@192.168.17.91: ~$ exit
Connection to 192.168.17.91 closed.
```

With each node no longer responsible for any token ranges, the `nodetool decommission` command should complete quickly. Repeat this exercise for all nodes within the target data center. Once complete on all nodes, the target data center will be effectively removed.

Backing up and restoring data

Apache Cassandra provides the ability to take a snapshot of all SSTable files on a node. The resulting snapshot files are essentially hard links or pointers to these files. Combining snapshots with the incremental backup feature helps to ensure that lost data can be restored in a quick and timely manner. For more information, refer to the *Backing up and restoring data* section of the Cassandra documentation, available at https://docs.datastax.com/en/cassandra/3.0/cassandra/operations/opsBackupRestore.html.

Taking snapshots

Snapshots can be taken system-wide, or focused on a single keyspace or table. Invoking a snapshot is done very easily with nodetool. To take a snapshot for all tables in a specific keyspace, simply type the name of that keyspace on the end of the command:

```
nodetool snapshot packt_chapter3

Requested creating snapshot(s) for [packt_chapter3] with snapshot name
[1538941504326] and options {skipFlush=false}
Snapshot directory: 1538941504326
```

To take a snapshot for a specific table, use the --table option. Follow that with the table and keyspace names:

```
nodetool snapshot --table security_logs_by_location packt_chapter3

Requested creating snapshot(s) for [packt_chapter3] with snapshot name
[1538941525101] and options {skipFlush=false}
Snapshot directory: 1538941525101
```

 It is advisable to move snapshot files to a location that is off the node, because they are usually required when the node is completely offline.

Enabling incremental backups

Incremental backups instruct Apache Cassandra to create links to newly flushed memtables since the last snapshot was taken. This has the effect of keeping point-in-time snapshots up-to-date with the latest writes. Incremental backups are disabled by default, but can be enabled by editing the following line in the `cassandra.yaml` file of each node:

```
incremental_backups: true
```

 As with snapshot files, it is a good idea to move incremental backups to another instance for storage.

Recovering from snapshots

A table can be restored from snapshot files with these simple steps:

> 1. `TRUNCATE` the table. This is necessary in the case of an accidental delete operation. If the snapshot files are restored without the table having been truncated, then the timestamp on the prevailing tombstone will still be more recent than anything saved via the snapshot process. Truncating the table ensures that the restored data takes precedence.
>
> 2. Copy the files from the most recent snapshot and backups directories into the table's `data` directory. Snapshot files are no different from normal SSTable files. Simply copy them into the `data` directory for your table. If you move your snapshots to another storage location, make sure you copy over files that are applicable to the node that requires them. Snapshot files are specific to the node on which they were taken.
>
> 3. Run `nodetool refresh`. This will load the recently copied snapshot or backup files into the cluster. A restart is not required.

An example of this process is as follows:

```
cqlsh 192.168.0.101 -u cassdba -p flynnLives
Connected to PermanentWaves at 192.168.0.101:9042.
[cqlsh 5.0.1 | Cassandra 3.11.2 | CQL spec 3.4.4 | Native protocol v4]
Use HELP for help.
cassdba@cqlsh> use packt_chapter3 ;
cassdba@cqlsh:packt_chapter3> TRUNCATE TABLE security_logs_by_location ;
cassdba@cqlsh:packt_chapter3> SELECT * FROM security_logs_by_location ;
```

```
   location_id | day | time_in | employee_id | mailstop
-------------+-----+---------+-------------+----------

(0 rows)
cassdba@cqlsh:packt_chapter3> exit

cd
data/data/packt_chapter3/security_logs_by_location-20a4acc0ca6911e88a728b22
637f8cc7
cp snapshots/1538941525101/* .
nodetool refresh packt_chapter3 security_logs_by_location

cqlsh 192.168.0.101 -u cassdba -p flynnLives
Connected to PermanentWaves at 192.168.0.101:9042.
[cqlsh 5.0.1 | Cassandra 3.11.2 | CQL spec 3.4.4 | Native protocol v4]
Use HELP for help.
cassdba@cqlsh> use packt_chapter3 ;
cassdba@cqlsh:packt_chapter3> SELECT * FROM security_logs_by_location ;

 location_id | day       | time_in                          | employee_id |
mailstop
-------------+-----------+----------------------------------+-------------+--
--------
       MPLS2 | 20180723 | 2018-07-23 15:49:11.754000+0000 |        samb |
M266
       MPLS2 | 20180723 | 2018-07-23 16:04:22.432000+0000 |     aploetz |
M266
       MPLS2 | 20180723 | 2018-07-23 16:08:24.682000+0000 |       johno |
M261
       MPLS2 | 20180723 | 2018-07-23 16:17:38.268000+0000 |  jblanchard |
M266
       MPLS2 | 20180723 | 2018-07-23 16:55:45.911000+0000 |        tedk |
M266
       MPLS2 | 20180723 | 2018-07-23 18:04:59.377000+0000 |   tmalepati |
M266

(6 rows)
```

Maintenance

With most databases, there are a number of routine and ad hoc activities to be completed periodically. Apache Cassandra is no exception.

Replacing a node

Sometimes, instead of removing a bad node and adding a new one, you want to replace a node. In larger clusters, this becomes important, in that a new node can be designated as a replacement to a prior, down node. This means that, when the node starts up, it will contact the seed nodes and receive the same token ranges as the previous node.

Let's say that 192.168.0.103 goes down, and I need to replace it. I can re-instance a new node, say, 192.168.0.105. To ensure that 105 gets the same token ranges as 103 had, I can add this one line to the end of the cassandra-env.sh file at 105:

```
JVM_OPTS="$JVM_OPTS -Dcassandra.replace_address=192.168.0.103"
```

Now, when 105 starts up, it will be assigned the same token ranges that 103 had.

> Remember to make sure that the new node has the same data center and rack names as the node being replaced.

Repair

As Apache Cassandra is an eventually consistent database, it knowingly sacrifices consistency. Sometimes, network conditions, hardware/instance failures, or periods of extremely high load can cause issues with data replication. To remedy these possible scenarios, you should run weekly repairs on your cluster.

Simply running this statement without any parameters will invoke a full repair on all keyspaces and tables in the cluster:

```
nodetool repair -full
```

As the system keyspaces shouldn't need to be repaired regularly, this command can be focused on repairing all tables in a particular keyspace:

```
nodetool repair -full packt_chapter3
```

Likewise, you can also specify a particular table to be repaired as follows:

```
nodetool repair -full packt_chapter3 security_logs_by_location
```

If you're in a multi-region cluster, you may want to restrict repairs to certain nodes. This helps to avoid heavy cross-region streaming:

```
nodetool -h 192.168.0.101 repair -full packt_chapter3 -hosts 192.168.0.101
-hosts 192.168.0.102 -hosts 192.168.0.103
```

When specifying a list of hosts to limit a repair, be sure to include your current node, and to include all nodes necessary to cover all token ranges!

A warning about incremental repairs

The idea behind incremental repairs is pretty simple—mark certain data as repaired, and don't bother repairing it until it changes. However, incremental repairs are still inherently broken, and there have been consistency issues reported with its use. They should be fixed with the release of Apache Cassandra 4.0, but the current warning with incremental repairs is to use them only at your own risk! When in doubt, use -full repairs.

Cassandra Reaper

Within the last year, an open source tool for managing Apache Cassandra repairs has emerged. Its name is **Cassandra Reaper**, and it can be downloaded from http://cassandra-reaper.io/.

Reaper takes all the guesswork out of running repairs with Apache Cassandra. In the past, repair had to be invoked manually, or via cron jobs that you hope complete on time. Reaper allows you to support many clusters with easily managed repair schedules.

This tool is a life-saver! Hats-off to the *Last Pickle* team who adopted and worked on the project!

Forcing read repairs at consistency – ALL

The type of repair isn't really part of the Apache Cassandra repair paradigm at all. When it was discovered that a read repair will trigger 100% of the time when a query is run at ALL consistency, this method of repair started to gain popularity in the community. In some cases, this method of forcing data consistency provided better results than normal, scheduled repairs.

Let's assume, for a second, that an application team is having a hard time logging into a node in a new data center. You try to cqlsh out to these nodes, and notice that you are also experiencing intermittent failures, leading you to suspect that the system_auth tables might be missing a replica or two. On one node you do manage to connect successfully using cqlsh. One quick way to fix consistency on the system_auth tables is to set consistency to ALL, and run an unbound SELECT on every table, tickling each record:

```
use system_auth ;
consistency ALL;
consistency level set to ALL.

SELECT COUNT(*) FROM resource_role_permissons_index ;
SELECT COUNT(*) FROM role_permissions ;
SELECT COUNT(*) FROM role_members ;
SELECT COUNT(*) FROM roles;
```

This problem is often seen when logging in with the default cassandra user. Within cqlsh, there is code that forces the default cassandra user to connect by querying system_auth at QUORUM consistency. This can be problematic in larger clusters, and is another reason why you should never use the default cassandra user.

The original idea for this approach goes back to a Python script written by Apache Cassandra MVP Christos Kalantzis. His cassTickler code iterates through all rows in a table, tickling each one with the ALL consistency, and forcing a read repair. Christos' code can be found at https://github.com/ckalantzis/cassTickler.

Clearing snapshots and incremental backups

While snapshots and incremental backups form a complete backup system, their use can increase overall disk usage. This is because the links, created to the SSTable files, prevent them from being cleaned up by the compaction process. Left unchecked, snapshots and incremental backups can fill a whole disk, causing node failure.

Snapshots

Clearing snapshots is a simple matter, and can be done via nodetool:

```
nodetool clearsnapshot
```

Running `clearsnapshot` without any parameters instructs Apache Cassandra to remove all snapshot files on a node. It can also be focused for a particular keyspace, like the following:

```
nodetool clearsnapshot -- packt_chapter3
```

Additionally, `clearsnapshot` can be focused even further, by specifying a snapshot by name:

```
nodetool clearsnapshot -t 1538941504326
```

The `nodetool clearsnapshot` command is very helpful, and can be useful to quickly clear disk space in a pinch. However, many DBAs find it much more helpful to write a script to traverse the `snapshot` directories and purge old snapshot files instead, keeping only the latest two or three per table. Running a periodic script to keep those files in check can provide a viable, long-term solution for snapshot file management.

Incremental backups

Similar to snapshots, incremental backup files have the same problem. But presently, there exists no way to quickly clean them up through nodetool. The preceding tip for snapshots becomes the only really viable option. It is advised to manually monitor/delete the files, or to write a script to traverse the `backup` directories, to prevent incremental backup files from growing uncontrollably.

Compaction

As discussed in prior chapters, compaction is the process by which similarly sized underlying SSTables are joined together. This process reclaims space used by obsolete (overwritten) data, including tombstones. Although compaction can constrain system resources, it is generally something you want to run. After all, queries that require seeks/reads from multiple SSTable files are much slower than queries that only hit one file.

Why you should never invoke compaction manually

Remember that compaction works by finding multiple SSTable files that are similarly-sized. When you force compaction, you merge SSTable files together, regardless of their size, or whether or not there is a qualifying number of them. This often results in one large SSTable file. The likelihood of other SSTable files growing large enough to be compacted with that big file is very minimal. Essentially, running `nodetool compact` could cause compaction to pretty much never run again.

> As previously mentioned, the best advice is to let Cassandra figure out when it wants to run compaction. Don't get in its way!

Adjusting compaction throughput due to available resources

As mentioned at the beginning of this section, compaction can consume a large amount of resources if left unchecked. A symptom of this would be an application experiencing query timeouts or consistency failures. When investigating the offending node, you may find that the CPU usage is maxed out, and several compactions (`nodetool compactionstats`) may be pending. A common way to remedy this problem is to lower the compaction throughput, as follows:

```
nodetool getcompactionthroughput
Current compaction throughput: 256 MB/s
```

Woah! Allowing compaction to consume 256 Mbps (megabits per second) is a sure way to saturate your instance's resources. Let's lower that, and monitor our node's progress:

```
nodetool setcompactionthroughput 8
nodetool getcompactionthroughput
Current compaction throughput: 8 MB/s
```

> Remember, you want compaction to run. Setting the compaction throughput value too low will cause compactions to backup, and probably never complete. The idea is to find the right value that allows you to keep your files compacted, while still allowing nodes to serve requests.

Summary

This chapter covered a broad range of subjects related to the Apache Cassandra nodetool utility. The commands covered here will help you to scale your cluster horizontally, as well as to remove and replace failed nodes. If you support a cluster that has nodes deployed in public or private cloud instances, you will find that it is often much faster to replace a failed node, than to try and resurrect it. To that end, you will find yourself using these tools and techniques often.

We discussed things such as taking snapshots, and incremental backups, as well as the maintenance associated with cleaning them up. It's important to remember that snapshots and backups taken are only valid for the data stored on a particular node. If the number of nodes exceeds your replication factor, you will likely have to maintain separate sets of off-cluster backup files for each node. This can be especially complex when a cluster gets big. It is often a good idea to do a sanity check with your application team. Remind them that Apache Cassandra isn't a consistent data store in the first place, and then ask if they are loading their data from an upstream source, which may lend itself to taking backups more easily than Apache Cassandra does.

Finally, we discussed some maintenance tasks and issues that you may face on your cluster. Remember to run your repairs weekly, especially if your application team is using deletes. And sometimes, quick and simple repairs can be made by tickling a record. Be sure to investigate Cassandra Reaper as a means to take some of the grunt work out of repair scheduling. Keep an eye on your compactions, take a set-and-monitor approach to finding the ideal compaction throughput, and don't let your pending compaction count get too high.

In the next chapter, we'll discuss tips and tools for monitoring your cluster. Combined with this chapter, you should have plenty of good information as a reference for managing and troubleshooting your production Apache Cassandra cluster.

7
Monitoring

This chapter will cover monitoring, logging, and administration. With large-scale datasets on distributed architectures comes the problem of providing a reliable service, which makes it more complex to keep an eye on all servers. As DataStax OpsCenter is no longer an option for use with Apache Cassandra, this chapter concentrates only on the open source toolset. Specifically, this chapter will cover the following topics:

- The **Java Management Extension** (**JMX**) interface: JConsole, JMXTerm
- Nodetool
- Metrics: **JMXTrans**, **Telegraf**, **InfluxDB**, **Grafana**, **Alerting**
- Logging: Filebeat, Kibana
- Troubleshooting

By the end of this chapter, you will understand different monitoring and logging tools, and how they provide more insight for problem solving on your cluster. You will be able to make decisions using reliable out-of-the-box applications from the open source community, including installing, configuring, analyzing, and setting up alerting.

JMX interface

JMX is a Java technology that provides tools for managing and monitoring applications, services, components, devices, and settings. These settings are represented as Java objects, known as **Managed Beans** (**MBeans**). As Apache Cassandra is written in Java, all the required classes have exposed MBeans, through which we can manage/monitor them accordingly. Cassandra defaults its JMX port to 7199, hence it should be opened through firewalls and security groups to allow access over it.

MBean packages exposed by Cassandra

The following are the MBean packages exposed by Cassandra:

- `org.apache.cassandra.db`: Key Cassandra architectural metrics and management operations, you can get a compaction summary and perform a compaction operation for an entire node or restrict it to a table in a keyspace
- `org.apache.cassandra.hints`: Only operations related to the hints service, such as pause/resume, dispatch, and delete all hints or for an endpoint
- `org.apache.cassandra.internal`: Unlike the previous package, this contains metrics related to internal actions of Cassandra, such as the number of core and maximum threads used for flushing memtables, clearing the cache, dispatching hints, and so on
- `org.apache.cassandra.metrics`: All statistical metrics and operations, such as row/key cache, client read/write request count/latency, cross-node latency for all requests, or narrow it down to a table
- `org.apache.cassandra.net`: Stats on internal communication network metrics and operations for Cassandra cluster-management, such as number of down/up end points, streams, dropped messages, and assassinating nodes.
- `org.apache.cassandra.request`: As in the internal package, this gives the core and maximum threads being used for the read repair stage
- `org.apache.cassandra.service`: Similar to the request package, it provides statistical reset metrics related to the GC inspector

JConsole (GUI)

JConsole is a built-in utility for the JDK, which gives a graphical view of resource utilization for a Java process. It also provides an interface to view metrics and perform operations to manage applications. Refer to the JConsole docs for further information at Oracle *Java SE Documentation*:Using JConsole: `https://docs.oracle.com/javase/7/docs/technotes/guides/management/jconsole.html`.

Connection and overview

Invoking a JConsole connection is pretty simple. You can connect to a local or remote Java process. For local, just select the corresponding **Process Identifier (PID)**. To connect to a remote process, you can either use the hostname/IP and port combination, or the JMX service that runs Cassandra without JMX authentication and SSL:

Figure 7.1: JConsole connection

In certain implementations, a node would have both internal and external IPs. These would be set in the `Cassandra.yaml` config, with the `listen_address` and `rpc_address` parameters set to internal IPs, and the `broadcast_address` and `broadcast_rpc_address` parameters set to external IPs. Additionally, some additional parameters need to be updated in `Cassandra-env.sh` as follows:

```
LOCAL_JMX='no'

if [ "$LOCAL_JMX" = "yes" ]; then
  JVM_OPTS="$JVM_OPTS -Dcassandra.jmx.local.port=$JMX_PORT -
XX:+DisableExplicitGC"
else
  JVM_OPTS="$JVM_OPTS -Dcom.sun.management.jmxremote.port=$JMX_PORT"
  JVM_OPTS="$JVM_OPTS -Dcom.sun.management.jmxremote.rmi.port=$JMX_PORT"
  JVM_OPTS="$JVM_OPTS -Djava.rmi.server.hostname=127.0.0.1"
```

```
JVM_OPTS="$JVM_OPTS -Dcom.sun.management.jmxremote.ssl=false"
JVM_OPTS="$JVM_OPTS -Dcom.sun.management.jmxremote.authenticate=false"
fi
```

The following shows an of JConsole:

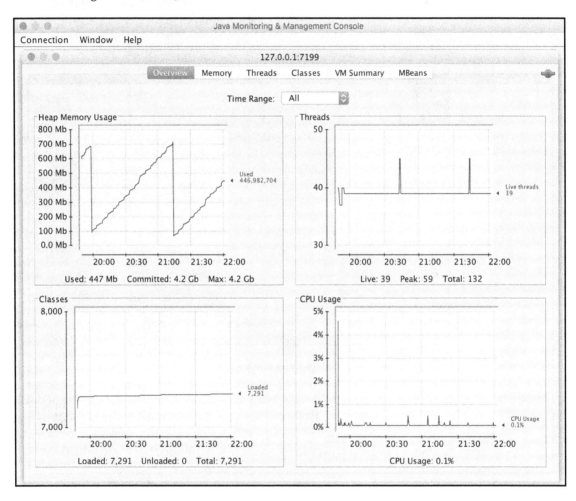

Figure 7.2: JConsole overview

Once a connection is successfully established, the **Overview** tab will be the homepage. It contains a view of key metrics for resources being utilized by the Java process, with more details under each tab for each corresponding metric.

Viewing metrics

The **MBeans** tab contains all the packages exposed by Cassandra, along with some Java-related packages exposed by default for any Java process. You can navigate to any of the nested methods to get a value of an attribute. In the following screenshot, the `DownEndpoint` metric can be viewed through `org.apache.Cassandra.net` | `FailureDetector` | `Attributes` | `DownEndpointCount`, which gives a count of the number of nodes that are down. Which is your favorite metric in Cassandra?

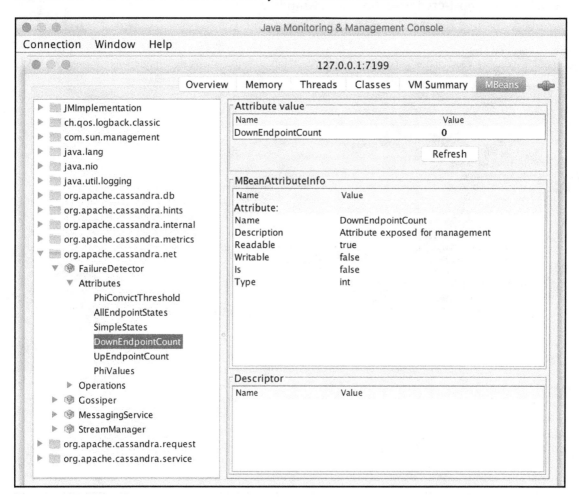

Figure 7.3: Viewing DownEndpointCount metrics on JConsole

Performing an operation

Instead of just getting a value for an attribute, you can perform an operation even without logging in to the server. This is the reason why we would recommend using JMX authentication/SSL, as the JMX port will be wide open. For example, you can invoke the `stopGossiping` operation from `org.apache.Cassandra.db` | `StorageService` | `Operations` | `stopGossiping`, which stops gossiping to other nodes.

Which is your most-used operation for Cassandra?

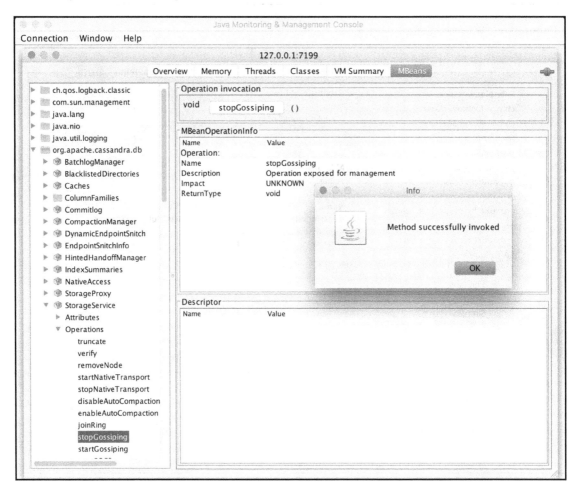

Figure 7.4: Performing the stopGossiping operation through JConsole

JMXTerm (CLI)

Unlike JConsole, JMXTerm is a command-line utility for any Java process with the JMX interface to view metrics and perform operations to manage applications. It's just a command-line tool, similar to JConsole, with an exception of graphical user interface. Refer to the JMXTerm docs for further information at *Apache-Confluence: JMXTerm Quick start*: https://cwiki.apache.org/confluence/display/KAFKA/jmxterm+quickstart.

Connection and domains

Download the JMXTerm jar from http://wiki.cyclopsgroup.org/jmxterm/download. html, then invoke JMXTerm from the CLI. Once you run the following command, Java just provides an interface to interact through JMX. This allows you to create a connection to the desired IP and port. If Cassandra is running on my local, 127.0.0.1:7199 can be used where JMX authentication and SSL are disabled on Cassandra:

```
java -jar <absolutePath>/jmxterm-1.0.0-uber.jar
open <IP>:7199
```

The preceding command will give the following output:

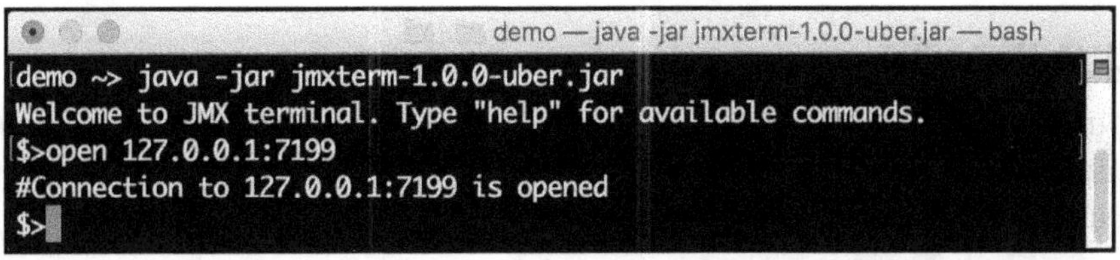

Figure 7.5: JMXTerm connection

The domains command gives all the MBean packages exposed by Cassandra, along with any Java-related packages exposed by default for any Java process:

```
domains
```

The output of the `domains` command is as follows:

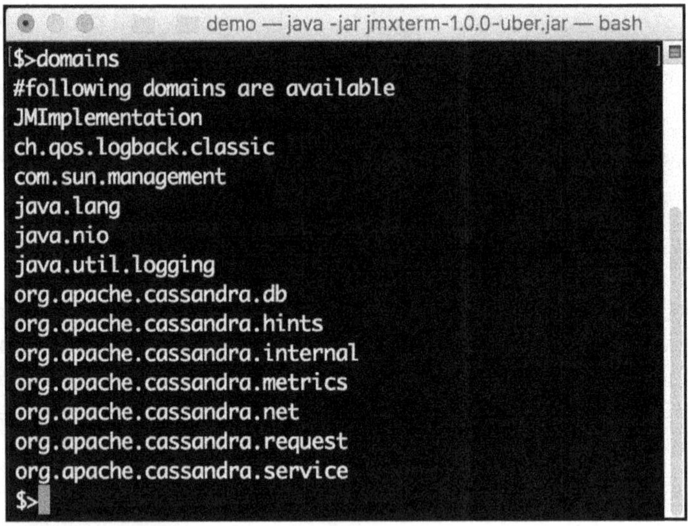

Figure 7.6: JMXTerm domains available for connected Java process

Getting a metric

To get a metric, such as `DownEnpointCount` in the `org.apache.Cassandra.net` package, the `get` command can be used as follows. This gives a count of nodes that are down via the CLI, which in turn can be used for alerting through a cron job.

Which is your most-used metric in Cassandra?

```
get -b org.apache.cassandra.net:type=FailureDetector DownEndpointCount
```

The output of the preceding command is as follows:

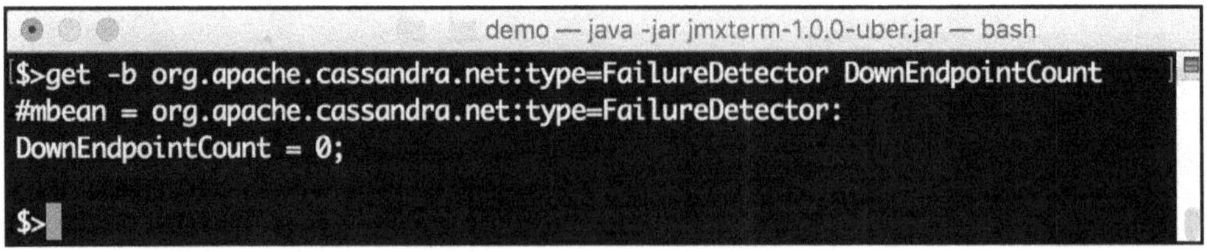

Figure 7.7: Getting the DownEndpointCount metric on JMXTerm

Performing an operation

Performing an operation is also possible through JMXTerm. For example, you can invoke the stopGossiping operation under the org.apache.Cassandra.db package using the following run command. This stops gossiping to other nodes.
Which is your favorite operation on Cassandra?

```
run -b org.apache.cassandra.db:type=StorageService stopGossiping
```

The output of the preceding command is as follows:

```
demo — java -jar jmxterm-1.0.0-uber.jar — bash
$>run -b org.apache.cassandra.db:type=StorageService stopGossiping
#calling operation stopGossiping of mbean org.apache.cassandra.db:type=StorageService with params □
#operation returns:
null
$>
```

Figure 7.8: Performing the stopGossiping operation through JMXTerm

Instead of the interactive CLI, you can run a list of commands using a file, as follows:

```
echo -e "open <IP>:7199\nrun -b org.apache.cassandra.db:type=StorageService
forceTerminateAllRepairSessions\nclose" > jmxcommands
java -jar<absolutePath>/jmxterm-1.0.0.-uber.jar -v silent -n < jmxcommands
```

Stopping a running repair process is similar on any production node. But invoking the preceding kind of operation would gracefully stop the repair process without restarting Cassandra. This can be used at the start of business hours to reduce the impact of a repair process.

The nodetool utility

Nodetool is an inbuilt CLI utility tool by Apache Cassandra for monitoring and managing Cassandra clusters. It even includes the ability to trigger commands on a remote node, as long as remote JMX has been enabled along with the required firewalls. Running a nodetool command remotely is very helpful as it wouldn't require SSH. But at the same time, it would be more prone to a security risk if endpoints are wide open to the public. The remote command can be triggered with the -h parameter through nodetool:

```
$CASSANDRA_HOME/bin/nodetool -h <ipAddress of host> ring
```

Based on the kind of installation, nodetool can be found in corresponding bin directories. Refer to the nodetool docs for further information at Apache-Cassandra: *Nodetool Usage*: http://Cassandra.apache.org/doc/4.0/tools/nodetool/nodetool.html.

Monitoring using nodetool

Monitoring Apache Cassandra clusters using nodetool has multiple parameters that can be passed based on the use case through the CLI. This is very good for checking on a single node, but when there are more nodes, it's hard to keep track of this setup across all nodes, as it is a tedious process.

The following are the most popular nodetool commands.

describecluster

As name suggests, it gives details about name of the cluster, the snitching type, the partitioner type, schema version, and the dynamic endpoint snitch flag. The schema version will display all the nodes along with nodes that have any schema version mismatches between nodes, resulting in an easier way of identifying faulty nodes:

```
$CASSANDRA_HOME/bin/nodetool describecluster
```

The output of the preceding command is as follows:

```
                                        @csapp1-0:/ — docker — bash
[root@csapp1-0 /]# nodetool describecluster
Cluster Information:
        Name: NoNameCluster
        Snitch: org.apache.cassandra.locator.GossipingPropertyFileSnitch
        DynamicEndPointSnitch: enabled
        Partitioner: org.apache.cassandra.dht.Murmur3Partitioner
        Schema versions:
                ea63e099-37c5-3d7b-9ace-32f4c833653d: [127.0.0.1]

[root@csapp1-0 /]#
```

Figure 7.9: describecluster

gcstats

This displays key garbage-collection statistics for the Apache Cassandra JVM and those stats are related to garbage collection, which have run since the last time the `nodetool gcstats` command was executed:

```
$CASSANDRA_HOME/bin/nodetool gcstats
```

The output of the preceding command is as follows:

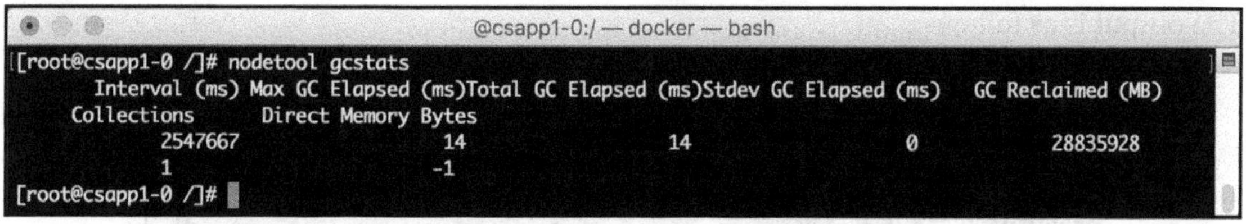

Figure 7.10: gcstats

getcompactionthreshold

This provides minimum and maximum thresholds for compaction on a table in a keyspace. This can be configured, but would require a restart of Cassandra for that config to be reflected. This can also be increased using `setcompactionthreshold`, but it would be reset when Cassandra is restarted. But it can be used as a quick fix during issues with nodes or while bootstrapping a node:

```
$CASSANDRA_HOME/bin/nodetool getcompactionthreshold <keyspaceName>
<tableName>
```

The output is as follows: 

Figure 7.11: getcompactionthreshold

getcompactionthroughput

This provides the current throughput for all compactions, irrespective of the table and keyspace. This can be configured but would require a restart of Cassandra for that config to be reflected. This can also be increased using `setcompactionthroughput`, but it would be reset when Cassandra is restarted, so it can be used as a quick fix during issues with nodes or while bootstrapping a node:

```
$CASSANDRA_HOME/bin/nodetool getcompactionthroughput
```

The output is as follows:

Figure 7.12: getcompactionthroughput

getconcurrentcompactors

This provides the number of possible concurrent compactions for Cassandra. This can be configured, but would require a restart of Cassandra for that config to be reflected. This can also be increased using `setconcurrentcompactors`, but it will also be reset when Cassandra is restarted. It can be used as a quick fix during issues with nodes or while bootstrapping a node:

```
$CASSANDRA_HOME/bin/nodetool getconcurrentcompactors
```

The output of the preceding command is as follows:

Figure 7.13: getconcurrentcompactors

getendpoints

This provides all the endpoints owned by a partition key for a table in a keyspace across the Cassandra cluster. During inconsistencies across a Cassandra cluster, it provides an easier way to find a faulty node for random partitions by checking the LOCAL_ONE consistency on all those replicas, and resolve the issue by running a repair only on that node or datacenter:

```
$CASSANDRA_HOME/bin/nodetool getendpoints <keyspaceName> <tableName>
<partitionKey>
```

The output of the preceding command is as follows:

```
● ● ●                        @csapp1-0:/ — docker — bash
[[root@csapp1-0 /]# nodetool getendpoints system_auth roles cassandra
127.0.0.1
[[root@csapp1-0 /]#
```

Figure 7.14: getendpoints

getlogginglevels

This provides all the logging levels set for the current Cassandra node. This can be configured, but would require a restart of Cassandra for that config to be reflected. It can also be increased using setlogginglevel, but it would be reset when Cassandra is restarted, so it can be used as a quick fix during issues with nodes or while troubleshooting a node:

```
$CASSANDRA_HOME/bin/nodetool getlogginglevels
```

The output of the preceding code is as follows:

```
● ● ●                        @csapp1-0:/ — docker — bash
[[root@csapp1-0 /]# nodetool getlogginglevels

Logger Name                                          Log Level
ROOT                                                      INFO
com.thinkaurelius.thrift                                 ERROR
org.apache.cassandra                                     DEBUG
[root@csapp1-0 /]#
```

Figure 7.15 getlogginglevels

getstreamthroughput

This provides the Mbps (megabits per second) limit for any streaming on the current Cassandra node. This can be configured, but would require a restart of Cassandra for that config to be reflected. It can also be increased using `setsteamthroughput`, but it would be reset when Cassandra is restarted, so it can be used as a quick fix during issues with node or while bootstrapping a node:

```
$CASSANDRA_HOME/bin/nodetool getstreamthroughput
```

The output of the preceding command is as follows:

```
@csapp1-0:/ — docker — bash
[root@csapp1-0 /]# nodetool getstreamthroughput
Current stream throughput: 200 Mb/s
[root@csapp1-0 /]#
```

Figure 7.16: getstreamthroughput

gettimeout

This provides the timeout in milliseconds for `read`, `range`, `write`, `counterwrite`, `cascontention`, `truncate`, `steamingsocket`, and `rpc` on the current Cassandra node. This can be configured, but would require a restart of Cassandra for that config to be reflected. This can also be increased using `settimeout`, but it would be reset when Cassandra is restarted. However, it can be used as a quick fix during issues with nodes or while bootstrapping a node:

```
$CASSANDRA_HOME/bin/nodetool gettimeout <timeoutType>
```

The output of the preceding code is as follows:

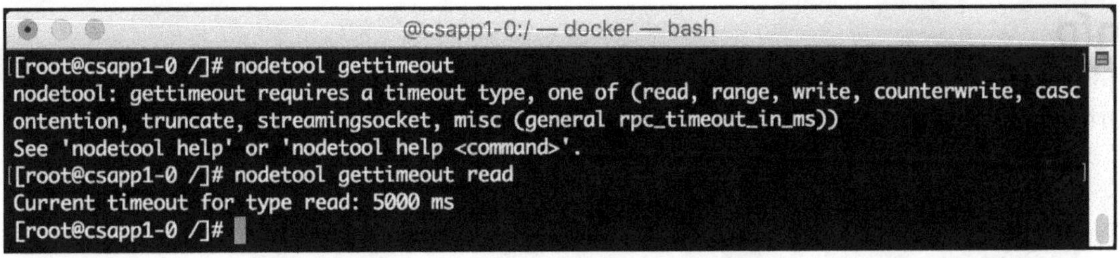

```
 ●  ●  ●                    @csapp1-0:/ — docker — bash
[root@csapp1-0 /]# nodetool gettimeout
nodetool: gettimeout requires a timeout type, one of (read, range, write, counterwrite, casc
ontention, truncate, streamingsocket, misc (general rpc_timeout_in_ms))
See 'nodetool help' or 'nodetool help <command>'.
[root@csapp1-0 /]# nodetool gettimeout read
Current timeout for type read: 5000 ms
[root@csapp1-0 /]#
```

Figure 7.17: gettimeout

gossipinfo

This provides all the gossip information for a Cassandra node, and contains the status, load, schema version, dc, rack, Cassandra version, listen, and RPC addresses:

```
$CASSANDRA_HOME/bin/nodetool gossipinfo
```

The output of the preceding code is as follows:

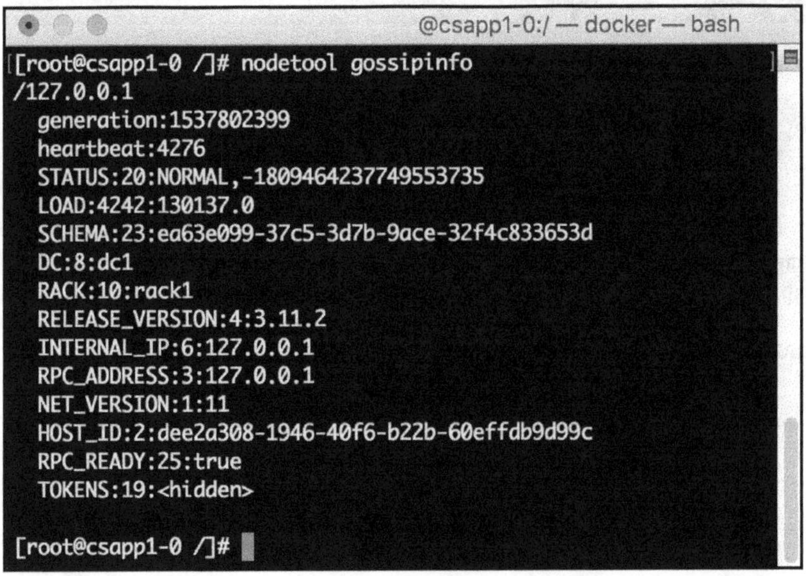

```
 ●  ●  ●                    @csapp1-0:/ — docker — bash
[root@csapp1-0 /]# nodetool gossipinfo
/127.0.0.1
    generation:1537802399
    heartbeat:4276
    STATUS:20:NORMAL,-1809464237749553735
    LOAD:4242:130137.0
    SCHEMA:23:ea63e099-37c5-3d7b-9ace-32f4c833653d
    DC:8:dc1
    RACK:10:rack1
    RELEASE_VERSION:4:3.11.2
    INTERNAL_IP:6:127.0.0.1
    RPC_ADDRESS:3:127.0.0.1
    NET_VERSION:1:11
    HOST_ID:2:dee2a308-1946-40f6-b22b-60effdb9d99c
    RPC_READY:25:true
    TOKENS:19:<hidden>

[root@csapp1-0 /]#
```

Figure 7.18: gossipinfo

info

This provides all the internal information of a Cassandra node, and contains ID, gossip, thrift, native transport, and other statuses, along with key and row-cache details:

```
$CASSANDRA_HOME/bin/nodetool info
```

The output of the preceding code is as follows:

```
@csapp1-0:/ — docker — bash
[root@csapp1-0 /]# nodetool info
ID                          : 61bc005d-be87-45ab-8180-488b32007e3d
Gossip active               : true
Thrift active               : true
Native Transport active     : true
Load                        : 99.28 KiB
Generation No               : 1537770324
Uptime (seconds)            : 2582
Heap Memory (MB)            : 271.34 / 1000.00
Off Heap Memory (MB)        : 0.00
Data Center                 : dc1
Rack                        : rack1
Exceptions                  : 0
Key Cache                   : entries 14, size 1.08 KiB, capacity 50 MiB, 78 hits, 98 requests, 0.796 recent hit rate, 14400 save period in seconds
Row Cache                   : entries 0, size 0 bytes, capacity 0 bytes, 0 hits, 0 requests, NaN recent hit rate, 0 save period in seconds
Counter Cache               : entries 0, size 0 bytes, capacity 25 MiB, 0 hits, 0 requests, NaN recent hit rate, 7200 save period in seconds
Chunk Cache                 : entries 15, size 960 KiB, capacity 218 MiB, 27 misses, 145 requests, 0.814 recent hit rate, NaN microseconds miss latency
Percent Repaired            : 100.0%
Token                       : (invoke with -T/--tokens to see all 16 tokens)
[root@csapp1-0 /]#
```

Figure 7.19: info

netstats

This provides all network information for a Cassandra node, and contains Mode, Large messages, Small messages, Gossip messages that are Active, Pending, Completed, and Dropped:

```
$CASSANDRA_HOME/bin/nodetool netstats
```

The output is as follows:

```
                                    @csapp1-0:/ — docker — bash
[root@csapp1-0 /]# nodetool netstats
Mode: NORMAL
Not sending any streams.
Read Repair Statistics:
Attempted: 0
Mismatch (Blocking): 0
Mismatch (Background): 0
Pool Name                    Active    Pending         Completed    Dropped
Large messages                 n/a           0                 0          0
Small messages                 n/a           0                 2          0
Gossip messages                n/a           0                 0          0
[root@csapp1-0 /]#
```

Figure 7.20: netstats

proxyhistograms

This provides histograms of latencies for read, write, range, CAS read, CAS write, and view write calls at the coordinator Cassandra node, and different percentiles (50%, 75%, 95%, 98%, 99%, Min, Max):

```
$CASSANDRA_HOME/bin/nodetool proxyhistograms
```

The output of the preceding code is as follows:

```
                                    @csapp1-0:/ — docker — bash
[root@csapp1-0 /]# nodetool proxyhistograms
proxy histograms
Percentile      Read Latency    Write Latency    Range Latency   CAS Read Latency   CAS Write Latency  View Write Latency
                     (micros)         (micros)         (micros)           (micros)            (micros)            (micros)
50%                      0.00             0.00             0.00               0.00                0.00                0.00
75%                      0.00             0.00             0.00               0.00                0.00                0.00
95%                      0.00             0.00             0.00               0.00                0.00                0.00
98%                      0.00             0.00             0.00               0.00                0.00                0.00
99%                      0.00             0.00             0.00               0.00                0.00                0.00
Min                      0.00             0.00             0.00               0.00                0.00                0.00
Max                      0.00             0.00             0.00               0.00                0.00                0.00

[root@csapp1-0 /]#
```

Figure 7.21: proxyhistograms

status

This provides information about a Cassandra cluster from a Cassandra node's perspective. It includes details such as `Datacenter`, `Status`, `Address`, `Load`, `Tokens`, `Owns (effective)`, `Host ID`, and `Rack` for each and every node part of its cluster:

```
$CASSANDRA_HOME/bin/nodetool status
```

The output is as follows:

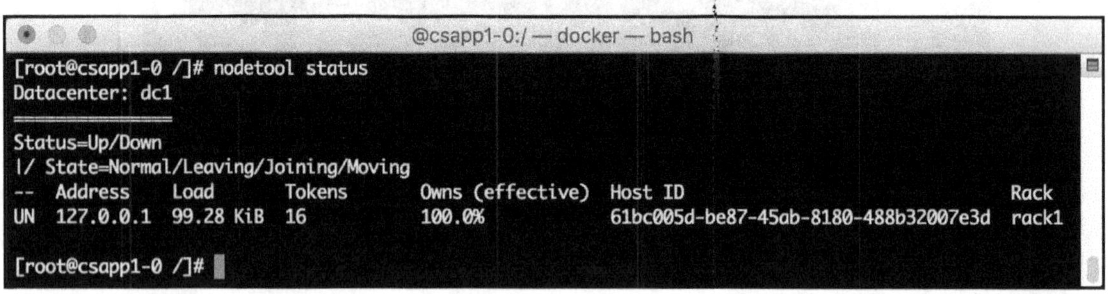

Figure 7.22: status

tablestats

This provides all statistical internal information about a table in a keyspace of Cassandra on that node. It displays properties such as read/write counts, latencies, SSTable, disk size, number of partitions, and off-heap memory used:

```
$CASSANDRA_HOME/bin/nodetool tablestats <keyspaceName>.<tableName>
```

The following is the output:

```
●  ●  ●                         @csapp1-0:/ — docker — bash
[root@csapp1-0 /]# nodetool tablestats system_auth.roles
Total number of tables: 36
----------------
Keyspace : system_auth
        Read Count: 2
        Read Latency: 0.338 ms
        Write Count: 1
        Write Latency: 0.194 ms
        Pending Flushes: 0
                Table: roles
                SSTable count: 0
                Space used (live): 0
                Space used (total): 0
                Space used by snapshots (total): 0
                Off heap memory used (total): 0
                SSTable Compression Ratio: -1.0
                Number of partitions (estimate): 0
                Memtable cell count: 1
                Memtable data size: 139
                Memtable off heap memory used: 0
                Memtable switch count: 0
                Local read count: 2
                Local read latency: NaN ms
                Local write count: 1
                Local write latency: NaN ms
                Pending flushes: 0
                Percent repaired: 100.0
                Bloom filter false positives: 0
                Bloom filter false ratio: 0.00000
                Bloom filter space used: 0
                Bloom filter off heap memory used: 0
                Index summary off heap memory used: 0
                Compression metadata off heap memory used: 0
                Compacted partition minimum bytes: 0
                Compacted partition maximum bytes: 0
                Compacted partition mean bytes: 0
                Average live cells per slice (last five minutes): NaN
                Maximum live cells per slice (last five minutes): 0
                Average tombstones per slice (last five minutes): NaN
                Maximum tombstones per slice (last five minutes): 0
                Dropped Mutations: 0

----------------
[root@csapp1-0 /]# █
```

Figure 7.23: tablestats

tpstats

This stands for **Thread Pool Stats** (**TPS**), and provides all statistical information related to different tasks for thread pools of a Cassandra node. It displays active, pending, completed, blocked, and all-time blocked stats for things such as the compaction executor, hints dispatcher, read repair, anti-entropy, read stage, misc stage, memtables, and gossip:

```
$CASSANDRA_HOME/bin/nodetool tpstats
```

The output is as follows:

```
● ● ●                    @csapp1-0:/ — docker — bash
[root@csapp1-0 /]# nodetool tpstats
Pool Name                      Active   Pending   Completed   Blocked   All time blocked
ReadStage                           0         0           3         0                  0
MiscStage                           0         0           0         0                  0
CompactionExecutor                  0         0        1513         0                  0
MutationStage                       0         0           1         0                  0
MemtableReclaimMemory               0         0          26         0                  0
PendingRangeCalculator              0         0           1         0                  0
GossipStage                         0         0           0         0                  0
SecondaryIndexManagement            0         0           0         0                  0
HintsDispatcher                     0         0           0         0                  0
RequestResponseStage                0         0           0         0                  0
Native-Transport-Requests           0         0           0         0                  0
ReadRepairStage                     0         0           0         0                  0
CounterMutationStage                0         0           0         0                  0
MigrationStage                      0         0           4         0                  0
MemtablePostFlush                   0         0          40         0                  0
PerDiskMemtableFlushWriter_0        0         0          26         0                  0
ValidationExecutor                  0         0           0         0                  0
Sampler                             0         0           0         0                  0
MemtableFlushWriter                 0         0          26         0                  0
InternalResponseStage               0         0           1         0                  0
ViewMutationStage                   0         0           0         0                  0
AntiEntropyStage                    0         0           0         0                  0
CacheCleanupExecutor                0         0           0         0                  0

Message type            Dropped
READ                          0
RANGE_SLICE                   0
_TRACE                        0
HINT                          0
MUTATION                      0
COUNTER_MUTATION              0
BATCH_STORE                   0
BATCH_REMOVE                  0
REQUEST_RESPONSE              0
PAGED_RANGE                   0
READ_REPAIR                   0
[root@csapp1-0 /]#
```

Figure 7.24: tpstats

verify

This provides verification of the SSTable or cell-level checksum for one or more tables in a keyspace on a Cassandra node. It displays whether checksums are different, and returns empty if the checksums match. This command provides a better picture of whether the node has consistent data:

```
$CASSANDRA_HOME/bin/nodetool verify <keyspaceName> <tableName>
```

The output is as follows: 

Figure 7.25: verify

Administering using nodetool

Similar to JMXTerm, nodetool provides the ability to perform some operations on Cassandra nodes that have multiple parameters. These can be passed based on the use case through the CLI. This is very good for running on a single node. But for multiple nodes, it's very hard to keep track of this setup across all nodes, as it is a tedious process.

cleanup

While scaling an Apache Cassandra cluster, data is streamed to new nodes or data is streamed from nodes based on scaling up or down. But once the data is streamed to new nodes after token allocation, Cassandra doesn't actually delete the data that is not owned by that node. In order to clean up all that data, nodetool has the following operation:

```
$CASSANDRA_HOME/bin/nodetool cleanup
```

drain

This next operation drains the node completely, by flushing all memtables to disk and stopping all connections from the client and nodes. Hence this operation will definitely require a restart in order to bring it back up. `nodetool drain` is generally used while upgrading a Cassandra process:

```
$CASSANDRA_HOME/bin/nodetool drain
```

Monitoring

flush

Unlike the drain operation, flush just flushes all memtables to disk without stoping all connections from the client and nodes, hence this operation will just clear memtables and generate new SSTable. This command has the ability to specify a table and keyspace instead of flushing memtables for all of them:

```
$CASSANDRA_HOME/bin/nodetool flush
```

resetlocalschema

When a particular node's schema is out of sync with the others, resetlocalschema will resynchronize it with other nodes that have the correct schema. Once the operation is triggered, it will truncate all schema-related stables and re-stream this data from other nodes, so it will lose meta data during this process. Schema disagreements might occur due to very high tombstones, such as 100,000+. This is very handy when a node is down during a schema change, and then brought up after three hours, as hints will have cleared and this node won't have been notified:

```
$CASSANDRA_HOME/bin/nodetool resetlocalschema
```

stopdaemon

This operation just stops the Cassandra daemon, resulting in closing all connections with clients and nodes abruptly. It will definitely cause errors on the app side based on the consistency levels being used:

```
$CASSANDRA_HOME/bin/nodetool stopdaemon
```

truncatehints

This operation triggers the truncating of hints on the local Cassandra node, or even on a remote Cassandra node. If there are more compactions happening for hints due to nodes going down frequently, it can be reduced by triggering it, which clears it and stabilizes the Cassandra cluster:

```
$CASSANDRA_HOME/bin/nodetool truncatehints
```

upgradeSSTable

This operation triggers the rewriting of SSTables that are not running on the current Cassandra version, which also ensures compatibility of SSTable with running versions of Cassandra. This is generally used during upgrade processes. It has some limitations, such as version 2.0.x of Cassandra cannot directly upgrade to 3.11.x. Therefore 2.0.x has to be first upgraded to 2.1.x, and then the 3.11.x version. Moreover, it has to be done across all the nodes to make it consistent across the cluster:

```
$CASSANDRA_HOME/bin/nodetool upgradeSSTable
```

Metric stack

Let's discuss a potential metrics stack to make tasks related to monitoring much easier. This metrics stack uses only open source community tools. Hence, there should be no concern over licensing for their use:

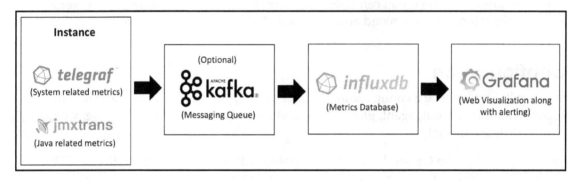

Figure 7.26: Metric stack built with all open source community tools

Even though there are more components, this is a reliable metric stack that can be used across all applications, irrespective of type.

Telegraf

Telegraf is a plugin-driven server in the Go language that acts as a collector and publisher of metrics to different types of metrics databases based on the format they accept. It offers the minimum utilization of memory and other resources. As it's a plugin-driven system, it is very easy to plug in a new input and output. Refer to the Telegraf docs for further information at *InfluxData-Telegraf: Installing*: `https://docs.influxdata.com/telegraf/v1.7/introduction/installation/`.

Installation

There are multiple ways to install Telegraf, based on the operating system. The following is a general RPM installation for CentOS or Red Hat:

```
rpm -ivh
https://dl.influxdata.com/telegraf/releases/telegraf-1.7.4-1.x86_64.rpm
```

For other flavors of Linux, you can refer to the previous docs. Make sure your server has access to the internet to download and install this RPM.

Configuration

By default, there will be a config file at `/etc/telegraf/telegraf.conf` that has all supported input, output, agent, global_tags, and so on. So based on our use case, we can customize it accordingly.

> Apache Cassandra can be integrated with Jolakia, which is a JMX-HTTP bridge. But all metrics aren't accessible through Jolakia, and it needs Cassandra to be restarted for a change in the config. Hence, JMXTrans is a more flexible option for Java-related apps.

Here is a sample `telgraf.conf` that collects and publishes all network-related metrics:

```
[global_tags]
  env = "sandbox"
  app = "mastering apache cassandra"
  region = "central"
  ip = "127.0.0.1"

[agent]
  interval = "10s"
  round_interval = true
  metric_buffer_limit = 1000
  flush_buffer_when_full = true
  collection_jitter = "0s"
  flush_interval = "60s"
  flush_jitter = "0s"
  debug = false
  quiet = false
  hostname = ""
  omit_hostname = false

[[outputs.influxdb]]
  urls = ["http://127.0.0.1:8086"]
  database = "telegraf"

# # optional
# [[outputs.kafka]]
# brokers = ["<broker>:9092"]
# topic = "<topicname>"
# compression_codec = 0
# required_acks = 0
# max_retry = 3
# data_format = "influx"

[[inputs.http_listener]]
  service_address = "127.0.0.1:5100"
  read_timeout = "10s"
  write_timeout = "10s"

[[inputs.net]]
```

After updating `telegraf.conf` with the desired parameters, you can start the Telegraf service using `service telegraf start`.

Conf file with all those metrics good to have can be found at
`https://github.com/malepati/book/blob/master/MasteringApacheCassandra3rdEdition/docker/cassandra-spark-jupyter/files_to_copy/telegraf.conf`

JMXTrans

JMXTrans is a powerful attribute-transformation tool written in Java. It bridges several JVMs over JMX on one side and monitoring tools on the other, without your writing a line of Java code. All Java-related metrics are exposed via JMX, which in turn can be transformed to the desired format for the metric system. This will have minimum utilization of memory and other resources. Refer to the JMXTerm docs for further information at *JMXTrans-Introduction to JMXTrans*: `https://github.com/jmxtrans/jmxtrans/wiki`.

Installation

There are multiple ways to install JMXTrans based on the operating system. The following is a general RPM installation for CentOS and Red Hat; for other Linux flavors you can refer to the preceding docs. Make sure your server has access to the internet to download and install this RPM:

```
rpm -ivh
http://central.maven.org/maven2/org/jmxtrans/jmxtrans/270/jmxtrans-270.rpm
```

Configuration

By default, JMXTrans refers the to config at `/var/lib/jmxtrans/`, which can have multiple files. It supports the JSON and YAML formats. So based on our flexibility, we can customize it accordingly.

This `jmxtrans.yaml` transforms `DownEndpointCount` from `FailureDetector` MBean metrics, to the InfluxDB format and writes to the local Telegraf HTTP port for publishing to InfluxDB:

```
servers:
  - port: 7199
    host: 127.0.0.1
    queries:
      - outputWriters:
        - "@class":
com.googlecode.jmxtrans.model.output.InfluxDbWriterFactory
```

```
            url: "http://127.0.0.1:5100/"
            username: admin
            password: admin
            database: jmxDB
    obj: org.apache.Cassandra.net:type=FailureDetector
    attr:
      - DownEndpointCount
    resultAlias: FailureDetector
```

After adding `jmxtrans.yaml` with the desired parameters, you can start the JMSTrans service using `service jmxtrans start`.

Config file with all those Metrics good to have can be found at `https://github.com/malepati/book/blob/master/MasteringApacheCassandra3rdEdition/docker/cassandra-spark-jupyter/files_to_copy/jmxtrans.yaml.`.

InfluxDB

InfluxDB is a time-series database, with no external dependencies, written in Go and optimized for fast, highly-available, and efficient data recording and retrieval in use cases such as monitoring metrics, performing real-time analytics, and IoT. Any metric with a text datatype can be written and read from it, along with a custom retention policy at the metric level. It allows tagging, which makes it a piece of cake for querying in a SQL-like query language. Refer to the InfluxDB docs for further information at *InfluxData-InfluxDB: Installing*: `https://docs.influxdata.com/influxdb/v1.6/introduction/`.

Installation

There are multiple ways to install InfluxDB based on the operating system. Following is a general RPM installation for CentOS Red Hat; for other flavors of Linux you can refer to the preceding docs. Make sure your server has access to the internet to download and install this RPM:

```
rpm -ivh
https://dl.influxdata.com/influxdb/releases/influxdb-1.6.2.x86_64.rpm
```

Configuration

By default, the config file is located at /etc/influxdb/influxdb.conf and has config parameters such as bind-address, metadata, data location, and InfluxDB logs. So based on our flexibility, we can customize it accordingly.

 Kafka can be used as a queueing application between Telegraf and InfluxDB as a more rigid framework for production work loads to reduce downtime if InfluxDB is down due to a performance load, which in turn prevents us from debugging during that timeline as those messages would be lost.

You can start the InfluxDB service using systemctl start influxd.

InfluxDB CLI

InfluxDB Query Language (**IFQL**) is used to interact with InfluxDB to retrieve data that has data written in the *InfluxDB Line Protocol*. Refer to the docs for more information at InfluxData-InfluxDB: *InfluxDB Line Protocol:* https://docs.influxdata.com/influxdb/v1.6/write_protocols/line_protocol_tutorial/ and InfluxData-InfluxDB: *InfluxDB command line interface (CLI/shell):* https://docs.influxdata.com/influxdb/v1.6/tools/shell/.

```
# initialize CLI and connect to local InfluxDB
influx
# create database telegraf
create database telegraf
# show list of databases
show databases
# use telegraf database
use telegraf
# show list of measurements
show measurements
# show series from cpu
show series from cpu
```

The corresponding output is as follows:

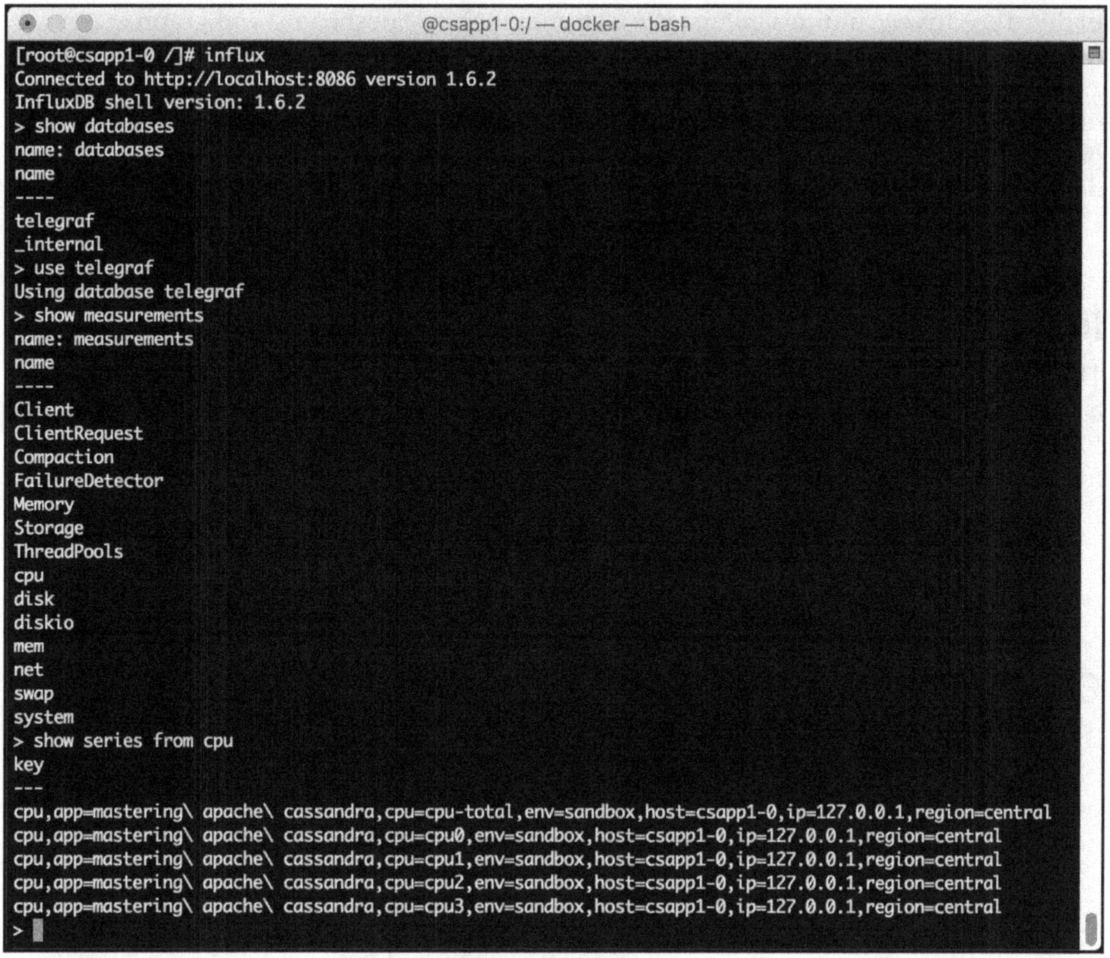

```
                        @csapp1-0:/ — docker — bash
[root@csapp1-0 /]# influx
Connected to http://localhost:8086 version 1.6.2
InfluxDB shell version: 1.6.2
> show databases
name: databases
name
----
telegraf
_internal
> use telegraf
Using database telegraf
> show measurements
name: measurements
name
----
Client
ClientRequest
Compaction
FailureDetector
Memory
Storage
ThreadPools
cpu
disk
diskio
mem
net
swap
system
> show series from cpu
key
---
cpu,app=mastering\ apache\ cassandra,cpu=cpu-total,env=sandbox,host=csapp1-0,ip=127.0.0.1,region=central
cpu,app=mastering\ apache\ cassandra,cpu=cpu0,env=sandbox,host=csapp1-0,ip=127.0.0.1,region=central
cpu,app=mastering\ apache\ cassandra,cpu=cpu1,env=sandbox,host=csapp1-0,ip=127.0.0.1,region=central
cpu,app=mastering\ apache\ cassandra,cpu=cpu2,env=sandbox,host=csapp1-0,ip=127.0.0.1,region=central
cpu,app=mastering\ apache\ cassandra,cpu=cpu3,env=sandbox,host=csapp1-0,ip=127.0.0.1,region=central
>
```

Figure 7.27: InfluxDB CLI

Grafana

In this data-driven culture, Grafana is a feature-rich metric dashboard and graph editor with the ability to support 30+ data sources, such as InfluxDB, Elasticsearch, Prometheus, and Graphite. It allows you to query, visualize, alert, and understand data with different forms of visualizations, such as table, bar/line graph, heat map, pie chart, and worldmap pannel. Even LDAP can be integrated for authentication for secure handling of confidential data. Refer to the Grafana docs for further information at Grafana Labs: *Grafana Documentation*: `http://docs.grafana.org/`.

Installation

There are multiple ways to install Grafana based on the operating system. The following is a general RPM installation for CentOS and Red Hat. For other Linux flavors, you can refer to the previous docs. Make sure your server has access to the internet for downloading and installing this RPM:

```
rpm -ivh
https://s3-us-west-2.amazonaws.com/grafana-releases/release/grafana-5.2.4-1
.x86_64.rpm
```

Configuration

By default, Grafana refers to the config location at `/etc/grafana/`, which even has a default LDAP configuration, along with saved dashboards and data sources under the provisioning directory. Even importing of JSON dashboards is possible; they are saved here. So based on our flexibility, we can customize it accordingly.

You can start the Grafana service using `service grafana-server start`.

By default, it creates `admin` and `admin` as the username and password and then gives you the ability to change them.

Visualization

Once the Grafana server is up-and-running, you can access it using a web browser to port `3000`. For example `http://127.0.0.1:3000` where it would navigate to login page. Upon authentication, we have to add a data source through the UI/CLI.

The following screenshot shows adding data sources through the web UI:

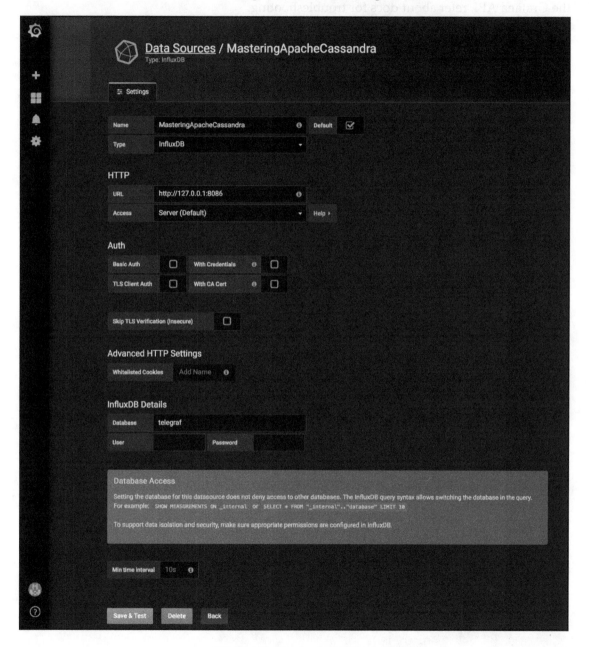

Figure 7.28: Adding data sources through the web UI

Through the CLI, we have to prepare a JSON file with all parameters. Then, we can post to the Grafana API, refer about docs for troubleshooting.

The following code shows adding a data source through the API:

```
cat > /tmp/grafanaDataSource.json <<EOF
{
  "id": 1,
  "orgId": 1,
  "name": "MasteringApacheCassandra",
  "type": "influxdb",
  "typeLogoUrl":
"public/app/plugins/datasource/influxdb/img/influxdb_logo.svg",
  "access": "proxy",
  "url": "http://127.0.0.1:8086",
  "password": "",
  "user": "",
  "database": "telegraf",
  "basicAuth": false,
  "isDefault": true,
  "jsonData": {
    "keepCookies": []
  },
  "readOnly": false
}
EOF

# As username and password are not changed
curl -X "POST" "http://localhost:3000/api/datasources" -H "Content-Type:
application/json" --user admin:admin --data-binary
@/tmp/grafanaDataSource.json
```

Secondly, we have to add a new dashboard, similarly to a data source; both are possible. Through the web UI, it is easy to set it up and navigate across dashboards and data sources, along with the types of panels available for visualization. A fully-built dashboard is shown and explained later.

The following screenshot shows adding a dashboard through the web UI:

Figure 7.29: Adding dashboard through web UI

Similar to data-source creation, dashboard creation is also required, hence a JSON file with all required parameters is prepared, then posted to the Grafana API with that file.

The following code shows adding a dashboard through the API:

```
cat > /tmp/grafanaDashboard.json <<EOF
{
  "dashboard": {
    "id": null,
    "uid": null,
    "title": "Production Overview",
    "tags": [ "templated" ],
    "timezone": "browser",
    "schemaVersion": 16,
    "version": 0
  },
  "folderId": 0,
  "overwrite": false
}
EOF

curl -X "POST" -i "http://localhost:3000/api/dashboards/db" -H "Content-
Type: application/json" --user admin:admin --data-binary
@/tmp/grafanaDashboard.json
```

Here is a sample panel showing the number of down nodes in Cassandra:

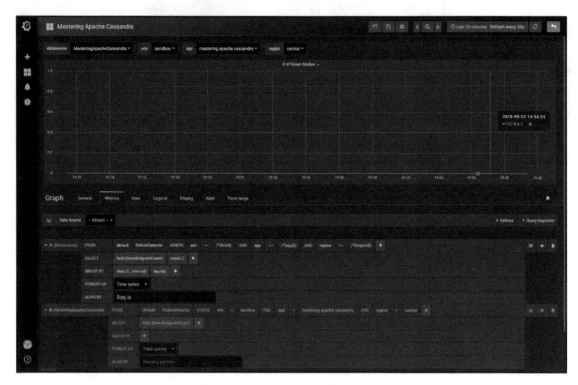

Figure 7.30: Example metric of DownEndpointCount with dynamic (visualization) and static (alerting) query

Alerting

Grafana has the inbuilt capability to alert even when the web UI is not being used. When an alert in a dashboard is saved, it is extracted into dedicated storage for validation on the server side, and scheduled accordingly. During the alert setup, there are multiple options for an alert to be triggered, along with different integrations, such as email, Kafka, **PagerDuty**, and Slack.

But the template variable is not compatible with alerting, which is the biggest drawback on the part of Grafana's architecture for the alerting process. As in the preceding screenshot, we can see both dynamic and static ways to query the same result is used due to this drawback. Moreover, instead of duplicating that visualization, disabling is possible by just clicking on the eye symbol on the right of the query. This is useful for alerting and not visualization. But this will not help when you have multiple clusters on the same dashboard; for this, we need to have a dedicated panel for each cluster.

Custom setup

Alerting is incomplete without the notification setup, so first we have to set up a new notification channel. Go to **Notification channels,** which is at the left bell symbol:

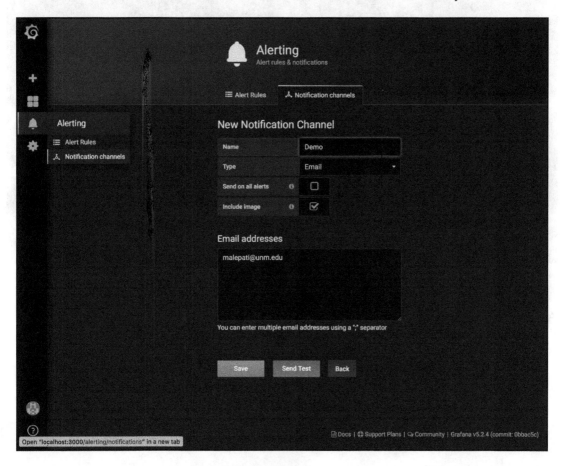

Figure 7.31: New notification channels setup for Grafana alerting

Based on the notification channel, additional configurations on the Grafana server are required. This is detailed in the Grafana docs, as in-depth configuration is beyond the scope of this book. For example, email-notification setup, SMTP, needs to be configured, and Slack notifications (URL, recipient, mention, and token) need to be updated. Once this is configured, created, and validated with a test message, navigate to the **Alert** tab under the desired panel and complete the remaining setup of alerts for that particular metric:

Figure 7.32: Grafana alert example for Number of nodes down in a cluster

As seen in the preceding screenshot, the B query is being used for the alert rather than A due to the incompatibility of its template variables for alerting.

Log stack

During an issue, logging on to each node and checking its logs is tiresome. Instead, we can use a logging stack or a built, custom logging stack with tools available based on our use case. The following stack is a subset of the **Elasticsearch, Logstash, Kibana** (**ELK**) stack. We wouldn't require a complex aggregation of logs across nodes, so logstash can be eliminated and we can use a simple Filebeat for log-forwarding, Elasticsearch for storage and querying, and Kibana for visualization and filtering. Moreover, this entire stack can be integrated with any application stack and all the logs across stacks can be visualized on a centralized backend with a single frontend along with all open source community tools. This wouldn't require a license as this logging stack is more of a replacement for a proprietary log aggregator:

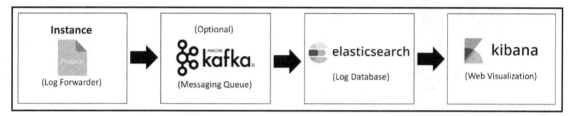

Figure 7.33: Log stack built with all open source community tools

Even though there are more components, it is a reliable logging stack that can be used to identify faulty nodes as querying through logs is pretty simple with regex integrations.

The system/debug/gc logs

Based on configurations set in $CASSANDRA_HOME/conf/logback.xml, the system.log and debug.log files are generated. But by default, logs related to the repair, storage, and streaming services have INFO level logs. These can be switched to WARN by adding the following lines at the end, just to reduce chattiness for efficient troubleshooting:

```
<logger name="org.apache.Cassandra.service.StorageService"
  level="WARN"/>
<logger name="org.apache.Cassandra.streaming.StreamResultFuture"
  level="WARN"/>
<logger name="org.apache.Cassandra.repair" level="WARN"/>
</configuration>
```

GC logs for Cassandra are configured in `$CASSANDRA_HOME/conf/Cassandra-env.sh` or `jvm.options`, and by default they are disabled. Although we have JVM-related metrics, it would be good to have as a second line of defence during any Cassandra-related issue for troubleshooting. In order to enable that, it's as simple as uncommenting required lines:

```
# Setting Log Dir
CASSANDRA_LOG_DIR=/usr/lib/Cassandra/logs
JVM_OPTS="$JVM_OPTS -DCassandra.logdir=${CASSANDRA_LOG_DIR}"

# GC logging options
JVM_OPTS="$JVM_OPTS -XX:+PrintGCDetails"
JVM_OPTS="$JVM_OPTS -XX:+PrintGCDateStamps"
JVM_OPTS="$JVM_OPTS -XX:+PrintHeapAtGC"
JVM_OPTS="$JVM_OPTS -XX:+PrintTenuringDistribution"
JVM_OPTS="$JVM_OPTS -XX:+PrintGCApplicationStoppedTime"
JVM_OPTS="$JVM_OPTS -XX:+PrintPromotionFailure"
JVM_OPTS="$JVM_OPTS -XX:PrintFLSStatistics=1"

JVM_OPTS="$JVM_OPTS -Xloggc:${CASSANDRA_LOG_DIR}/gc.log"
JVM_OPTS="$JVM_OPTS -XX:+UseGCLogFileRotation"
JVM_OPTS="$JVM_OPTS -XX:NumberOfGCLogFiles=10"
JVM_OPTS="$JVM_OPTS -XX:GCLogFileSize=10M"
```

For reflecting `gc.log` parameters, the Cassandra service needs to be restarted, as they are JVM parameters that need to be passed on to the process.

Filebeat

Filebeat is one of the most widely-used log shippers for all simple use cases that do not require aggregation. The idea is to keep things simple by forwarding logs to a custom desired backend storage, making it a very lightweight shipper for logs. Due to its simplicity, it is very robust and never misses a beat; that is a line in the log file. If it's interrupted, it resumes from where it left off, which reduces the amount of load once the process is started back up. As it is a lightweight shipper, it would use many of your resources, which makes your instance more efficient. Refer to the Filebeat docs for further information at Elastic-Docs: *Filebeat Reference*: `https://www.elastic.co/guide/en/beats/filebeat/current/filebeat-overview.html`.

Installation

There are multiple ways to install Filebeat based on the operating system. Here is a general RPM installation for CentOS or Red Hat; for other Linux flavors, you can refer to the previous docs. Make sure your server has access to the internet for downloading installing this RPM:

```
rpm -ivh
https://artifacts.elastic.co/downloads/beats/filebeat/filebeat-6.4.1-x86_64
.rpm
```

Configuration

By default, Filebeat would have a config file at /etc/filebeat/filebeat.yml. This contains all the required parameters related to input, tags, output, and more. It even has a set of predefined modules that can be enabled/disabled in filebeat.yml for getting all Cassandra-related logs to be shipped as follows:

```
filebeat.inputs:
- type: log
  enabled: true
  paths: - /usr/lib/Cassandra/logs/*.log
  multiline.pattern: '^[[:space:]]'
  multiline.negate: false
  multiline.match: after
```

So based on our flexibility, we can customize it accordingly for all the logs that need to be shipped. Moreover, it has compatibility of multiline, because during exceptions it would be annoying if they are not part of same message being shipped to the backend. There are other config parameters, which can be referred to from the preceding docs.

You can start the Filebeat service using service filebeat start.

Elasticsearch

The heart of ELK (our custom stack) is Elasticsearch, which is distributed like Apache Cassandra with a different architecture, a RESTful search, and an analytics storage engine. This is where all the logs shipped from Filebeat and are stored, based on our retention policy. Logs are retained to discover faulty nodes and the reason for their faultiness. The best part is its capability to manage unstructured and structured numbers and text, on a single datastore. Refer to the Elasticsearch docs for more information at Elastic-Docs: *Elasticsearch*: `https://www.elastic.co/products/elasticsearch`.

Installation

There are multiple ways to install Elasticsearch based on the operating system. Here is a general RPM installation for CentOS and Red Hat; for other Linux flavors you can refer to the preceding docs. Make sure your server has access to the internet for downloading and installing this RPM:

```
rpm -ivh
https://artifacts.elastic.co/downloads/elasticsearch/elasticsearch-6.4.1.rp
m
```

Configuration

By default, Elasticsearch has a config file at `/etc/elasticsearch/elasticsearch.yml`. This contains all the required parameters related to metadata, data paths, network, memory, and so on. It even has a set of predefined parameters, which can be disabled when not being used. The key parameters we would change are as follows:

```
cluster.name: <applicationName>
node.name: <hostname>
node.attr.rack: <rack/az>
path.data: /var/lib/elasticsearch
path.logs: /var/log/elasticsearch
network.host: 127.0.0.1
http.port: 9200
```

Once these parameters are configured, you can start the Elasticsearch service by using: `service elasticsearch start`.

Kibana

Kibana is an open source frontend/data-visualization plugin for data stored and indexed in Elasticsearch (for the ELK stack). Even Kibana has different panel formats for text data or transformed text data based on custom querying and filtering. This is a kind of data-access layer for the ELK stack, which has a regex way of filtering along the indexed files that contains logs. Kibana makes it easier to understand and visualize large volumes of unstructured, structured, alphanumeric data. Refer to the Kibana docs for further information: `https://www.elastic.co/guide/en/kibana/6.4/install.html`.

Installation

There are multiple ways to install Kibana based on operating systems. Here is a general RPM installation for CentOS Red Hat; for other Linux flavors you can refer to the previous docs. Make sure your server has access to the internet for downloading and installing this RPM:

```
rpm -ivh
https://artifacts.elastic.co/downloads/kibana/kibana-6.4.1-x86_64.rpm
```

Configuration

By default, Kibana would have a config file at `/etc/kibana/kibana.yml` that contains all the required parameters related to metadata, Elasticsearch, logging, and more. It even has a set of predefined parameters, which can be disabled when not being used. The key parameters we would change are:

```
server.port: 5601
server.host: "127.0.0.1"
elasticsearch.url: "http://127.0.0.1:9200"
# If authentication is enabled on elasticsearch cluster
#elasticsearch.username: "user"
#elasticsearch.password: "pass"
```

Once these parameters are configured, you can start the Elasticsearch service using `service kibana start`. After a successful startup, you can access it using the web browser on port 5601, for example, `http://127.0.0.1:5601`:

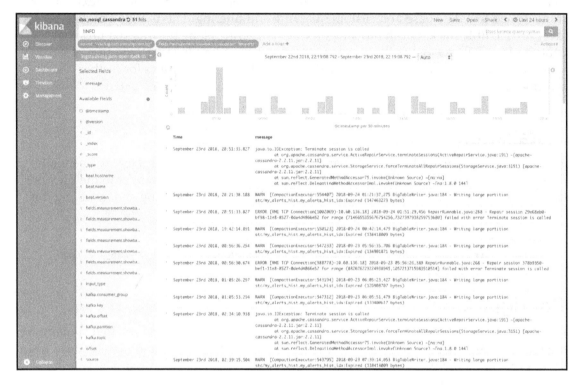

Figure 7.34: Filtering non INFO logs for troubleshooting across all datacenters in a cluster

From the preceding screen, we can easily figure out that sessions are getting terminated. From the app side, this should be fixed using long-lasting connections, instead of opening and closing it for every call.

Troubleshooting

We have learned a lot about monitoring, alerting, and logging tools, which can be used for troubleshooting an unexpected issue and resolving it faster and more easily. In distributed systems such as Cassandra, it would be very hard to find which node has the issue and whether it's related to the application, resource cap, resource steal, network outage, disk corruption, inappropriate Cassandra parameters, and so on. Going through all the nodes with a checklist is also tiresome. But with this kind of setup, we would be notified of any key issues that get triggered with alerting, and we can pinpoint the corresponding node. This reduces the effort of digging through all the nodes. With all this set up, it would a piece of cake to run productions environments without any outage, which in turn wouldn't cause any business loss. But once issues come up, based on the type of issue we will be working on a resolution, which in turn gives us good evidence for **Root Causal Analysis (RCA)** and we can proactively work on resolving other nodes that might have similar issues in the near future.

Apart from all these dependencies, we may encounter other issues related to specific Apache Cassandra versions. For example, version 2.1.5 had a memory-leak bug, where the commit log wasn't getting flushed. So GC wasn't happening, which in turn grows used head size then at max heap size it would get into the **Stop The World** (**STW**) scenario, where the node would become unresponsive for a period of time. Another one is Apache Cassandra version 3.11.3, which had a bug with deletes. For these kind of issues, the best option is to upgrade to a more stable minor version than going directly to a major version upgrade, which would require some effort for the traffic shift during the upgrade to reduce the impact. Another example would be if an SSL certificate expired, during restart it would come up with just a warning that the cert has expired. But that node is not able to gossip with any others, which makes it as an isolated node in cluster. The quick fix would be to fix the certs and join back to ring.

If this kind of setup is available across the entire stack across all applications, it would be very easy to identify the faulty layer and fix it sooner, rather than creating a ripple effect in certain scenarios.

High CPU usage

Before going to the solution, what are the first thoughts which come up when you see the following screenshot for a Cassandra cluster which is running in the cloud and balanced across three **Available Zones** (**AZs**) with three replication factor? Is it that a few nodes are being hit hard? More compactions? Smaller nodes than the rest? Repairs? Bulk loading? Bad network layer?

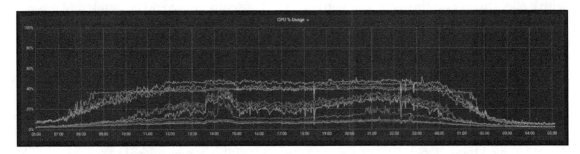

Figure 7.35: High CPU usage on a few nodes

In order to compare apples to apples, let's first make sure all the nodes are the same size, including the CPU architecture, because different CPU architectures in the same cluster might perform differently. There are higher chances of different architectures within a region; when it's spread across multiple AZs, it might be due to older hardware in those AZs or due to a high demand in provisioning older hardware for HA. When you are pinning a corresponding architecture across all AZs, you have a better understanding of eliminating instance types.

But here, the instance type was the issue, all those very high CPU percentages are from a very old architecture. These nodes had a very high CPU, and in turn got migrated or decommissioned as these nodes were provisioned a while ago. So the best practice is to proactively have random internal audits for comparison across the cluster and datacenters, along with the type of disk being used, so that all nodes in a cluster are consistent in terms of resources.

Different garbage-collection patterns

What are your initial thoughts when you look at the following screenshot showing a Cassandra cluster which is running in the cloud and balanced across three AZs with a replication factor three, instance types and architectures are the same across them all? Is it that a few nodes are being hit hard? More compactions? The parameters are not consistent? Different versions of Cassandra? Bad hosts?

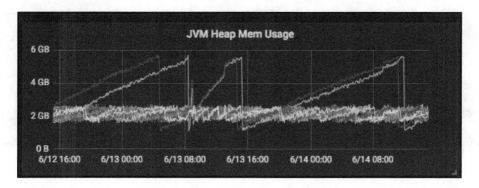

Figure 7.36: Two nodes are having different GC patterns than the rest

As we know that all the nodes have same instance type and architecture, we are comparing similar things. If you know different types of GCs are being used, then this would be a piece of cake. Even though configuration-management tools are used across clusters for maintaining a consistent state of configuration parameters on all nodes, there might be an integration among the configuration management tools that might config different values. We can be more confident about such an edge case, where this would have happen as the majority of nodes have the same pattern, except those two.

That expectation is absolutely right; those two nodes are on the CMS GC whereas rest are on G1. This was caused due to an integration error that came up during startup. This in turn used the default GC type, which is CMS, and caused the max heap size to be calculated dynamically based on the resources available. A simple fix is to re-run that configuration-management tool to fix the config inconsistency across the faulty nodes.

Hotspots

Now for the following screenshot; this Cassandra cluster is running in the cloud and balanced across three AZs with replication three factor, instance types, architectures and even the config parameters are also consistent across the cluster. What are the first guesses of the issue? Is it that a few nodes are being hit hard? Different versions of Cassandra? Bad calculations in the metric system?

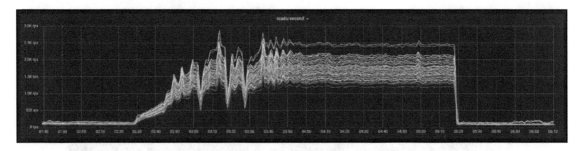

Figure 7.37: A few nodes are having higher reads than the rest

Here, the majority of inconsistencies on Cassandra's server side are eliminated, as this clearly shows a few nodes have 500-1,000 reads per second more than the rest, and a higher probability of hotspots. But before that, it is important to ask whether the Cassandra versions are the same. If so, then was this cluster recently upgraded and are SSTables still being upgrade for those nodes? But none of these would be related to application reads, which for sure it would be related to hot spots, or a few apps are not properly load balancing across the cluster. But this pattern is not observed for smaller loads, and only applies to higher loads.

This is due to large partitions on those nodes, which have a higher amount of reads. Even though they are load-balanced, replicas would be available on them, resulting in handling more reads than the rest, and this occurs only when there is clustering and read queries are happening with partition and clustering keys. This issue was not observed with a low load, but as the scale increases, it can be clearly seen.

Disk performance

Even before looking at the following screenshot, what are the metrics that come to your mind when you want to know more about disk performance? How do you capture them? What are the use cases for those metrics being used? If you expected the following metrics, you are definitely on the right track for understanding the importance of these metrics. For the following screenshot, this Cassandra cluster is running in the cloud and balanced across three AZs with a replication factor three; instance types and architectures are the same and even the config parameters are also consistent across the cluster, along with no hot spots or large partitions. What are your first guesses about the issue if all entire schema is size-tiered compaction strategy? Is it that a few nodes are being hit hard? Different versions of Cassandra? Bad calculations in the metric system?

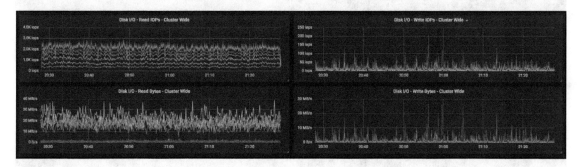

Figure 7.38: Read and write disk IOPs and data rate

Among them, which metric is a little suspicious? Clearly it's read disk IOPs rate. When everything is the same and only a few have higher read IOPs rate. But the write IOPs rate is pretty consistent across the cluster. It might be due to compactions, but over a period of time they should come back to normal – but this is seen consistently for a few days. Read/write IOPs are also consistent, along with the write IOPs rate, which means that writing is balanced, but reads are unbalanced.

This was due to new nodes that were added to the cluster. Data was streamed and a cleanup was run on all of them. Old nodes would have a larger number of SSTables to scan during a read, whereas new nodes would have more efficient SSTables due to being newly added. But as time passes, those new nodes also would get to that state and this is not an issue, but just a different pattern observed to different up-time nodes.

Node flakiness

Have you ever seen node flakiness when a Cassandra cluster is expanded across different domains through a **Virtual Private Network** (**VPN**)? This Cassandra cluster is expanded across two domains through VPN, `phi_convict_threshold` is set to `10`; it was upgraded a few days back. But this flakiness existed before the upgrade as well. The instance types and architectures are the same and even the config parameters are consistent across the cluster. What are your first guesses about the flakiness shown in the following screenshot? Bad calculation in the metric system? A bad network-layer integration? A bad VPN?

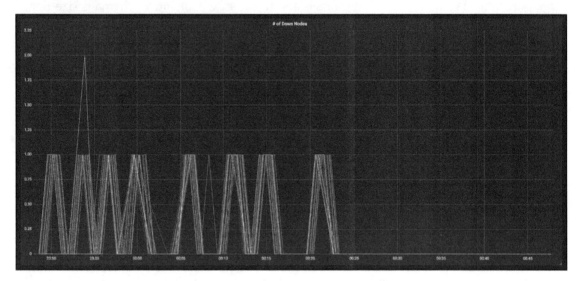

Figure 7.39: Nodes going up and down due to gossip issue

If this gossip flakiness existed even before the upgrade, some people might think that bumping `phi_convict_threshold` to `12` might fix it. As we all know, when DCs are across domains, there are many factors to consider that might be the reason for this. But definitely there are parameters on the Cassandra side that can be tweaked to resolve this. But finding the RCA would be far better than just investing effort on work arounds, and when it comes back up, we would be in same position again. But this was observed only on bigger clusters, where some of the nodes would be off with others. It would totally depend on the gossip process, as and when it gets an update, it would update its local state as well.

This was due to some network configuration through VPN. When this cluster was only on one domain, it worked like a charm, without any flakiness. During the upgrade, different nodes were on different versions of Cassandra for certain periods of time. Once all the upgrades are done, just rolling the restart of all nodes actually fixed it. So just a rolling restart of all nodes has fixed this flakiness, which might be due to network integrations between domains.

All-in-one Docker

All the preceding applications are really hard to get working with all the integrations locally. To make it simple for testing locally, a Docker image is built with all the monitoring setup, except logging. An Elasticsearch cluster is a heavy application, which would not be sufficient for running log stack with this. This all-in-one Docker is built on CentOS 7 community Docker with all the following applications with corresponding versions:

- Cassandra 3.11.2
- Influxdb 1.6.2
- Grafana 5.2.4
- Telegraf 1.7.4
- JMXTrans 270
- Spark 2.3.1
- Python 2.7.15
- R 3.5.1

 Prerequisite: Docker should be installed. Refer to Docker CE (Community Edition) installation at *Docker-Get Docker CE for CentOS*: `https://docs.docker.com/install/linux/docker-ce/centos/`.

All the required configs for the preceding applications are already preconfigured. This makes it very simple to run this complex metric stack with Apache Cassandra, along with a prebuilt Grafana dashboard containing all of the key metrics required for easier troubleshooting, and eliminating all the dependencies for brining it up locally. This Docker image also includes R, Spark, and Jupyter installations, which are discussed in further chapters. By default, CASSANDRA, SPARK, and SPARK_CLI are enabled and MONITOR is disabled. Based on these flags, the corresponding components would be started. Cassandra would be installed at `/usr/lib/apache-cassandra-3.11.2`.

Creating a database and other monitoring components locally

To create a database locally, along with other monitoring components, there are two options. Either pull the image directly from the Docker Hub, or build locally from the source. The following are the steps for both ways:

```
# Pull from dockerhub
docker pull malepati/cassandra-spark-jupyter:latest

# Build from source
# Clone git repo https://github.com/malepati/book
git clone git@github.com:malepati/book.git
cd book/MasteringApacheCassandra3rdEdition/docker
docker build -t malepati/cassandra-spark-jupyter:latest cassandra-spark-
jupyter/.

# Running docker container locally
docker run \
--name demo \
--hostname 'csapp1-0' \
-p 3000:3000 \
-p 7199:7199 \
-p 8086:8086 \
-p 9042:9042 \
-e 'MONITOR=true' \
-e 'SPARK=false' \
--rm -it malepati/cassandra-spark-jupyter:latest
```

This would first start Influxdb, followed by Grafana, Telegraf, JMXTrans, and finally Cassandra. Just give it two minutes to bring up all the services.

Web links

The Grafana web ui can be accessed using the web browser on port `3000`; for example, `http://127.0.0.1:3000`. As the server has just started, give it five minutes to see the metrics flowing through the stack, and finally to Grafana. This even includes an alert about the number of nodes down, where no notification channel is set up for this Docker image.

The following screenshot shows an overview of the custom Cassandra Grafana dashboard, part one:

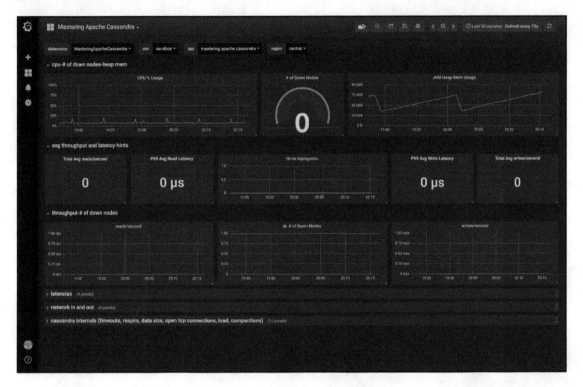

Figure 7.40: Final Grafana dashboard with all key metrics-1

The following screenshot demonstrates an overview of the custom Cassandra Grafana dashboard, part two:

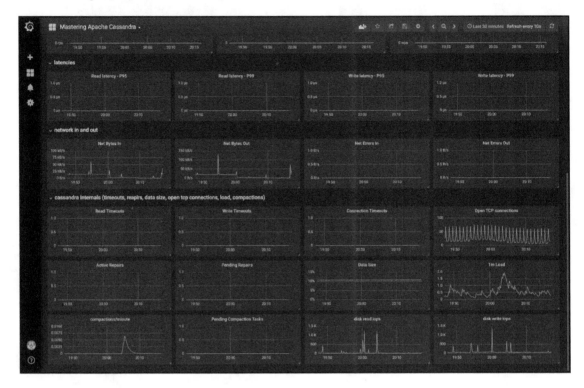

Figure 7.41: Final Grafana dashboard with all key metrics-2 (internal)

From these screenshots, you can see several panels that give in-depth details of debugging or analysis and act accordingly. For example, *Data Size* panel shows as at 10% for which, due to our historical load, it might spike up to 75% and if majority have a size-tiered compaction strategy then either we have to expand the disk or add more nodes based on the load averages. With this setup, we can clearly identify the problem, such as a bad host or network issue. Adding alerting on top of this would help even more by setting a threshold for disk % used and dynamically grow the disk if that alert is triggered in a cloud infrastructure.

When you have multiple Apache Cassandra clusters, it is a hassle to maintain multiple dashboards. If a metric panel has been added for one cluster on a dashboard, then it is a tedious process to get it propagated to every cluster's dashboard. In this kind of situation, the template variables are there to help us. Variables can be created based on a dynamic selection of those variables.

The following screenshot shows variables for a custom Cassandra Grafana dashboard:

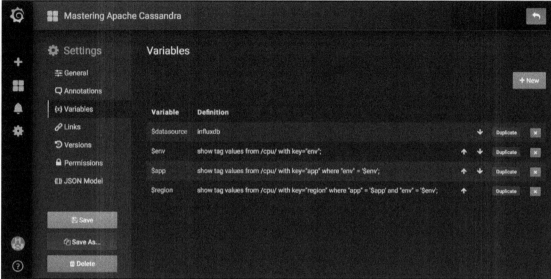

Figure 7.42: List of template variables

Summary

Apache Cassandra is based on a peer-to-peer architecture, which makes it difficult to manage and monitor when we have more nodes. This chapter provides a wide variety of options available for monitoring and logging for Apache Cassandra, which will help in identifying issues proactively. We started with a single-node GUI-based monitoring with JConsole, followed by a CLI utility, JMXTerm, which can easily be integrated to jobs/scripts for any kind of operation. These two are really handy for monitoring or managing in the current state, but neither of them would help historical data-analysis when there is an outage. Inbuilt tools from Cassandra also would not solve this, because nodetool would just be a wrapper to JMXTerm.

The introduction of a metric stack is important. It would contain a metrics publisher, Telegraf for system metrics, and JMXTrans for JVM-related metrics, followed by InfluxDB as metric storage, and Grafana for visualization. But Grafana has another cool feature in alerting, which has notification capabilities based on our custom filter and notification channel setup.

Logs are just as important as metrics. But filtering or digging through logs over a period of time is a hassle on multiple Cassandra nodes through the CLI. This results in the introduction of a logging stack, which contains Filebeat as lightweight log shipper/forwarder, followed by Elasticsearch for log storage, and Kibana for visualization with the capability of filtering using regex patterns and building dashboards for a better understanding. General troubleshooting use cases were also discussed, and we closed with an all-in-one Docker that contains Apache Cassandra and the entire metric stack (Telegraf, JMXTrans, InfluxDB, and Grafana) to test and build Cassandra locally.

8
Application Development

In this chapter, we will discuss the development of applications backed by Apache Cassandra. This subject is one of the most misunderstood areas of Cassandra. Too often, developers assume that their years of developing with relational databases have prepared them for working with a distributed database such as Apache Cassandra. Unfortunately, their familiar, relational foundations lead them down the wrong path.

In this chapter, we will discuss the following topics:

- Common mistakes made at the application and data model levels
- Driver selection
- Appropriate connection properties
- Handling simple and complex result sets in Java
- Loading data without overwhelming your nodes

By the end of this chapter, you will understand how to build Java applications to work with Apache Cassandra. These example applications will start small and simple, and grow in complexity as the chapter progresses.

The ideas and patterns presented here should help you understand how to properly architect applications to work with your own use cases and data models.

Getting started

The first steps to building an application for use with Apache Cassandra are both important to get right, and easy to get wrong. Here we will cover some fundamental questions about whether or not Cassandra is even the correct data store for the application in question.

But first, let's start with an overview of what the wrong path looks like.

The path to failure

As most developers are used to working with relational databases, the typical path to failure starts with a data model that closely resembles one found in a RDBMS. A loading job is then written, which only succeeds in crashing their nodes every couple of hours.

Finally, once the data is there, they build their application around a RDBMS framework driver (because their team has experience with a specific framework) that was augmented to (rather than designed to) work with Cassandra.

In the end, the app team blames the DBAs for an application with high latency, a trainwreck of a data loader, and request timeouts about as common as firecrackers in the U.S. in early July.

All of these issues are preventable. What's more, responsibility for them falls squarely on the application team.

The way to avoid getting started incorrectly is to ensure that, as a developer, you are properly educated as to how working with Apache Cassandra is different. There are many resources available to help developers get started (including this book). Often, all it takes is a Google search to find them.

Forget everything you learned about working with relational databases, as it will not help you. Assuming a learning mindset is key to getting started correctly.

Is Cassandra the right database?

Too often, the decision to use Cassandra is made for the wrong reasons. This usually results in hacks and extra engineering to make Cassandra meet requirements, and ultimately leads to more work and headaches once the application starts storing large amounts of data.

If Apache Cassandra is indeed the correct data store for your application, then you shouldn't need to do much extra work to get it to behave as expected.

Often, teams select Apache Cassandra because they need a highly-available data store. While that is a strength of Cassandra, that single reason by itself is not sufficient. As we learned in earlier chapters, Apache Cassandra achieves high availability by making key architecture decisions that can severely cripple certain types of query patterns.

Apache Cassandra was designed to solve problems associated with storing and serving large amounts of data. When you reach the max capacity of your hardware in the RDBMS world—whether storage, throughput, or some other resource limitation—the common solution is to scale up, or vertically. Vertical scaling is achieved by adding additional resources to the machine, such as more CPU, RAM, or disks.

Cassandra is designed to be scaled out, horizontally. Horizontal scaling is achieved by simply adding more machines to the cluster. So, when three instances aren't enough to hold your data or meet your performance requirements, add more. This linear scalability is one of the main advantages of Apache Cassandra.

However, linear scalability comes at the cost of consistency and query flexibility. With Cassandra, you should seek to avoid the extra network time incurred when having to query more than one node. This is why designing tables so that requests can be served by a single node is so important.

Many databases are capable of efficiently handling things such as unbound queries (queries without `WHERE` clauses including `SELECT COUNT`), tables that need to be queried multiple ways, or query patterns anchored by multiple keys. Unfortunately, Apache Cassandra is not one of them. These types of usage patterns do not perform well at scale.

As previously discussed, there are many well-documented use cases where Apache Cassandra is just not a good idea:

- Data search functionality
- Frequently deleting and/or updating data in place (building a queue)
- Data model requirements for allowing every column to be queryable
- Data model requirements for querying all data in a table
- Updates to primary key components
- Querying data that may not exist

 That last one is a fairly common problem. Remember from the earlier chapters how Apache Cassandra's read path works. If data is not found in certain structures, the path gets longer. Thus, querying for a key that may not exist will perform poorly.

Stay away from these types of use cases! If you must support one of the preceding requirements, then you should look at another data store product.

There is a difference between deleting a row or updating a row in place a few times versus hundreds or thousands of times. The first should not be a problem, while the latter most likely will be!

Good use cases for Apache Cassandra

Good use cases for Apache Cassandra are those that work with the underlying storage engine, instead of fighting against it.

Remember, Cassandra has a log-based storage engine, the SSTable files underneath are immutable, and all data is not necessarily stored on every node (depending on your RF). Keep those points in mind, and you'll start to recognize good use cases quite easily:

- Large, growing datasets that require high performance and availability
- Data based on time or sequential events, such as log or time series data
- Data models requiring specific, narrow query patterns
- Data models serving ranges of multiple, sorted results

Often, modeling problems with Apache Cassandra can be solved by understanding the difference between **querying** and **searching**. When executing a query, we are giving the data store specific parameters for where to look for data. It either finds it, or it does not.

When executing a search, we are giving the data store a pattern to look for, and sometimes a vague notion of how or where to apply that pattern. Quite often, a search operation results in a scan of a large percentage of the dataset, which is definitely something we don't want to be doing a lot of with Cassandra.

Apache Cassandra is not a good tool for searching for data. It doesn't have the proper toolset to allow for searching, and it's not designed to work well with full table scans. With Cassandra, you need to know your specific query parameters up-front.

Use and expectations around application data consistency

Applications will vary in their consistency requirements by use case. The key thing to remember is that Apache Cassandra is (by design) not a consistent database. It is designed around achieving high levels of performance and availability.

There are steps you can take to improve the consistency of your application's data, but you will trade performance to achieve it.

It is important to also understand how many nodes your cluster contains, as well as what **replication factor (RF)** is used on your keyspace. Too often, these aspects are abstracted from application developers, who in turn end up making ill-informed decisions around their choice of consistency level. In fact, the most common mistake that developers make is to assume that they need QUORUM consistency levels.

For modern applications, querying at ONE is often sufficient. Queries at ONE only wait for a response from a single replica, making it the highest-performing level of consistency.

Sometimes, there are applications and use cases that may require a higher level of consistency. In these cases, using a QUORUM consistency level will wait for a quorum of replicas (usually two) to respond. As incurring network time for contacting two replicas increases latency, performance suffers by comparison.

 I always encourage my development teams to start their applications with LOCAL_ONE consistency. As testing and implementation progresses, they may find scenarios where LOCAL_ONE doesn't work for them. Increasing consistency at that point on an as-needed basis is a good approach to start with.

For an example, assume that you are running on a small, two-node cluster. Given the constraints due to the number of nodes, your keyspace is also configured with a RF of two. In this exact scenario, I have seen developers elect for a default consistency level of LOCAL_QUORUM.

So, you might ask, what is the problem with that? Well, let's examine how quorum is computed. Essentially, quorum is a **majority**, so it is computed as *Replication factor* divided by *2*, plus *1*:

$$QUORUM \ of \ replicas \ to \ query \ = (\frac{Replication \ factor}{2}) + 1$$

Now, plug in our RF of 2, and the problem should be apparent:

$$QUORUM \ of \ replicas \ to \ query \ = (\frac{2}{2}) + 1 = 2$$

That's right, QUORUM consistency with a *RF* of 2 will require a response from all replicas.

Mistakes like this are made because of assumptions that developers make about their cluster implementation. When deciding which consistency level to use, your use case, requirements, and your cluster's architecture all come into play.

Choosing the right driver

There are drivers available for many languages to work with Cassandra. Your best chance for success is in using the open source (non-enterprise) drivers written by DataStax. Avoid using framework drivers, such as Spring Data, Hibernate, JDBC, ODBC, and others. These typically take longer to implement new features and bug fixes.

This happens because these types of drivers are usually dependent on a specific version of the DataStax drivers themselves, and have to issue a new release to keep up with the features and fixes offered in the base driver. The best option here is to cut out the middleman, and use the recommended DataStax driver for your language.

There are drivers available for several languages to work with Cassandra, including (but not limited to) the following:

Language	URL
C	https://github.com/datastax/cpp-driver
C#	https://github.com/datastax/csharp-driver
C++	https://github.com/datastax/cpp-driver
Go	https://github.com/gocql/gocql
Java	https://github.com/datastax/java-driver
Node.js	https://github.com/datastax/nodejs-driver
PHP	https://github.com/datastax/php-driver
Python	https://github.com/datastax/python-driver
Ruby	https://github.com/datastax/ruby-driver

Cassandra drivers for multiple languages

Hector (now deprecated) was the first Java driver available for Apache Cassandra, and it used the Thrift protocol to connect. Recent versions of Cassandra disable the Thrift protocol, and Apache Cassandra 4.0 removes it completely. Additionally, the last pull request to the Hector project was three years ago, which was to change the the README to mark it as inactive. DO NOT CREATE ANY NEW PROJECTS USING HECTOR!

For our examples in this chapter, we will use the open source DataStax Java driver, refer docs for further information *DataStax(2018)-Java Driver for Apache Cassandra 3.6*, which was retrieved on 2018/09/22 at `https://docs.datastax.com/en/developer/java-driver/3.6/manual/`.

Building a Java application

In this section, we will build a Java application to interact with our Apache Cassandra cluster. We will start with some simple examples, and build our way up to something more complex.

Finally, we will cover writing a job to load data, and discuss adjustments to allow it to work at a large scale.

Driver dependency configuration with Apache Maven

Inside our **integrated developer environment** (**IDE**), we will create a new Maven Java project. I'll specify the package as `PacktCassDev`. Then, we'll need to make sure that our `pom.xml` file is configured with the desired version of the DataStax Java driver:

```
<dependencies>
    <dependency>
        <groupId>com.datastax.cassandra</groupId>
        <artifactId>cassandra-driver-core</artifactId>
        <version>3.6.0</version>
    </dependency>
</dependencies>
```

We won't have any other dependencies, so this should be the only dependency listed (for now). With that in place, we can move on to writing a class to handle our connections.

 You are welcome to use the IDE of your choice. This chapter should work fine either with the latest version of Eclipse or NetBeans.

Connection class

Let's start by building a class to handle the connection to Apache Cassandra. We'll try to make this robust enough to be useful for each exercise to follow. First of all, let's specify our package (if it's not already specified), and import a few classes from the driver:

```
package PacktCassDev;

import com.datastax.driver.core.Cluster;
import com.datastax.driver.core.ConsistencyLevel;
import com.datastax.driver.core.Session;
import com.datastax.driver.core.policies.DCAwareRoundRobinPolicy;
import com.datastax.driver.core.policies.TokenAwarePolicy;
import com.datastax.driver.core.ResultSet;
import com.datastax.driver.core.BoundStatement;
import com.datastax.driver.core.QueryOptions;
```

 The name of your package may differ from the example—that's alright.

Now, let's define our class definition and constructor. Our constructor will accept inputs such as a node list, credentials, and a local data center:

```
public class CassandraConnection {
  private Cluster cluster;
  private Session session;

  public CassandraConnection(String[] nodes, String user, String
    pwd, String dc) {
    connect(nodes,user,pwd,dc);
  }
```

As one of our constructors is calling the connect method, let's make sure we define that, and have it accept the same parameters used by the constructor:

```
public void connect(String[] nodes, String user, String pwd, String dc) {
  QueryOptions qo = new QueryOptions();
  qo.setConsistencyLevel(ConsistencyLevel.LOCAL_ONE);

  cluster = Cluster.builder()
  .addContactPoints(nodes)
  .withCredentials(user,pwd)
  .withQueryOptions(qo)
  .withLoadBalancingPolicy(
  new TokenAwarePolicy(
```

```
    DCAwareRoundRobinPolicy.builder()
    .withLocalDc(dc)
    .build()
    ))
    .build();
    session = cluster.connect();
}
```

Of all the parts of this class, the `connect` method is by far the most important. Some things to note here—yes, we are setting all of the basic parameters: a list of node endpoints, a username, and a password. But we're also accepting a default, local data center. That data center name gets used as we define our load balancing policy.

If you look closely, you can see that this method is actually defining two load balancing policies. First, we want to use `TokenAwarePolicy`. This load balancing policy ensures that all queries with a partition key are sent directly to a node which is responsible for storing the requested data. It performs much faster than the other load balancing policies, because it bypasses the need for a coordinator node.

However, we also specify a nested load balancing policy as a parameter for `TokenAwarePolicy`. This is in case your application sends the cluster an unbound or keyless query. These types of queries use a coordinator node to pull together the data, and then build and return the result set.

We're using `DCAwareRoundRobinPolicy` as a fall-back policy, in case the query can't provide the information required for token awareness. `DCAwareRoundRobinPolicy` accepts a local data center name as a parameter, so it knows which nodes an unbound query should be restricted to.

Another thing worth noting is that we are also defining a `QueryOptions` object. With that object defined, we are then setting the default query consistency level of `LOCAL_ONE`. This is the first thing defined in our `connect` method, so that we can reference it from within our cluster builder.

 `LOCAL_ONE` is actually the default query consistency. We are specifying it for completeness, so that it is clear where it is configured.

With the `connect` method complete, we'll add five more methods to help round out our `CassandraConnection` class. These methods will help us expose other necessary functionalities for querying, writing, and working with our connection or `session` objects:

```
public ResultSet query(String strQuery) {
    return session.execute(strQuery);
}
public ResultSet query(BoundStatement bStatement) {
    return session.execute(bStatement);
}

public void insert(BoundStatement bStatement) {
    session.execute(bStatement);
}

public Session getSession() {
    return session;
}

public void close() {
    cluster.close();
}
}
```

The `query` methods allow for two ways in which to send queries to your cluster. Sometimes, an application may need to send a simple, static query. Other (most) times, your application will want to ensure that it is using a prepared statement with bound variables.

The `insert` method is an example of that, which is why it only accepts a `BoundStatement`. If there are times when you might need some more finely-tuned control of your `session` object, it can be accessed via this class.

Lastly, there is a `close` method which will cleanly shut things down.

 The query in this code was done in a single-threaded, synchronous (blocking) manner. Asynchronous queries will be covered later in this chapter.

Other connection options

There are additional options (not shown previously) that can be accessed via the `Cluster` class, that play important roles in managing the connection to your cluster.

For most of these options, the default settings should suffice. But for those of you looking to optimize your driver to account for an edge case issue, additional connection options can be defined, as follows.

> Depending on the version of the DataStax Java driver, some of these options and their syntax may change. Please consult the appropriate documentation for the most recent information.

Retry policy

Earlier versions of the driver allowed you to specify a retry policy. That is, if the attempted query should fail, the driver would automatically retry it under certain conditions.

Newer versions of the driver are deprecating some often-used policies, such as `DowngradingConsistencyRetryPolicy`. The reason for this is that query retry logic tends to be specific to the business requirements or use case, and should really be handled at the application level, not with the driver.

Default keyspace

A default keyspace can be defined for each session created off the main connection object. Without this option, each table will need its corresponding keyspace specified with each query. This option is useful for clusters which have only one (non-system) keyspace.

To set this option, the `keyspace name` can be provided as the `session` object is created during the cluster's `connect` method:

```
session = cluster.connect("keyspace_name");
```

> The recommended best practices for cluster and session objects, refer docs for more information *Popescu A(2014)-4 simple rules when using the DataStax drivers for Cassandra,* which was retrieved on 2018/09/22 at `https://www.datastax.com/dev/blog/4-simple-rules-when-using-the-datastax-drivers-for-cassandra`, is to use a single, long-lived cluster object for your application. Within that, no more than a single session should be used per keyspace. If your application is fully asynchronous, only one `session` object should be used in the application.

Port

If necessary, a different port for the native binary protocol can be specified. By default, `9042` is used, and this does not need to be specified if it has not changed. Adding it can be done by specifying it as another option with the cluster builder:

```
.withPort(9042)
```

SSL

If your cluster uses SSL, there are a few different ways to specify the keystore holding your SSL certificate. The easiest is to simply add it to your JRE's cacerts file.

You can also set a specific Java keystore and its password via **Java Secure Socket Extension (JSSE)** properties:

```
-Djavax.net.ssl.keyStore=/usr/local/myfiles/.keystore
-Djavax.net.ssl.keyStorePassword=reindeerFlotilla
```

Once this is complete, you can simply invoke SSL as a part of your cluster builder:

```
.withSSL()
```

Connection pooling options

The DataStax Java driver abstracts managing connections through its connection pool, and by abstracting those details from the developer. However, a more finely-tuned configuration of the connection pool settings are available by creating a `PoolingOptions` object.

Its creation and subsequent invocation through the cluster builder are similar to the `QueryOptions` instantiation shown previously:

```
PoolingOptions po = new PoolingOptions();
...
Cluster.builder().withPoolingOptions(po)
.build();
```

The capabilities and default settings of the connection pool can vary greatly according to whichever version of the CQL native binary protocol is used. The following table shows a protocol version compatibility comparison refer docs for further information at *DataStax(2018)-Java Driver for Apache Cassandra 3.0-Native Protocol*, which was retrieved from `https://docs.datastax.com/en/developer/java-driver/3.0/manual/native_protocol/` between different versions of the driver and Apache Cassandra.

	Driver 2.0 to 2.1.1	Driver 2.1.1 to 2.1.x	Driver 3.0+
Apache Cassandra 2.0	v2	v2	v2
Apache Cassandra 2.1	v2	v3	v3
Apache Cassandra 2.2	v2	v3	v4
Apache Cassandra 3.0+	v2	v3	v4

Protocol versions compatible with specific combinations of DataStax Java driver and Apache Cassandra version

Apache Cassandra officially removed protocol v1 and v2 with Cassandra 3.0. While the newest drivers may still connect to older versions of Apache Cassandra 2.0 and 2.1, they will operate with reduced functionality.

Several settings in the connection pool allow for a differentiation between connections to local and remote hosts (determined by host distance). The number of initial and maximum connections can be set as such:

```
po.setConnectionsPerHost(HostDistance.LOCAL, 2, 8);
po.setConnectionsPerHost(HostDistance.REMOTE, 1, 2);
```

The preceding settings are the default for version 2 of the CQL native binary protocol. For versions 3 and up, the defaults are set as follows:

```
po.setConnectionsPerHost(HostDistance.LOCAL, 1, 1);
po.setConnectionsPerHost(HostDistance.REMOTE, 1, 1);
```

Version 3 of the CQL native binary only needs a single connection per host. This is because the number of requests per connection that v3 can handle is much higher.

Therefore, while v2 is forced to handle 128 requests per connection, v3's defaults are as follows:

```
po.setMaxRequestsPerConnection(HostDistance.LOCAL, 1024)
po.setMaxRequestsPerConnection(HostDistance.REMOTE, 256);
```

One important setting within the connection pool is that of the heartbeat interval. Setting the heartbeat interval keeps long-running connections from being killed, by simply sending a small heartbeat at a pre-configured interval. The default setting is 30 seconds.

It can be adjusted as follows:

```
po.setHeartbeatIntervalSeconds(10);
```

The connection pooling options are things that most developers shouldn't need to change. If you're having a problem with connections dropping or queries timing out, the problem will most likely be solved with adjustments to your data model, as opposed to the connection pool.

Starting simple – Hello World!

Now that we have our connection class defined, let's work on our main class. Similar to the above, let's start with our package definition and imports:

```
package PacktCassDev;

import com.datastax.driver.core.ResultSet;
import com.datastax.driver.core.Row;
```

Next, we'll define our class along with our `main` method:

```
public class CassHelloWorld {
  public static void main(String[] args) {
    String[] nodes = {"192.168.0.101"};
    CassandraConnection conn = new CassandraConnection();
    conn.connect(nodes, "cassdba", "flynnLives", "ClockworkAngels");
```

In the previous code, we also instantiated our local `CassandraConnection` object as `conn`, and invoked the `connect` method with our endpoints, username, password, and local data center name.

In the code for this chapter, passwords are shown hardcoded in the clear. This was done to keep the subject of this chapter focused on development with Apache Cassandra. Obviously, for actual production applications, you will want to use a secure password store to inject any required credentials at runtime. Also, be sure not to store passwords or endpoints in Git repositories.

Next, we'll define and execute our query, and build our result set:

```
String strSELECT ="SELECT cluster_name,data_center,"
  + "listen_address,release_version,dateof(now()) "
  + "FROM system.local WHERE key='local'";
ResultSet rows = conn.query(strSELECT);
```

As we're building our query to be a string without any dynamic parameters, the `query(String strQuery)` method will work just fine.

Next, we'll begin presenting our output, and process the result set. Since we're querying the `system.local` table, there will only be one row returned.

We could use the `RowSet.one()` method—but iterating through your result set is a good habit to get into, regardless of what you know about your target tables:

```
System.out.println("Hello from:");

for (Row row : rows) {
  System.out.print(
    row.getString("cluster_name") + " " +
    row.getString("data_center") + " " +
    row.getString("release_version") + "\n" +
    row.getTimestamp("system.dateof(system.now())")
  );
}
```

Essentially, this section will query the cluster name, data center, and version of Apache Cassandra (as well as the system time) from whichever node it connects to.

As the result set is processed, these properties are referenced via the `row.getString` method, and sent to the console output.

> The `row.getString` method will accept either a column name or a zero-based ordinal column index as a parameter. It's a good idea to use the column name, to avoid any ambiguity over what is being returned and referenced.

Finally, we'll close our connection before the `main` method completes:

```
conn.close();
  }
}
```

Running this program should result in output similar to this:

```
Hello from:
PermanentWaves ClockworkAngels 3.11.2
Sat Sep 22 14:51:08 CDT 2018
```

 If your output contains a warning about slf4j failing to load a class, it can be ignored.

Using the object mapper

For this application, we will also use the DataStax object mapper. The object mapper makes it easier for Java developers to serialize results as Java objects, and vice versa.

This feature set is often why developers select a framework driver instead. But the DataStax Java driver does indeed have one.

To get access to the additional libraries required to use the object mapper, we will need to add another dependency to pom.xml:

```
<dependency>
  <groupId>com.datastax.cassandra</groupId>
  <artifactId>cassandra-driver-mapping</artifactId>
  <version>3.6.0</version>
</dependency>
```

Our goal here will be to build a service layer using the CassandraConnection class. We'll utilize the security_logs_by_location table created back in Chapter 3, *Effective CQL*.

Go ahead and create that table (if you haven't already), and add data to it as follows:

```
CREATE TABLE IF NOT EXISTS packt_ch3.security_logs_by_location (
  location_id text,
  day int,
  time_in timestamp,
  employee_id text,
  mailstop text,
  PRIMARY KEY ((location_id, day), time_in, employee_id)
) WITH CLUSTERING ORDER BY (time_in ASC, employee_id ASC);

INSERT INTO packt_ch3.security_logs_by_location_desc
(location_id,day,time_in,employee_id,mailstop)
VALUES ('MPLS2',20180723,'2018-07-23 9:04:59.377','tejam','M266');
```

```
INSERT INTO packt_ch3.security_logs_by_location_desc
(location_id,day,time_in,employee_id,mailstop)
VALUES ('MPLS2',20180723,'2018-07-23 7:17:38.268','jeffb','M266');
INSERT INTO packt_ch3.security_logs_by_location_desc
(location_id,day,time_in,employee_id,mailstop)
VALUES ('MPLS2',20180723,'2018-07-23 7:01:18.163','sandrak','M266');
INSERT INTO packt_ch3.security_logs_by_location_desc
(location_id,day,time_in,employee_id,mailstop)
VALUES ('MPLS2',20180723,'2018-07-23 6:49:11.754','samb','M266');
INSERT INTO packt_ch3.security_logs_by_location_desc
(location_id,day,time_in,employee_id,mailstop)
VALUES ('MPLS2',20180723,'2018-07-23 7:08:24.682','johno','M261');
INSERT INTO packt_ch3.security_logs_by_location_desc
(location_id,day,time_in,employee_id,mailstop)
VALUES ('MPLS2',20180723,'2018-07-23 7:55:45.911','tedk','M266');
INSERT INTO packt_ch3.security_logs_by_location_desc
(location_id,day,time_in,employee_id,mailstop)
VALUES ('MPLS2',20180723,'2018-07-23 11:04:22.432,'aaronp','M266');
```

Next, we'll create an entity class for the `security_logs_by_location` table. Name it `SecurityLogsByLocation`.

Make sure that it is a part of the `PacktCassDev` package, and that it has the required inputs:

```
package PacktCassDev;

import com.datastax.driver.mapping.annotations.ClusteringColumn;
import com.datastax.driver.mapping.annotations.PartitionKey;
import com.datastax.driver.mapping.annotations.Table;
import java.text.DateFormat;
import java.text.SimpleDateFormat;
import java.util.Date;
```

Now, we'll define our class with the `@Table` annotation, so that the object mapper knows what to do with it. The first part of the class will contain the (private) property definitions for the columns in the table, complete with applicable key annotations:

```
@Table(keyspace="packt_ch3", name="security_logs_by_location",
 readConsistency="LOCAL_ONE", writeConsistency="LOCAL_QUORUM",
 caseSensitiveKeyspace=false, caseSensitiveTable=false)
public class SecurityLogsByLocation {
 @PartitionKey(0)
 private String location_id;

 @PartitionKey(1)
 private int day;
```

```
@ClusteringColumn(0)
private Date time_in;

@ClusteringColumn(1)
private String employee_id;
private String mailstop;
```

Now, we'll define three constructors for this class. The first constructor will accept values for all properties. The second constructor will accept the same properties as the first, minus date-related parameters (day,time_in), as those will be computed.

Finally, we will also define a default, empty, basic constructor:

```
public SecurityLogsByLocation(String locationId, int day, Date timeIn,
    String employeeId, String mailstop) {
  this.location_id = locationId;
  this.day = day;
  this.time_in = timeIn;
  this.employee_id = employeeId;
  this.mailstop = mailstop;
}

 public SecurityLogsByLocation(String locationId, String employeeId, String
mailstop) {
   Date rightNow = new Date();
   DateFormat dateFormat = new SimpleDateFormat("yyyyMMdd");
   this.location_id = locationId;
   this.day = Integer.parseInt(dateFormat.format(rightNow));
   this.time_in = rightNow;
   this.employee_id = employeeId;
   this.mailstop = mailstop;
 }

 public SecurityLogsByLocation() {
 }
```

If the default, empty constructor is not defined, code execution will throw a NoSuchMethodException SecurityLogsByLocation.<init>.

At this point, we will also define public getters and setters for our properties. These definitions will be omitted for brevity. Plus, most IDEs allow you to auto-generate getters and setters.

We will, however, overload the default `toString()` method to format our output concisely:

```
public String toString() {
    StringBuilder returnValue = new StringBuilder();
    returnValue.append(this.location_id);
    returnValue.append(" - ").append(this.time_in.toString());
    returnValue.append(" - ").append(this.employee_id);
    returnValue.append(" - mstp=").append(this.mailstop);
    return returnValue.toString();
  }
}
```

We'll also create a service class that uses our entity class. Name this class `SecurityLogService`. As with our previous class, create it in the `PacktCassDev` package, and ensure that it has the required inputs:

```
package PacktCassDev;

import com.datastax.driver.mapping.Mapper;
import com.datastax.driver.mapping.MappingManager;
import com.datastax.driver.mapping.Result;
import com.datastax.driver.mapping.annotations.Accessor;
import com.datastax.driver.mapping.annotations.Param;
import com.datastax.driver.mapping.annotations.Query;
import java.util.Date;
import com.datastax.driver.core.Session;
```

Before defining the class, we will define the `SecurityLogsAccessor` interface, and lead it with the `@Accessor` annotation. Its contents will be a method named `getAllByLocationDay`, prefaced with the `@Query` annotation.

The method will also specify its required parameters of `location_id` and `day`:

```
@Accessor
interface SecurityLogsAccessor {
 @Query("SELECT * FROM packt_ch3.security_logs_by_location WHERE
location_id=:location_id AND day=:day")
 Result<SecurityLogsByLocation> getAllByLocationDay(@Param("location_id")
String locationId,
   @Param("day") int day);
}
```

The `SecurityLogService` class will contain a single constructor (taking an active session as a parameter), as well as our public query methods.

Now, we could just make the `mapper` object public, but there are probably things in the `mapper` class that we don't want publicly accessible to just anyone. Here, we'll start with the private definitions for `mapper` and `accessor` (defined previously), as well as the constructor:

```
public class SecurityLogService {
  private Mapper<SecurityLogsByLocation> mapper;
  private SecurityLogsAccessor accessor;

  public SecurityLogService(Session session) {
    MappingManager manager = new MappingManager(session);
    mapper = manager.mapper(SecurityLogsByLocation.class);
    accessor = manager.createAccessor(SecurityLogsAccessor.class);
  }
```

To finish the service class, we will define three public query methods. The first will get a single security log entry, which will require parameters for all of the table's primary key components.

The next query method will leverage our `accessor` to get all security log entries for a specific `location_id` and `day`.

Finally, we will include a method to write a single security log entry to our table, accepting the entity class as its lone parameter. These definitions can be seen as follows:

```
  public SecurityLogsByLocation getSecurityLogEntry(String locationId,
    int day, Date timeIn, String employeeId) {
      return mapper.get(locationId,day,timeIn,employeeId);
  }

  public Result<SecurityLogsByLocation> getAllForDay(String locationId, int
day) {
    return accessor.getAllByLocationDay(locationId,day);
  }

  public void saveSecurityLogEntry(SecurityLogsByLocation entry) {
    mapper.save(entry);
  }
}
```

Now that we have those two class files, we'll create a main class to call the new service layer and send operations to that table.

Create a new file called `CassSecurityLogMapper`, ensure that it is created inside the `PacktCassDev` package, and that it has `Result` as its lone import:

```
package PacktCassDev;
import com.datastax.driver.mapping.Result;
```

The `CassSecurityLogMapper` class will start similarly to how we started the `CassHelloWorld` class earlier. We will define the class name, along with our `main` method containing our node list and connection object instantiation:

```
public class CassSecurityLogMapper {

  public static void main(String[] args) {
    String[] nodes = {"192.168.0.101"};
    CassandraConnection conn = new CassandraConnection(nodes,
      "cassdba", "flynnLives", "ClockworkAngels");
```

With that complete, we will also instantiate an object for the `SecurityLogService` class, and pass it our connection's `session` object:

```
    SecurityLogService securityLogSvc = new
    SecurityLogService(conn.getSession());
```

We'll start by instantiating a new `SecurityLogsByLocation` object for employee `scottb`. Once created, we'll invoke our `saveSecurityLogEntry` method to write this new entry to our table:

```
    SecurityLogsByLocation scottB = new
    SecurityLogsByLocation("MPLS2","scottb","M266");
    securityLogSvc.saveSecurityLogEntry(scottB);
```

Next, we'll build a result set meant to hold query results for location `MPLS2` on `20180723`. Following that query, we will iterate through the results and send them to the console output:

```
    Result<SecurityLogsByLocation> resultsFor0723 =
    securityLogSvc.getAllForDay("MPLS2", 20180723);
    for (SecurityLogsByLocation entry : resultsFor0723) {
      System.out.println(entry);
    }
```

Finally, we'll query the single entry we created for user `scottb`, and also send those results to the console output:

```
    SecurityLogsByLocation newEntry =
    securityLogSvc.getSecurityLogEntry(scottB.getLocation_id(),
      scottB.getDay(), scottB.getTime_in(), scottB.getEmployee_id());
```

```
System.out.println(newEntry);
conn.close();
  }
}
```

Running this program should yield results similar to the following:

```
MPLS2 - Mon Jul 23 06:49:11 CDT 2018 - sblowers - mstp=M266
MPLS2 - Mon Jul 23 07:01:18 CDT 2018 - skue - mstp=M266
MPLS2 - Mon Jul 23 07:08:24 CDT 2018 - jolson - mstp=M261
MPLS2 - Mon Jul 23 07:17:38 CDT 2018 - jblanchard - mstp=M266
MPLS2 - Mon Jul 23 07:55:45 CDT 2018 - tknutson - mstp=M266
MPLS2 - Mon Jul 23 09:04:59 CDT 2018 - tmalepati - mstp=M266
MPLS2 - Mon Jul 23 11:04:22 CDT 2018 - aaronp - mstp=M266
MPLS2 - Mon Sep 24 07:39:56 CDT 2018 - scottb - mstp=M266
```

At this point, it should be apparent that utilizing the object mapper of the DataStax Java driver can avoid some of the tedious work associated with data querying and serialization. Simple operations require very little work, while more complex queries (requiring an accessor) will likely take some extra effort.

Building a data loader

For some implementations, application teams simply use Apache Cassandra as a high-performance cache for data imported from another system. These types of use cases typically have short bursts of high-write throughput, followed by prolonged periods of read activity.

Use cases such as this require a way to load a lot of data at once, usually as frequently as every day or so.

Asynchronous operations

Querying and writing data from a distributed database such as Apache Cassandra can be tricky at times. Often, write-heavy usage patterns can cause performance bottlenecks, and force applications to wait for operational completion. With the DataStax Java driver, both read and write operations can be executed in an asynchronous, non-blocking fashion.

A common problem with periods or bursts of high-write throughput is that the nodes can become overloaded with traffic. When this happens, it is usually because data is being written faster than Cassandra can keep up with. It typically results in a plethora of problems including high CPU, dropped requests, connection timeouts, constant compaction, and system resources so consumed that read requests cannot be served.

While scaling horizontally by adding more nodes can solve the problem, that is usually expensive and time-consuming. One thing that developers can do to help control this situation is to both use asynchronous write operations and limit the number of active threads at any given time.

This technique is known as **throttling**, and it will be at the center of our data loading example.

Data loader example

First of all, let's start by making an adjustment to our CassandraConnection class. Start by importing ResultSetFuture and PreparedStatement:

```
import com.datastax.driver.core.ResultSetFuture;
import com.datastax.driver.core.PreparedStatement;
```

Then we will add two new methods to allow for listenable, asynchronous operations:

```
public ResultSetFuture asyncOp(BoundStatement bStatement) {
  return session.executeAsync(bStatement);
}

public PreparedStatement prepare(String strCQL) {
  return session.prepare(strCQL);
}
```

The asyncOp method is similar to the query method used in the last example. The difference is that the asyncOp method returns ResultSetFuture instead of ResultSet. This way, the query can be executed, and our application can continue to run other tasks. We can generate a result set based on the response later, once we are ready to listen for it.

The prepare method allows us to invoke our session to prepare a CQL statement. This puts our statement into the prepared statement cache, and allows us to bind different variables to it before we send it to asyncOp.

 If you have a lot of data to iterate through and write, make sure to prepare your statements outside of any loop constructs. Bind your variables to the prepared statement inside the loop, and then execute. This prevents the prepared statement cache from being overwhelmed with requests for the same statement.

With that complete, we'll create a new main class named `CassSecurityDataLoader`. It will need to be in the `PacktCassDev` package, with the following imports:

```
package PacktCassDev;

import java.util.ArrayList;
import java.util.Date;
import java.util.List;
import com.datastax.driver.core.BoundStatement;
import com.datastax.driver.core.PreparedStatement;
import com.datastax.driver.core.ResultSetFuture;
```

Next, name the class as `CassSecurityDataLoader`, and define the maximum number of threads that can be inserting to Cassandra at any one time:

```
public class CassSecurityDataLoader {
  private final static int maxThreads = 10;
```

With that complete, we will define our main class and our node list and instantiate our connection class:

```
public static void main(String[] args) {
   String[] nodes = {"192.168.0.101"};
   CassandraConnection conn = new CassandraConnection(nodes,
     "cassdba", "flynnLives", "ClockworkAngels");
```

Here, we will define a list structure of type `ResultSetFuture` to contain threads controlling writes to our cluster. Additionally, we'll initialize our thread counter to 0:

```
   List<ResultSetFuture> listenableFutures = new
 ArrayList<ResultSetFuture>();
   int threadCount = 0;
```

Next, we'll define our query string with a multi-line `StringBuilder` (to avoid word wrap). With that complete, we'll invoke the public `prepare` method that we created on our connection class to enter the query into our cluster's prepared statement cache:

```
   StringBuilder insertQuery = new StringBuilder
     ("INSERT INTO packt_ch3.security_logs_by_location ");
   insertQuery.append("(location_id,day,time_in,employee_id,mailstop) ");
   insertQuery.append("VALUES (?,?,?,?,?)");
   PreparedStatement statement = conn.prepare(insertQuery.toString());
```

At this point in the code, we will start to define some of the defaults for our example. We're going to make sure that all rows written (for this model) end up in the partition at location MKE0 on Pi Day 2020.

We'll implement a `for` loop construct, iterating through a counter 1,000 times, and using that counter as the employee name/ID.

Inside the loop, we'll use the current value of `threadCount` as a suffix to the mail stop, just to set some off-the-cuff cardinality to that column:

```
String location = "MKE0";
int day = 20200314;
for (Integer employeeName = 0; employeeName < 1000; employeeName++){
    StringBuilder mailstop = new StringBuilder("MK").append(threadCount);
```

With the `for` loop begun, and our variables randomized/set, we'll bind our variables to our prepared statement (making it a `BoundStatement`). Then, we'll use the `asyncOp` method on our connection class to send the write asynchronously to our cluster.

That method will return a `ResultSetFuture`, which we'll add to our list of `listenableFutures`. Finally, we'll increment our `threadCount`:

```
BoundStatement boundStatement = statement.bind(location,day,
    new Date(),employeeName.toString(),mailstop.toString());
ResultSetFuture future = conn.asyncOp(boundStatement);
listenableFutures.add(future);
threadCount++;
```

At this point in the loop, our insert operation has been fired off asynchronously, and we've taken care of our defined structures to track it. Having just incremented `threadCount`, we'll check to see if it exceeds or matches the defined maximum number of allowed threads (`maxThreads`). If it does not, the loop will start over.

If our `threadCount` has reached the allowed threshold, we'll output which employee has triggered the max, and then iterate through our list of `listenableFutures` blocking while we ensure that they all complete.

When they do complete, we'll clear our `listenableFutures`, reset `threadCount` to zero, and restart the loop as shown here:

```
    if (threadCount >= maxThreads) {
        System.out.println(employeeName + " sent! Max threads in-flight,
waiting ");
        listenableFutures.forEach(ResultSetFuture::getUninterruptibly);
        listenableFutures = new ArrayList<ResultSetFuture>();
        threadCount = 0;
    }
}
```

As our loop is complete, we'll block here and listen for any extra write threads that are yet to complete. With that done, we'll signal completion to the console output and close the cluster connection:

```
listenableFutures.forEach(ResultSetFuture::getUninterruptibly);
System.out.println("Loader complete!");
conn.close();
 }
}
```

The code for this loader was inspired by Ryan Svihla's blog post refer docs for more information at *Svihla R(2016)-Cassandra: Batch Loading Without the Batch - Nuanced Edition*, which was retrieved on 2018/09/23 from `https://dzone.com/articles/cassandra-batch-loading-without-the-batch-the-nuan`, entitled **Batch Loading Without the Batch**. The previous example was meant to be simplistic, and by no means covers all the ways to limit the number of threads in-flight. I highly recommend reading Svihla's article (full reference, is available in the *Appendix*) to attain more detailed control of your threads and the application's behavior.

When nodes are overwhelmed with write activity, limiting the number of threads in-flight is a good approach that can be quickly implemented. The optimal max thread count will vary by application, use case, and write payload size.

You should thoroughly test any solution (including the preceding code) before using it under production-level, high-write throughput conditions.

The complete code to this section can be found at:
`https://github.com/aploetz/PacktCassDev`

If you see an error indicating that `method references are not supported in -source...`, try adding the following options to the `build` section of the `pom.xml` file:

```
<build>
    <plugins>
        <plugin>
            <groupId>org.apache.maven.plugins</groupId>
            <artifactId>maven-compiler-plugin</artifactId>
            <version>3.8.0</version>
            <configuration>
                <source>1.8</source>
```

```
            <target>1.8</target>
        </configuration>
      </plugin>
    </plugins>
  </build>
```

Summary

This chapter was designed with a specific goal in mind—that of bridging the knowledge gap between Apache Cassandra DBAs and software developers. Often, developers only have experience with relational databases, and sometimes not even that much.

This chapter was as much about educating developers as it was about providing perspective for the DBAs. That is to say, as a DBA sometimes it is important to see the world through the eyes of your dev team.

We started out in this chapter by covering correct use cases and database selection. Then we began to discover the DataStax Java driver, its behaviors and configurations, and how it interacts with Apache Cassandra.

Finally, we built a series of short programs of increasing complexity. Each program used the same connection class, and iteratively explained how to get from problem definition to program execution.

Integration with Apache Spark

9

This chapter will provide different options for a SQL interface for the Apache Cassandra NoSQL database using Spark CLIs. With distributed, non-relational databases such as Apache Cassandra, it's really hard to run ad hoc analytical queries (that require data aggregation). These types of queries require both a relational interface and an aggregation capability, and there are out-of-the-box options, among which Spark is one. This chapter will provide an overview of Spark architecture with its installation and configuration, along with different CLIs to perform **Create, Read, Update, and Delete (CRUD)** operations using any relational queries. Additionally, there is a web UI for multiple components that are integrated into the Spark architecture to understand the in-depth working of all of the tasks behind the scenes for any query with visualization. Specifically, this chapter will cover the following topics:

- Spark (architecture, installation, and configuration)
- PySpark
- SparkR
- Read, transform, and write
- The Jupyter web interface

Spark

Spark is a powerful, open source, general-purpose, unified cluster-computing analytics framework for large-scale data-processing. It's known for high performance, in-memory processing with an efficient engine and query optimizer. The four most widely-used interpreters for Spark are Python, Scala, Java, and R, including their interactive CLI. Spark is built on a foundation of **Resilient Distributed Dataset** (**RDD**) spread across the cluster of nodes. This eliminates computational limitations due to a cap of maximum resources that can be on a single machine, theoretically making it an infinitely scalable system. With all this, it is no surprise that it is the largest open source project in the data-processing community. Refer to Apache Spark docs for further information at *Spark-Spark Overview*: http://spark.apache.org/docs/2.3.1/.

Architecture

Spark's architecture is based on a master-slave relationship, where all of the APIs interact only with the master in order to establish a connection the cluster. Once the connection is established, the application talks (through the Spark context) directly to the slaves (known as workers in the Spark architecture). Once the connection with the cluster is established, a Spark context is allocated and it becomes the master of the Spark application. Then, the master manages te amount of resources allocated for the tasks to the slaves, and acknowledges clients accordingly. There are two modes of deployment:

- **Local mode**: This is the simplest of all deployments as it's similar to pseudo-cluster mode where master and workers run on a single machine with a non-distributed JVM as master, and all slaves are running on the same JVM. This is generally used for development and testing purposes.
- **Cluster mode**: This is similar to *Local mode* but with distributed architecture, where workers run on different instances. The workers run on a distributed JVM with tasks and resources managed by a master. This is generally used for production workloads.

In cluster mode, the current system supports multiple Cluster Managers, because Spark has a built-in Cluster Manager along with the capability to be embedded into an existing ecosystem that already has a Resource Manager. Hence, Spark can work with its Cluster Manager or with other Cluster Managers, such as Mesos, Yarn, or Kubernetes:

- **Standalone**: The simplest Cluster Manager, which comes built-in with Spark, making it easy to set up a cluster across multiple instances
- **Apache Mesos**: One of the open source Cluster Managers, which also manages resources along with compatibility for Hadoop MapReduce and service applications
- **Hadoop YARN**: A cluster and resource manager in Hadoop, with compatibility for all components provided by Hadoop
- **Kubernetes**: An open source, containerized resource and Cluster Manager with automated deployment, scaling, and management of those containerized applications

Nomad is another Cluster Manager, which is a third-party project without support by the Apache Spark project.

The following image shows the architecture of Spark cluster:

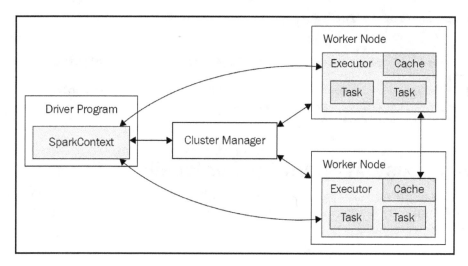

Figure 9.1: Spark cluster manager

Installation

Generally Spark can be installed from the source or prebuilt binaries. The following examples demonstrate how to use the binaries with prebuilt Hadoop 2.7 installation for any Linux, and for other kinds you can refer to the Spark docs at *Spark-Spark Overview*: http:// spark.apache.org. Make sure your server has access to the internet for downloading the binary and installing it accordingly:

```
# Assuming on a Centos 7 instance
# Java Installation.Refer OpenJDK Docs for further information at OpenJDK:
Download and Install, which
# was retrieved from http://openjdk.java.net/install/
yum install java-1.8.0-openjdk

# Spark Installation
curl -#
https://archive.apache.org/dist/spark/spark-$SPARK_VERSION/spark-$SPARK_VER
SION-bin-hadoop2.7.tgz | tar zx -C /usr/lib

# Setting Spark environment
cat > /etc/profile.d/spark.sh << EOF
SPARK_VERSION=2.3.1
SPARK_HOME=/usr/lib/spark-\$SPARK_VERSION-bin-hadoop2.7
PATH=\$PATH:\$SPARK_HOME/bin:\$SPARK_HOME/sbin
```

```
EOF

# Sourcing profile for setting env variables
source /etc/profile

# Generating log4j.properties from log4j.properties.template to reduce
chattiness
sed "s/log4j.rootCategory=.*/log4j.rootCategory=ERROR, console/g"
$SPARK_HOME/conf/log4j.properties.template >
$SPARK_HOME/conf/log4j.properties
```

Running custom Spark Docker locally

As discussed in previous chapters, this custom all-in-one Docker image is built on the CentOS 7 community Docker, with all of the following applications with their corresponding versions:

- Cassandra 3.11.2
- InfluxDB 1.6.2
- Grafana 5.2.4
- Telegraf 1.7.4
- JmxTrans 270
- Spark 2.3.1
- Python 2.7.15
- R 3.5.1

It even has the PySpark, SparkR, and Jupyter CLIs installed with the required configuration. They can be triggered with corresponding parameters through `SPARK_CLI` flags with PySpark, SparkR, or Jupyter, but PySpark would be the default if it's not passed. All of the required configs for the preceding applications are already preconfigured. This makes it very simple to run this complex custom Spark for easier troubleshooting and eliminates all the dependencies from running locally. For creating the PySpark shell locally connecting to an Apache Cassandra cluster, along with web UI components, there are two options. Either pull the image directly from Docker Hub or build locally from the source.

 Prerequisite: Docker should be installed. Refer to Docker CE (Community Edition) installation at Docker – *Get Docker CE for CentOS*: `https://docs.docker.com/install/linux/docker-ce/centos/`.

The following are the steps for both ways:

```
# Pull from dockerhub
docker pull malepati/cassandra-spark-jupyter:latest

# Build from source
# Clone git repo https://github.com/malepati/book
git clone git@github.com:malepati/book.git
cd book/MasteringApacheCassandra3rdEdition/docker
docker build -t malepati/cassandra-spark-jupyter:latest cassandra-spark-
jupyter/.

# Running docker container locally based on
#SPARK_CLI(pyspark/jupyter/sparkR)
docker run \
--name demo \
-p=4040:4040 \
-p=4041:4041 \
-p=7077:7077 \
-p=8080:8080 \
-p=8081:8081 \
-p=8082:8082 \
-p=9042:9042 \
-e 'CS_HOST=127.0.0.1' \
-e 'CS_DC=dc1' \
-e 'CS_UNAME=cassandra' \
-e 'CS_PWD=cassandra' \
--rm -it malepati/cassandra-spark-jupyter:latest
```

This Docker image would have a predefined dataset, which consists of demo keyspaces with offers and orders tables and a small amount of data, which can be found at https://github.com/malepati/book/blob/master/ MasteringApacheCassandra3rdEdition/docker/cassandra-spark-jupyter/files_to_ copy/demo.cql. It would first start Cassandra without monitoring, then a master is started, followed by a worker with a corresponding master URL and build extra parameters for final PySpark, SparkR, Jupyter CLI. Spark would be installed at /usr/lib/spark-2.3.1-bin-hadoop2.7. CS_HOST and CS_DC are mandatory for getting PySpark to work, and CS_UNAME and CS_PWD are optional parameters. Local Cassandra has authentication enabled that requires these, but if you're connecting to other clusters that don't have authentication enabled, those corresponding parameters can be ignored.

Configuration

With the binaries installation, the `conf` folder is located in the `$SPARK_HOME/conf` parent directory, which contains all of the templates related to environment, config parameters, slaves, metrics, logging, scheduler, and Docker. Based on the use case, we can copy to the same location and rename to corresponding names without *.template* suffix to the filename. Then those would be picked up during our initialization. There are some sets of parameters that can be passed without config during initialization; these need not be set and can be passed as parameters. An example format for `spark-defaults.conf` is as follows:

```
spark.master spark://127.0.0.1:7077
spark.serializer org.apache.spark.serializer.KryoSerializer
spark.driver.memory 5g
spark.executor.extraJavaOptions -XX:+PrintGCDetails
```

The web UI

The web UI or Spark UI is a web interface for Spark components to monitor, analyze, and inspect job executions in a web browser. This allows for the monitoring of task progress and the timeline with the amount of resources given. Each and every component has its own web API, which has in-depth tracking of tasks in pending, processing, and completed statuses along with config, timeline, and logs. Make sure all of the required firewalls are opened to access the corresponding ports from all the instances in Spark cluster.

Port numbers and their usage:

- `4040`: PySpark application port that is used to access in-depth details of an application that is running on a Spark cluster
- `4041`: SparkR application port that is used to access in depth details of an application that is running on a Spark cluster
- `7077`: Job submissions are directed to this port; it can be even the interactive CLI shell for any language that needs to be using this port for end-to-end tasks or job-execution
- `8080`: Master port that is used to access details of the master and to get an overview of the Spark cluster, such as the number of worker nodes and how many application are running at that point in time
- `8081`: Worker port that is used to access details of the worker and to get an overview of all of the executions that worker node has pending, processing, and completed tasks at that point of time

If proper firewalls are configured, redirecting links from the master UI would be seamless, which is very helpful for navigating between and among the APIs.

Master

Master is the first component that is started for bootstrapping other worker nodes to form a distributed Spark cluster. You can start a standalone master server by executing the following:

```
$SPARK_HOME/sbin/start-master.sh -h 127.0.0.1
```

Once it starts, it will print out spark://127.0.0.1:7077, which can be used to connect worker nodes or even pass as a parameter argument to SparkContext; the same will be displayed on the master's web UI (http://127.0.0.1:8080):

Figure 9.2: Master web UI

As seen in the previous screenshot, demo, sparklyr, and PySparkShell are the active applications that are using the Spark cluster displayed under the **Running Applications** section, whereas some_app_name1 is an application that has been completed under **Completed Applications**. This is shown along with other details, such as corresponding durations, which gives the time since they have been running.

Worker

The worker is the following component, which is started after master nodes, and it's bootstrapped to form a distributed Spark cluster. You can start a standalone worker server by executing the following:

```
$SPARK_HOME/sbin/start-master.sh -h 127.0.0.1 spark://127.0.0.1:7077
```

Once it starts, check the master's web UI. You should see a new worker node added to it and listed under the worker section, along with its instance configuration idle on the OS. This new worker node will be hyperlinked to redirect to the worker web UI, and can be navigated to with the following URL (`http://127.0.0.1:8081`):

Figure 9.3: Worker web UI

Application

The application is the final component that is connected to master nodes to start interacting with data on this newly-built distributed Spark cluster. The application can be a job submit or even an interactive CLI shell of any language. You can start a PySpark shell and connect to an Apache Cassandra cluster by executing the following:

```
$SPARK_HOME/bin/pyspark \
--packages com.datastax.spark:spark-cassandra-connector_2.11:2.3.0 \
--master spark://127.0.0.1:7077 \
--conf spark.driver.memory=<1/4th of memory in GB>g \
--conf spark.executor.memory=<1/2th of memory in GB>g \
--conf spark.driver.maxResultSize=<1/4th of memory in GB>g \
--conf spark.cassandra.connection.host=<cassanra contact point> \
--conf spark.cassandra.connection.local_dc=<dc name> \
--conf spark.cassandra.auth.username=<cassandra username> \
--conf spark.cassandra.auth.password=<cassandra password> \
--conf spark.cassandra.input.consistency.level=<consistency level> \
--conf spark.cassandra.connection.ssl.enabled=true \
--conf
spark.cassandra.connection.ssl.trustStore.path=<absolutepath>/truststore \
--conf spark.cassandra.connection.ssl.trustStore.password=<truststore
password>
```

This new application will be hyperlinked to redirect to the application web UI and can be navigated with following URL (http://127.0.0.1:4040):

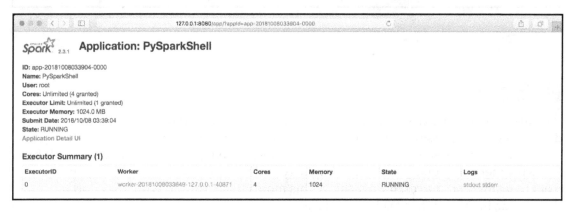

Figure 9.4: PySpark application overview web UI

Once it starts, check the master's web UI, you should see a new application, `PySparkShell`, added to it and listed under the application section, along with its progress and the stages of the tasks it has:

Figure 9.5: PySpark application event detailed timeline web UI

PySpark

PySpark is an interactive CLI, built-in with Spark, which provides the Python way of developing for processing large amounts of data, either from a single source or aggregating from multiple sources. This is one of the most widely-used CLIs for data interaction. It has a much wider community, due to its simplicity in developing data-processing applications from five different sources. It can achieve this more efficiently and with less effort for developing in Python than Scala, R, or Java.

PySpark can be found in the `bin` directory of the binary installations. Moreover, this can be directly run in `local` or `pseudo` mode, where all of the resources of an instance can be directly used. But as PySpark is an application CLI for spark, there wouldn't be any master or worker web UI. Only the application web UI would be accessible. Refer to the PySpark docs for further information at *Spark: Python on Spark*: `https://spark.apache.org/docs/latest/quick-start.html`.

The parameter to be passed to start PySpark shell in `local` mode is as follows:

```
--master local[*]
```

That is the only difference for connection or interacting to a `local` or `pseudo` mode and `cluster` mode.

Connection config

To start the PySpark CLI shell, we just need the `--master` parameter to connect to the desired cluster. Based on the use case, the connection parameters would be changing along with the packages being used for connection. To connect to an Apache Cassandra cluster with authentication and SSL encryption enabled, the following list of parameters need to be passed to the PySpark shell. If any of them are not enabled on the Cassandra side, those parameters need to be removed accordingly. An example format for connecting to a Cassandra node with authentication and SSL enabled is as follows:

```
# To Start PYSpark shell without master or slave.
# Remove authentication or ssl parameters based on cassandra side enabling
$SPARK_HOME/bin/pyspark \
--packages com.datastax.spark:spark-cassandra-connector_2.11:2.3.0 \
--master local[*] \
--conf spark.driver.memory=<1/4th of memory in GB>g \
--conf spark.executor.memory=<1/2th of memory in GB>g \
--conf spark.driver.maxResultSize=<1/4th of memory in GB>g \
--conf spark.cassandra.connection.host=<cassanra contact point> \
--conf spark.cassandra.connection.local_dc=<dc name> \
--conf spark.cassandra.auth.username=<cassandra username> \
--conf spark.cassandra.auth.password=<cassandra password> \
--conf spark.cassandra.input.consistency.level=<consistency level> \
--conf spark.cassandra.connection.ssl.enabled=true \
--conf
spark.cassandra.connection.ssl.trustStore.path=<absolutepath>/truststore \
--conf spark.cassandra.connection.ssl.trustStore.password=<truststore
password>
```

Accessing Cassandra data

Once configuration is all set, first we import a table locally into a DataFrame. A DataFrame is a datatype used in Spark that has an enhanced version of RDD, with additional structure (metadata) to it. For example, assume the preloaded schema and data for everything is in a Docker image. Let's say our marketing team wants to send personalized email notifications to all users who have purchased items that have offers currently. We need to join the `itemid` column from `orders` and the `offers` table in the `demo` schema. Refer to the PySpark API docs for further information at *Spark: Python API Docs*: `https://spark.apache.org/docs/latest/api/python/index.html`.

The commands are as follows:

```
_keyspace = 'demo'
offers =
sqlContext.read.format('org.apache.spark.sql.cassandra').load(table='offers
', keyspace=_keyspace)
orders =
sqlContext.read.format('org.apache.spark.sql.cassandra').load(table='orders
', keyspace=_keyspace)

temp = orders.join(offers, orders.itemid == offers.itemid)
result = temp.select(orders.userid, offers.offerid)

result.show(20, False)

result.distinct().sort('userid').show(20, False)
```

After loading the corresponding tables into their respective DataFrames, the `temp` DataFrame would have joined data with all of the columns. But we need only `userid` and `offerid` for promotions, hence we select only those columns. But they consist of duplicate offers for a user, hence `distinct` with `sort` of user would have the final DataFrame. This can be seen in the following screenshot of the PySpark CLI, displaying the result of the preceding commands:

```
● ● ●                                    @29bd443f60a3:/ — docker
Welcome to

      __         __
     / __/_____ / /__
    _\ \/ _ \/ _ `/  '_/
   /__/ .__/\_,_/_/ /_\   version 2.3.1
      /_/

Using Python version 2.7.5 (default, Jul 13 2018 13:06:57)
SparkSession available as 'spark'.
>>> _keyspace = 'demo'
>>> offers = sqlContext.read.format('org.apache.spark.sql.cassandra').load(table='offers', keyspace=_keyspace)
18/10/08 05:23:28 WARN ObjectStore: Version information not found in metastore. hive.metastore.schema.verification is not enabled so
  recording the schema version 1.2.0
18/10/08 05:23:28 WARN ObjectStore: Failed to get database default, returning NoSuchObjectException
18/10/08 05:23:29 WARN ObjectStore: Failed to get database global_temp, returning NoSuchObjectException
>>> orders = sqlContext.read.format('org.apache.spark.sql.cassandra').load(table='orders', keyspace=_keyspace)
>>> temp = orders.join(offers, orders.itemid == offers.itemid)
>>> result = temp.select(orders.userid, offers.offerid)
>>> result.show(20, False)
+------+-------+
|userid|offerid|
+------+-------+
|usr1  |ofr1   |
|usr1  |ofr1   |
|usr2  |ofr2   |
|usr3  |ofr2   |
|usr3  |ofr1   |
|usr2  |ofr4   |
|usr3  |ofr4   |
|usr1  |ofr2   |
|usr3  |ofr2   |
|usr1  |ofr3   |
|usr3  |ofr3   |
+------+-------+

>>> result.distinct().sort('userid').show(20, False)
+------+-------+
|userid|offerid|
+------+-------+
|usr1  |ofr1   |
|usr1  |ofr2   |
|usr1  |ofr3   |
|usr2  |ofr4   |
|usr2  |ofr2   |
|usr3  |ofr2   |
|usr3  |ofr3   |
|usr3  |ofr1   |
|usr3  |ofr4   |
+------+-------+

>>> ▉
```

Figure 9.6: PySpark CLI result section

SparkR

SparkR is an interactive CLI, built-in with Spark, which provides an R interface of developing for processing large amounts of data either from a single source or aggregating from multiple sources. This is the statisticians' CLI for data interaction. As R is a statistician's language, it is a little more complicated than Python, due to the limitations and architecture of R.

SparkR can be found in the `bin` directory of the binary installations. It also has support for running in `local` or `pseudo` mode and, based on which, there would/wouldn't be any master and worker web UI. But the application web UI would be accessible regardless. Refer to the SparkR docs for further information at *Spark: R on Spark*: `https://spark.apache.org/docs/latest/sparkr.html`.

Unlike PySpark, SparkR requires the R package to be installed, much like PySpark requires Python, which is built-in with CentOS. Hence, the R package needs to be installed for SparkR to be working, and the command to install the R package is as follows:

```
yum install epel-release
yum install openssl-devel
yum install libxml2-devel
yum install curl-devel
yum install R
```

Connection config

To start the SparkR CLI shell, we just need the `--master` parameter to connect to the desired cluster. Based on our use case, the connection parameters will change along with the packages being used for the connection. To connect to an Apache Cassandra cluster with authentication and SSL encryption enabled, the following list of parameters needs to be passed to the SparkR shell. If any of them are not enabled on the Cassandra side, those parameters need to be removed accordingly. An example format for connecting to a Cassandra node with authentication and SSL enabled is as follows:

```
# To Start SparkR shell with master or slave.
# Remove authentication or ssl parameters based on cassandra side enabling
$SPARK_HOME/bin/SparkR \
--packages com.datastax.spark:spark-cassandra-connector_2.11:2.3.0 \
--master local[*] \
--conf spark.driver.memory=<1/4th of memory in GB>g \
--conf spark.executor.memory=<1/2th of memory in GB>g \
--conf spark.driver.maxResultSize=<1/4th of memory in GB>g \
--conf spark.cassandra.connection.host=<cassanra contact point> \
--conf spark.cassandra.connection.local_dc=<dc name> \
--conf spark.cassandra.auth.username=<cassandra username> \
--conf spark.cassandra.auth.password=<cassandra password> \
--conf spark.cassandra.input.consistency.level=<consistency level> \
--conf spark.cassandra.connection.ssl.enabled=true \
--conf
spark.cassandra.connection.ssl.trustStore.path=<absolutepath>/truststore \
--conf spark.cassandra.connection.ssl.trustStore.password=<truststore
password>
```

Accessing Cassandra data

Once the configuration is all set, we import a table to `local` and register it as a table locally. This allows any kind of queries to be run. Refer to the SparkR API docs for further information at *Spark: R API Docs*: `https://spark.apache.org/docs/latest/api/R/index.html`.

The commands are as follows:

```
# for All in one docker its already installed
# install.packages(c("sparklyr","dplyr"), repos="http://cran.us.r-
#project.org")
library(sparklyr)

config <- spark_config()
config$sparklyr.defaultPackages = "com.datastax.spark:spark-cassandra-
connector_2.11:2.3.0"
config$spark.driver.host = '127.0.0.1'
config$spark.cassandra.connection.host = '127.0.0.1'
config$spark.cassandra.auth.username = 'cassandra'
config$spark.cassandra.auth.password = 'cassandra'
config$spark.cassandra.connection.local_dc = 'dc1'

sc <- spark_connect(
master = 'spark://127.0.0.1:7077',
spark_home = '/usr/lib/spark-2.3.1-bin-hadoop2.7',
config = config
)

offers_df <- sparklyr:::spark_data_read_generic(
  sc, "org.apache.spark.sql.cassandra", "format",
  list(keyspace = "demo", table = "offers")
  ) %>%
  invoke("load")

offers_tbl <- sparklyr:::spark_partition_register_df(
        sc, offers_df, name = "offers", repartition = 0, memory = TRUE)

offers_tbl
```

There are different packages that can be used for operations, such as `select`, `filter`, `summarize`, and `arrange`, at `https://dplyr.tidyverse.org/`, among which `dplyr` is a widely-used one. The following is a screenshot of the SparkR CLI displaying the simple result of the preceding commands:

```
                                    @1f32b1504611:/ — docker

Welcome to

      __       __
     / _/_____/ /__
    \ \/ _ \/ _ `/  _/
   /___/ .__/\_,_/ /_/\_\    version  2.3.1
       /_/

SparkSession available as 'spark'.
> library(sparklyr)
> config <- spark_config()
> config$sparklyr.defaultPackages = "com.datastax.spark:spark-cassandra-connector_2.11:2.3.0> config$spark.driver.host = '127.0.0.1'
> config$spark.cassandra.connection.host = '127.0.0.1'
> config$spark.cassandra.auth.username = 'cassandra'
> config$spark.cassandra.auth.password = 'cassandra'
> config$spark.cassandra.connection.local_dc = 'dc1'
> sc <- spark_connect(
+ master      = 'spark://127.0.0.1:7077',
+ spark_home = '/usr/lib/spark-2.3.1-bin-hadoop2.7',
+ config = config
+ )
> offers_df <- sparklyr:::spark_data_read_generic(
+   sc, "org.apache.spark.sql.cassandra", "format",
+   list(keyspace = "demo", table = "offers")
+ ) %>%
+   invoke("load")
> offers_tbl <- sparklyr:::spark_partition_register_df(
+        sc, offers_df, name = "offers", repartition = 0, memory = TRUE)
> offers_tbl
# Source: spark<offers> [?? x 2]
  offerid itemid
* <chr>   <chr>
1 ofr3    item8
2 ofr4    item9
3 ofr2    item6
4 ofr2    item7
5 ofr1    item1
6 ofr1    item2
7 ofr1    item3
8 ofr1    item4
9 ofr1    item5
>
```

Figure 9.7: SparkR CLI result

For example, if we need to filter all of the users who have ordered an item, then filtering from the `dplyr` library can be used, with all of the same config set as for the preceding example. Additionally, the `orders` table needs to be loaded, as follows:

```
library(dplyr)

orders_df <- sparklyr:::spark_data_read_generic(
  sc, "org.apache.spark.sql.cassandra", "format",
  list(keyspace = "demo", table = "orders")
) %>%
  invoke("load")

orders_tbl <- sparklyr:::spark_partition_register_df(
      sc, orders_df, name = "orders", repartition = 0, memory = TRUE)

filter(orders_tbl, itemid == 'item6')
```

On the same session, just importing the `dplyr` library would enable it to perform any kind of transformation on the corresponding table. This can be done locally on a Spark cluster:

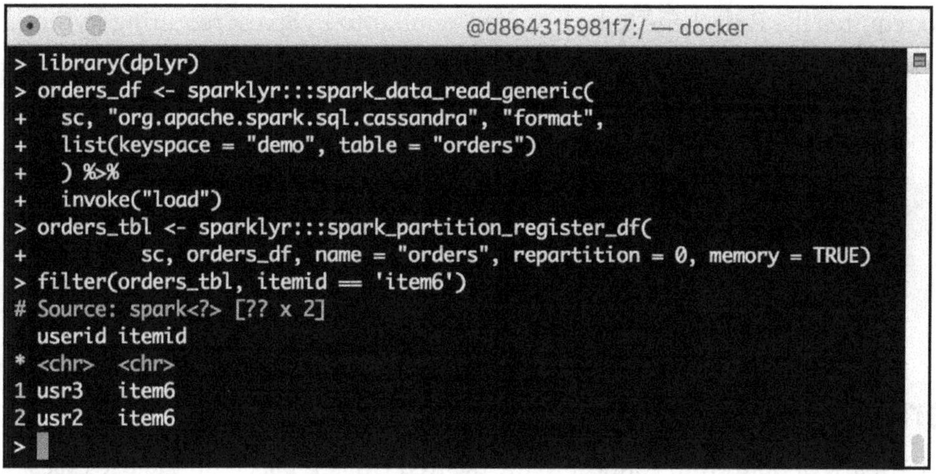

Figure 9.8: SparkR dplyr transformations

RStudio

RStudio is an open source IDE for the R programming language. It provides the GUI with a way of interacting with Spark. It also provides an R way of developing to process large amounts of data either from a single source or aggregating from multiple sources. This is just a GUI of the R CLI, which is also integrated with Spark. There are multiple ways to install it, based on the operating system in `pseudo` mode. Refer to the RStudio docs for further information about RStudio and to download it at `https://www.rstudio.com/products/rstudio/download/`.

 Prerequisite: R development tools should be installed along with other dependency packages, as CentOS requires the `yum install {epel-release, openssl-devel, libxml2-devel, curl-devel}` packages for successful working R installations, whereas Ubuntu requires `apt update` followed by `apt install {libxml2-dev, libghc-curl-dev, r-cran-httr, r-cran-openssl}` for successful working R-based installations.

RStudio requires the R package to be installed, similar to PySpark requiring Python, hence R development tools need to be installed for working on RStudio, and the command to install the RStudio package is as follows:

```
rpm -ivh https://download1.rstudio.org/rstudio-1.1.456-x86_64.rpm
```

 This would only work on GUI instances and not for a CLI, hence the desktop way of installation is required. This can be installed on local laptops as well with corresponding packages.

Connection config

Unlike PYSpark or SparkR to connect to the desired cluster, based on the use cases, connection parameters would be changing along with the packages being used for connection. To connect to an Apache Cassandra cluster with authentication and SSL encryption enabled, a list of the following parameters needs to be passed to the R shell. If any of them are not enabled on the Cassandra side, those parameters need to be removed accordingly. An example format for connecting to a Cassandra node with authentication and SSL enabled is as follows:

```
# Once RStudio is opened, R shell would be on left bottom where you can run
below commands.
# Remove authentication or ssl parameters based on cassandra side enabling
```

```
install.packages(c("sparklyr","dplyr"))
library(sparklyr)
library(dplyr)
spark_install("2.1.1")

config <- spark_config()
config$sparklyr.defaultPackages = "com.datastax.spark:spark-cassandra-
connector_2.11:2.0.1"
config$spark.cassandra.connection.host = '127.0.0.1'
config$spark.cassandra.auth.username = 'cassandra'
config$spark.cassandra.auth.password = 'cassandra'
config$spark.cassandra.connection.local_dc = 'dc1'

sc <- spark_connect(
master = 'local',
spark_home = spark_home_dir(),
config = config
)
```

Accessing Cassandra data

Once the configuration is all set, we import the table to `local`. We then register it as a table locally, so that any kind of queries can be run. The commands are as follows:

```
# Import to locally
cass_df <- sparklyr:::spark_data_read_generic(
  sc, "org.apache.spark.sql.cassandra", "format",
  list(keyspace = "system_auth", table = "roles")
  ) %>%
  invoke("load")

# Register as a table
cass_tbl <- sparklyr:::spark_partition_register_df(
        sc, cass_df, name = "roles", repartition = 0, memory = TRUE)

View(cass_tbl)
```

The following is a screenshot of RStudio on macOS. The bottom-left screen shows the CLI's way of displaying the `roles` table data. If you need a cleaner display, you can click the table icon on the right end of `roles`, at the top-right under the `Connections` section:

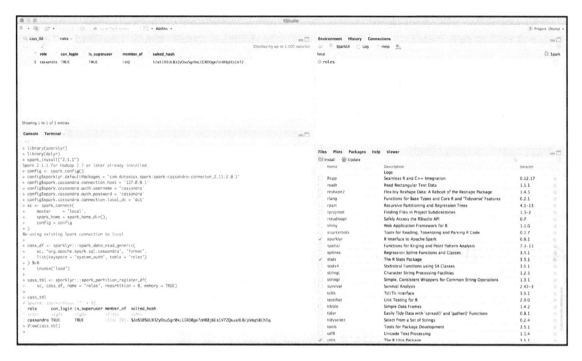

Figure 9.9: RStudio on macOS

Jupyter

Jupyter is an open source, open-standards, services project for interactive computing across many applications. Jupyter Notebook is a web application that allows you to create, view, modify, and delete documents with any compatible data, along with Python CLI shell interaction. Jupyter runs on many programming languages, but Python with pip is a mandatory requirement. Refer to the Jupyter docs for further information: `http://jupyter.org`.

Architecture

Notebook is a kind of frontend, which does something extra apart from running code. It stores the code and output with markdown nodes in an editable file known as Notebook. When actions are performed on that file, either at the client side through the web UI or on the server side, they are sent back and forth through the Notebook server. It also acts as an application and web server, which saves on disk as a JSON file with the `.ipynb` extension. Refer to the Jupyter documentation for more information:
`https://jupyter.readthedocs.io/en/latest/architecture/how_jupyter_ipython_work.html`.

The following image shows the architecture of a Jupyter Notebook:

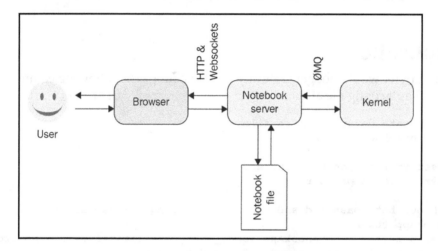

Figure 9.10: Jupyter Notebook architecture

As you can see, a user can directly interact with an instance's kernel through the web UI using the Jupyter Notebook server. This has code saved in Jupyter Notebook files, in which case, the user's ability can be locked down to a particular directory and not outside of it. This makes some set of use cases where we can interact with the instance directly from the web UI, rather than through SSH.

Installation

For Juptyer, a simple pip package needs to be installed. Be careful, as there are multiple Python and pip versions—based on the pip version linked to a Python version, Jupyter would be installed accordingly for that version.

Prerequisite: Python and pip should be installed.

The following is the command to install Jupyter:

```
pip install jupyter
```

Jupyter can be installed using the Anaconda/Conda distribution as well, refer *Jupyter Documentation: Installing Jupyter Using Anaconda and Conda, retrieved from* https://jupyter.readthedocs.io/en/latest/install.html#installing-jupyter-using-anaconda-and-conda.

Configuration

By default, Jupyter would not generate any default config. The following command would generate a default config file at /root/.jupyter/jupyter_notebook_config.py:

```
# To generate default config file
jupyter notebook --generate-config

# To set initial password instead of token
jupyter notebook password

# With out both password and token for testing purpose add --
NotebookApp.token=''
jupyter notebook --NotebookApp.iopub_data_rate_limit=1.0e10 --no-browser --
port 8082 --allow-root --ip=0.0.0.0 --NotebookApp.token=''
```

If you start Jupyter without a password, it creates a default token that can be used for the initial login. Then, it will prompt for password creation. But with the password command, it would prompt you to set an initial password from the CLI and then hash the password in a particular format to /root/.jupyter/jupyter_notebook_config.json. This should be used when you access the web UI through the browser.

Web UI

Once Jupyter Notebook is started and connected to port `8082`, you can access the web UI through any browser with the `http://127.0.0.1:8082` URL.

By default, it uses the `/` directory and displays all files, this can be restricted with the `--notebook-dir=<absolutepath>/dirname` parameter when starting Jupyter Notebook.

The commands for starting Jupyter are as follows:

```
# Creating parent directory for jupyter
mkdir /usr/lib/jupyter

jupyter notebook  --NotebookApp.iopub_data_rate_limit=1.0e10 --no-browser --port 8082 --allow-root --ip=0.0.0.0 --NotebookApp.token='' --notebook-dir=/usr/lib/jupyter
```

The following screenshot shows the homepage of the Jupyter web UI:

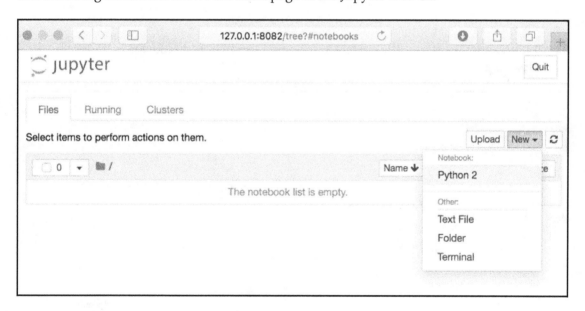

Figure 9.11: Jupyter homepage

The following screenshot shows how ad hoc Python commands can be run from Jupyter web UI:

Figure 9.12: Jupyter ad hoc python command

The following image shows the currently running terminals and Notebooks under the **Running** tab on Jupyter web UI:

Figure 9.13: Jupyter running tasks

This would restrict access to only `/usr/lib/jupyter`, which is a much safer approach. Here, as we have not saved that ad hoc Python command, Notebook shows as `untitled.ipynb` under the `Notebooks` section. As this terminal has been closed, it would not show under the **Terminals** section of the **Running** tab, but Jupyter Notebook would be retained unless deleted.

PYSpark through Juypter

If Spark is already installed on the machine and `SPARK_HOME` is set, then the `findspark` pip package will get information related to the installed Spark. It will then connect Jupyter to the Spark installation with this package, which needs to be installed as follows:

```
pip install findspark
```

Otherwise, pip would not have the PySpark package installed by default. Hence, for using PySpark through Jupyter, it is mandatory to install it with the following command:

```
pip install pyspark
```

For example, a business wants to know the total number of orders counted by user. As Cassandra doesn't have an aggregation ability, Spark gives us the ability to do all of the required transformation along with sorting for a cleaner report. Setting a custom Spark and Cassandra config after startup to Jupyter Notebook is done as follows:

```
import os
import sys
import findspark

findspark.init()
from pyspark import SparkContext, SparkConf
from pyspark.sql.functions import *
from pyspark.sql import *

os.environ['PYSPARK_SUBMIT_ARGS'] = '--packages com.datastax.spark:spark-
cassandra-connector_2.11:2.3.0 --master spark://127.0.0.1:7077 pyspark-
shell'
conf = SparkConf()
conf.set("spark.cassandra.auth.username", "cassandra")
conf.set("spark.cassandra.auth.password", "cassandra")
conf.set("spark.cassandra.connection.host", "127.0.0.1")
conf.set("spark.cassandra.connection.local_dc", "dc1")

conf.setAppName('demo')
```

```
sc = SparkContext(conf=conf)
sqlContext = SQLContext(sc)

_keyspace = 'demo'
orders =
sqlContext.read.format('org.apache.spark.sql.cassandra').load(table='orders
', keyspace=_keyspace)
result = orders.groupby(orders.userid).count()
result.sort('userid').show(20, False)
```

As in SQL, `groupby` can be used on a column, along with `count`, which gives the aggregation along with the count and stores it in a result DataFrame. But in order to sort, you can use `sort` on a corresponding column. `show` is for limiting number of rows to display, along with a flag for truncating a cell value, if it's very long:

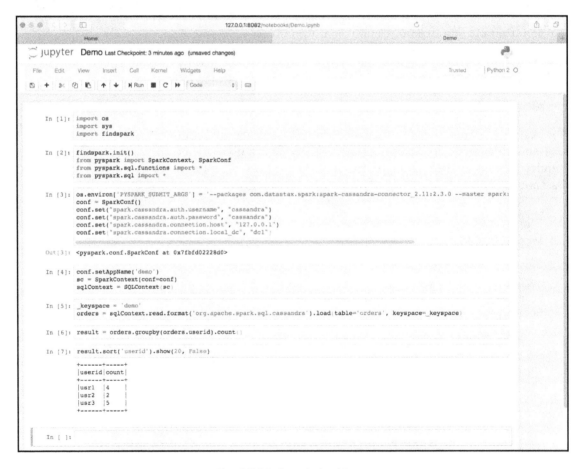

Figure 9.14: PySpark execution through Jupyter

Summary

Spark gives a SQL interface for a NoSQL Cassandra database that is running ad hoc tasks, such as generating business reports on the fly, data analysis, debugging, and finding data patterns. This chapter provided a brief overview of the Spark architecture, which stands on top among other sets of available tools; it offers ease of installation and a huge community, as well as backing up on Hadoop for data warehousing. It also discusses different ways of installation, along with a custom all-in-one Docker image, which has Apache Cassandra, a monitoring stack, and Spark including PySpark, SparkR, and Jupyter with their dependencies. The Docker image has several flags that can be enabled based on the use case or toolset to test locally along with their configurations.

Having a web UI is very helpful for debugging long-running tasks along with resources being available and allocated, with a brief display for the Spark master, worker, and applications running on a cluster. An in-depth description of PySpark, SparkR, RStudio, and Jupyter, which included connection configuration parameters in different ways, and Apache Cassandra data access from corresponding CLIs. Thanks for joining us on this adventure of learning!

This was followed by a discussion of some sets of examples that contain data extraction from Cassandra, then loading into a Spark cluster for any kind of transformations that can not be done at the Cassandra layer due to architectural constrains, and finally report in custom designed format. You will gain an in-depth working knowledge of all these CLIs (especially PySpark and Jupyter) as they are some of the most widely-used CLIs.

References

The following are the references mentioned in each chapter:

Chapter 1 – Quick Start

Decandia G., Hastorun D., Jampani M., Kakulapati G., Lakshman A., Pilchin A. (2007). *Dynamo: Amazon's Highly Available Key-value Store*. Proceedings of the Twenty-First ACM SIGOPS Symposium on Operating Systems Principles (pp. 205-220). Doi: 10.1145/1294261.1294281c

Chapter 2 – Cassandra Architecture

- Apache Software Foundation (2016). *Documentation – Adding, replacing, moving, and removing nodes*. Retrieved on April 18, 2018 from `http://cassandra.apache.org/doc/latest/operating/topo_changes.html`.
- Brewer E., Fox A. (1999). *Harvest, Yield, and Scalable Tolerant Systems*. University of California at Berkeley, Berkeley, CA. Retrieved on April 4, 2018 from `http://lab.mscs.mu.edu/Dist2012/lectures/HarvestYield.pdf`.
- DataStax (2018). *Apache Cassandra 3.0 for DSE 5.0*: *Understanding the Architecture*. Retrieved on April 4, 2018 from `https://docs.datastax.com/en/cassandra/3.0/cassandra/architecture/archTOC.html`.
- Kozliner E. (2017). *Merkle Tree Introduction*. Retrieved on June 3, 2018 from `https://medium.com/@evankozliner/merkle-tree-introduction-4c44250e2da7`.
- Ploetz A., Kandhare D., Kadamni S., Wu X. (2018). *Seven NoSQL Databases in a Week*. Packt Publishing.
- Saha S. (2017). *The Gossip Protocol: Inside Apache Cassandra*. Retrieved on April 22, 2018 from `https://www.linkedin.com/pulse/gossip-protocol-inside-apache-cassandra-soham-saha/`.
- Strickland R. (2014). *Cassandra High Availability*. Packt Publishing.
- Williams B. (2012). *Dynamic snitching in Cassandra: past, present, and future*. Retrieved on April 22, 2018 from `https://www.datastax.com/dev/blog/dynamic-snitching-in-cassandra-past-present-and-future`.

Chapter 3 – Effective CQL

- Apache (2018). *Apache JIRA Issue Tracker – Cassandra Project – CASSANDRA-10027*. Retrieved on July 23, 2018 from `https://issues.apache.org/jira/browse/CASSANDRA-10027`.
- DataStax (2015). *Putting some structure in the storage engine*. Retrieved on June 24, 2018 from `https://www.datastax.com/2015/12/storage-engine-30`.
- DataStax (2018). *CQL for Apache Cassandra 3.0: CQL limits*. Retrieved on July 8, 2018 from `https://docs.datastax.com/en/cql/3.3/cql/cql_reference/refLimits.html`.
- Haddad (2018). *Apache Cassandra Performance Tuning – Compression with Mixed Workloads*. Retrieved on August 8, 2018 from `http://thelastpickle.com/blog/2018/08/08/compression_performance.html`.
- Ploetz (2015). *Cassandra Compatible CQL Data Types*. Retrieved on July 23, 2018 from `http://www.aaronstechcenter.com/cassandra-compatible-types.php`.

Chapter 4 – Configuring a Cluster

- Birkman Y. (2016). *Why we use Terraform and not Chef, Puppet, Ansible, SaltStack, or CloudFormation*. Retrieved on May 14, 2018 from `https://blog.gruntwork.io/why-we-use-terraform-and-not-chef-puppet-ansible-saltstack-or-cloudformation-7989dad2865c`.
- Bonér J., Dean J., Norvig P. (2012). *Latency numbers every programmer should know*. Retrieved on April 26, 2018 from `https://gist.github.com/jboner/2841832`.
- DataStax (2018). *DSE 6.0 Administrator Guide: Recommended production settings*. Retrieved on April 28, 2018 from `https://docs.datastax.com/en/dse/6.0/dse-admin/datastax_enterprise/config/configRecommendedSettings.html`.
- Eichwald H. (2016). *Tuning the JVM for low pauses garbage collectors CMS and G1*. Retrieved on April 29, 2018 from `https://www.cakesolutions.net/teamblogs/low-pause-gc-on-the-jvm`.
- Ellis J. (2014). *Off-heap memtables in Cassandra 2.1*. DataStax Developer Blog. Retrieved on May 10, 2018 from `https://www.datastax.com/dev/blog/off-heap-memtables-in-cassandra-2-1`.
- Haddad J. (2018). *Cassandra Performance Tuning*. Presented at Data Day Texas 2018 – University of Texas at Austin, Austin, TX.

- Issues, Apache. (2016). *Cassandra ASF Jira: CASSANDRA-8150*. Retrieved on May 2, 2018 from `https://issues.apache.org/jira/browse/CASSANDRA-8150`.
- Tobey A. (2015). *Amy's Cassandra 2.1 tuning guide*. Retrieved on April 24, 2018 from `https://tobert.github.io/pages/als-cassandra-21-tuning-guide.html`.

Chapter 5 – Performance Tuning

- Dean J., Norvig P. (2012). *Latency Numbers Every Programmer Should Know*. Retrieved on September 4, 2018 from `https://gist.github.com/jboner/2841832`.
- Gilmore E. (2011). *Maximizing Cache Benefit with Cassandra*. DataStax Developer Blog. Retrieved on September 4, 2018 from `https://www.datastax.com/dev/blog/maximizing-cache-benefit-with-cassandra`.
- Haddad J. (2018). *Apache Cassandra Performance Tuning – Compression with Mixed Workloads*. The Last Pickle. Retrieved on September 4, 2018 from `http://thelastpickle.com/blog/2018/08/08/compression_performance.html`.
- Hobbs T. (2012). *When to Use Leveled Compaction*. DataStax Developer Blog. Retrieved on September 4, 2018 from `https://www.datastax.com/dev/blog/when-to-use-leveled-compaction`.
- Slater B. (2016). *Deep Diving Cassandra-Stress – Part 3 (Using YAML Profiles)*. Instaclustr. Retrieved on August 16, 2018 from `https://www.instaclustr.com/deep-diving-cassandra-stress-part-3-using-yaml-profiles/`.

Chapter 6 – Managing a Cluster

- Casares J. (2018). *Assassinate – A Command of Last Resort within Apache Cassandra*. The Last Pickle. Retrieved on October 7, 2018 from `http://thelastpickle.com/blog/2018/09/18/assassinate.html`.
- DataStax. (2018). *Backing up and restoring data*. DataStax. Retrieved on October 7, 2018 from `https://docs.datastax.com/en/cassandra/3.0/cassandra/operations/opsBackupRestore.html`.
- Kalantzis C. (2015). *Cassandra Tickler*. Retrieved on October 7, 2018 from `https://github.com/ckalantzis/cassTickler`.

Chapter 7 – Monitoring

- Oracle: SE Java Documentation: *Using JConsole*: Retrieved from `https://docs.oracle.com/javase/7/docs/technotes/guides/management/jconsole.html`.
- Apache: Confluence: *jmxterm quickstart*: Retrieved from `https://cwiki.apache.org/confluence/display/KAFKA/jmxterm+quickstart`.
- Apache: Cassandra: *Nodetool Usage*: Retrieved from `http://Cassandra.apache.org/doc/4.0/tools/nodetool/nodetool.html`.
- InfluxData: *Installing Telegraf*: Retrieved from `https://docs.influxdata.com/telegraf/v1.7/introduction/installation/`.
- JMXTrans: *Introduction to JMXTrans*: Retrieved from `https://github.com/jmxtrans/jmxtrans/wiki`.
- InfluxData: InfluxDB: *Introducing InfluxDB OSS*: Retrieved from `https://docs.influxdata.com/influxdb/v1.6/introduction/`.
- InfluxData: InfluxDB: *InfluxDB Line Protocol tutorial*: Retrieved from `https://docs.influxdata.com/influxdb/v1.6/write_protocols/line_protocol_tutorial/`.
- InfluxData: InfluxDB: *InfluxDB Command Line Interface (CLI/Shell)*: Retrieved from `https://docs.influxdata.com/influxdb/v1.6/tools/shell/`.
- Grafana Labs: *Grafana Documentation*: Retrieved from `http://docs.grafana.org/`.
- Elastic: Docs: *Filebeat Overview*: Retrieved from `https://www.elastic.co/guide/en/beats/filebeat/current/filebeat-overview.html`.
- Elastic: Docs: *Elasticsearch Reference*: Retrieved from `https://www.elastic.co/products/elasticsearch`.
- Elastic: Docs: *Kibana Reference*: Retrieved from `https://www.elastic.co/guide/en/kibana/6.4/install.html`.
- Docker: *Get Docker CE for CentOS*: Retrieved from `https://docs.docker.com/install/linux/docker-ce/centos/`.

Chapter 8 – Application Development

- DataStax. (2018). *Java Driver for Apache Cassandra 3.6.* Retrieved on September 22, 2018 from `https://docs.datastax.com/en/developer/java-driver/3.6/manual/`.
- DataStax. (2018). *Java Driver for Apache Cassandra 3.0 – Native Protocol:* `https://docs.datastax.com/en/developer/java-driver/3.0/manual/native_protocol/`
- McCall N. (2015). *Hector Git commit: Marking as non-active, adding link to Java Driver and thank you message.* Retrieved on September 16, 2018 from `https://github.com/hector-client/hector/commit/a302e68ca8d91b45d332e8c9afd7d98030b54de1`.
- Popescu A. (2014). *4 simple rules when using the DataStax drivers for Cassandra.* Retrieved on September 22, 2018 from `https://www.datastax.com/dev/blog/4-simple-rules-when-using-the-datastax-drivers-for-cassandra`.
- Svihla R. (2016). *Cassandra: Batch Loading Without the Batch – Nuanced Edition.* Retrieved on September 23, 2018 from `https://dzone.com/articles/cassandra-batch-loading-without-the-batch-the-nuan`.

Chapter 9 – Integration with Apache Spark

- Spark: Spark overview: Retrieved from `http://spark.apache.org`.
- OpenJDK: Download and install: Retrieved from `http://openjdk.java.net/install/`.
- Docker: Get Docker CE for CentOS: Retrieved from `https://docs.docker.com/install/linux/docker-ce/centos/`.
- Spark: Python on Spark: Retrieved from `https://spark.apache.org/docs/latest/quick-start.html`.
- Spark: Python API docs: Retrieved from `https://spark.apache.org/docs/latest/api/python/index.html`.
- Spark: R on Spark: Retrieved from `https://spark.apache.org/docs/latest/sparkr.html`.
- Spark: R API docs: Retrieved from `https://spark.apache.org/docs/latest/api/R/index.html`.

- DPLYR: Overview: Retrieved from `https://dplyr.tidyverse.org/`.
- RStudio: Download RStudio: Retrieved from `https://www.rstudio.com/products/rstudio/download/`.
- Jupyter Documentation, retrieved from `http://jupyter.org`
- Jupyter Documentation: How Jupyter Ipython Work: Retrieved from `https://jupyter.readthedocs.io/en/latest/architecture/how_jupyter_ipython_work.html`
- Jupyter Documentation: Installing Jupyter Using Anaconda and Conda: Retrieved from `https://jupyter.readthedocs.io/en/latest/install.html#installing-jupyter-using-anaconda-and-conda`.

Other Books You May Enjoy

If you enjoyed this book, you may be interested in these other books by Packt:

Learning Apache Cassandra - Second Edition
Sandeep Yarabarla

ISBN: 9781787127296

- Install Cassandra
- Create keyspaces and tables with multiple clustering columns to organize related data
- Use secondary indexes and materialized views to avoid denormalization of data
- Effortlessly handle concurrent updates with collection columns
- Ensure data integrity with lightweight transactions and logged batches
- Understand eventual consistency and use the right consistency level for your situation
- Understand data distribution with Cassandra
- Develop simple application using Java driver and implement application-level optimizations

Seven NoSQL Databases in a Week

Aaron Ploetz, Devram Kandhare, Sudarshan Kadambi, Xun (Brian) Wu

ISBN: 9781787288867

- Understand how MongoDB provides high-performance, high-availability, and automatic scaling
- Interact with your Neo4j instances via database queries, Python scripts, and Java application code
- Get familiar with common querying and programming methods to interact with Redis
- Study the different types of problems Cassandra can solve
- Work with HBase components to support common operations such as creating tables and reading/writing data
- Discover data models and work with CRUD operations using DynamoDB
- Discover what makes InfluxDB a great choice for working with time-series data

Leave a review - let other readers know what you think

Please share your thoughts on this book with others by leaving a review on the site that you bought it from. If you purchased the book from Amazon, please leave us an honest review on this book's Amazon page. This is vital so that other potential readers can see and use your unbiased opinion to make purchasing decisions, we can understand what our customers think about our products, and our authors can see your feedback on the title that they have worked with Packt to create. It will only take a few minutes of your time, but is valuable to other potential customers, our authors, and Packt. Thank you!

Index

www.ingramcontent.com/pod-product-compliance
Lightning Source LLC
Chambersburg PA
CBHW080619060326
40690CB00021B/4746

* 9 7 8 1 7 8 9 1 3 1 4 9 9 *